INQUIRY BY DESIGN

**THE BROOKS/COLE BASIC CONCEPTS
IN ENVIRONMENT AND BEHAVIOR SERIES**

Series Editors:

Irwin Altman, The University of Utah
Daniel Stokols, University of California, Irvine
Lawrence S. Wrightsman, The University of Kansas

AN INTRODUCTION TO ECOLOGICAL PSYCHOLOGY
Allan W. Wicker, Claremont Graduate School

CULTURE AND ENVIRONMENT
Irwin Altman, The University of Utah
Martin Chemers, The University of Utah

**INQUIRY BY DESIGN:
TOOLS FOR ENVIRONMENT-BEHAVIOR RESEARCH**
John Zeisel, Harvard University

**ENVIRONMENTAL EVALUATION:
PERCEPTION AND PUBLIC POLICY**
Ervin H. Zube, University of Arizona

ENVIRONMENTAL PROBLEMS/BEHAVIORAL SOLUTIONS
John D. Cone, West Virginia University
Steven C. Hayes, University of North Carolina

INQUIRY BY DESIGN: TOOLS FOR ENVIRONMENT-BEHAVIOR RESEARCH

JOHN ZEISEL

Harvard University

BROOKS/COLE PUBLISHING COMPANY
MONTEREY, CALIFORNIA

To Evan, Elizabeth, and Eva

Brooks/Cole Publishing Company
A Division of Wadsworth, Inc.

Printed in the United States of America

10 9 8 7 6 5 4 3 2 1

Library of Congress Cataloging in Publication Data

Zeisel, John.
    Inquiry by design.

    (The Brooks/Cole basic concepts in environment and
behavior series)
    Bibliography: p.
    Includes index.
    1. Environmental psychology—Research. 2. Archi-
tectural design—Psychological aspects. I. Title.
II. Series: Brooks/Cole basic concepts in environment
and behavior series.
BF353.Z44   155.9   80–14292
ISBN 0–8185–0375–0

Acquisition Editor: *William H. Hicks*
Project Development Editor: *Claire Verduin*
Manuscript Editor: *Rephah Berg*
Production Staff: *John Bergez and Jennifer Young*
Interior Design: *Jamie Sue Brooks*
Illustrations: *Lori Heckelman*
Cover Illustration: *Ascending and Descending* by M. C. Escher, © BEELDRECHT,
        Amsterdam/VAGA, New York, 1980. Collection Haags Gemeente museum.
Typesetting: *Graphic Typesetting Service, Los Angeles, California*

SERIES FOREWORD

The study of environment and behavior has shown a rapid development in recent decades; we expect that interest in this field will continue at a high level in the future. As a young and informative area, it has many exciting qualities. For example, the analysis of the relationship between human behavior and the physical environment has attracted researchers from many fields in the *social sciences,* such as psychology, sociology, geography, and anthropology, and from the *environmental design* fields, such as architecture, urban and regional planning, and interior design. The multidisciplinary character of this field has led to an atmosphere of stimulation, cross-fertilization, and, yes, even confusion and difficulty in communication. Furthermore, because of the diversity in intellectual styles and goals of its participants, research on environment and behavior has as often dealt with applied, real-world problems of environmental design as it has treated basic and theoretical issues.

These factors, coupled with the relatively young stage of development of the field, led us to believe that a series of short books on different areas of the environment and behavior field would be useful to students, researchers, and practitioners. Our view was that the study of environment and behavior had not yet firmed up to the point that a single volume would do justice to the wide range of topics now being studied or to the variety of audiences interested in the field. Furthermore, it became clear to us that new topical areas have emerged over the past decade and that some vehicle is necessary to facilitate the evolutionary growth of the field.

For these reasons, Brooks/Cole established the present series of books on environment and behavior with the following goals in mind: first, we endeavored to develop a series of short volumes on areas of research and knowledge that are relatively well established and are characterized by a reasonably substantial body of knowledge. Second, we have recruited authors from a diversity of disciplines who bring to bear a variety of perspectives on various subjects in the field. Third, we asked authors not only to summarize research and knowledge on their topic but also to set forth a "point of view," if not a theoretical orientation, in their book. It was our intention, therefore, that these volumes be more than textbooks in the usual sense of the term—that they not only summarize existing knowledge in an understandable way but also, we hope, advance the field intellectually. Fourth, we wanted the books in the series to be useful to a broad range of students and readers. We planned for the volumes to be educationally valuable to students and professionals from different fields in the social sciences and environmental-design fields and to be of interest to readers with different levels of formal professional training. As part of our broad and flexible strategy, the series will allow instructors in a variety of fields teaching a variety of courses to select different combinations of volumes to meet their particular course needs. In so doing, an instructor might select several books for a course or use a small number of volumes as supplementary reading material.

Because the series is open-ended and not restricted to a particular body of content, we hope that it will not only serve to summarize knowledge in the field of environment and behavior but also contribute to the growth and development of this exciting area of study.

Irwin Altman
Daniel Stokols
Lawrence S. Wrightsman

FOREWORD

Several Invitations to Several Groups of Readers

Donald T. Campbell

It gives me a special pleasure to invite several quite distinct groups of readers to this very fine book by my friend John Zeisel. Let me list all of you first before I explain why I extend each of these several invitations.

- Undergraduates, graduate students, and practitioners in architecture, industrial design, landscape architecture, interior design, and city planning.
- Policy scientists and program-evaluation professionals who are called upon to engage in environment-behavior studies.
- Instructors in research methods in the environment-behavior professions.
- Instructors in applied social-science research methods.
- Program-evaluation methodologists and advocates of an experimenting society.

For those of you who are or will be engaged in the professions of deliberate environmental change, and who do not at all aspire to be research methodologists even for your own field, this book has several distinct values. It invites you to treat each new project not only as an opportunity to apply the skill and wisdom you have already acquired but also as an exploration that can expand that skill and wisdom. From the title on—design itself as a mode of inquiry—it provides both inspiration and commonsense suggestions for learning from your innovations. It will encourage you to collaborate with your clients in still bolder explorations of alternatives that you and they might not otherwise dare try. It will even enable them and you to look with pride on a noble mistake—a mistake no more costly than the banalities you might otherwise commit in the name of timidity —for risking such mistakes is part of your duty to add to the wisdom of the profession you utilize.

This book does a remarkable job of teaching the whole scope of social-science methods, from philosophy of science to doorstep interviewing, without the prerequisites that would exclude many designers from the usual text (statistical methods, formal experimental design, sociological and psychological theories of human behavior, formal courses in philosophy of science). Zeisel's mode of instruction is to start where you are, with a concrete problem you understand, and to illustrate the methodological alternative in that setting before presenting it in abstract terms. Not only will this training help you to become practitioners of environmental change and intelligent readers of research literature, it will also be a resource for low-cost, informal ways of learning more from your own practice —even through efforts so obvious but so neglected as a two-year-later interview or a questionnaire directed to the occupants of a new environment you have designed.

Most of you have esthetic as well as utilitarian goals. This book will help you tell how well you and your client have done for all types of goals. Some of you will want to develop a unique personal style or "signature." Why not make it also a *tested* style, instead of stubbornly persisting in self-defeating idiosyncrasies? There are plenty of intelligent idiosyncrasies and intelligent versions of your favorite thematic emphasis.

This book can also bring home to you how ambiguous and equivocal are most judgments of effect in natural situations, how many recurrent "optical illusions" and illusions of judgment make our own evaluations of outcomes misleading in ways both overly encouraging and overly discouraging. Greater awareness of the equivocality of inference will help you become a more subtle judge of your project's impact.

This awareness will also, I hope, make you a more self-confident critic of studies presented as definitive social science applied to your area. You, with your site-specific wisdom, are the most competent critic of such studies. You can generate the most relevant and plausible "threats to validity" for a particular study in your field or on your project. Properly understood, this book will help you to keep from being mystified by computer output and elaborate statistical massagings based upon inappropriate assumptions and inadequately controlled and often irrelevant data, so that you will not be cowed into suppressing your doubts and your wise alternative explanations of the outcomes. (I hope it also leads you to demand graphic presentation of the data in its least massaged form as one of the final data presentations.)

Those of you already teaching research methods for the environmental-change professions can improve your teaching by supplementing your present statistical-tools-and-abstractions-first textbook with this text, which reverses the order and presents the need for methodology in concrete settings of obvious professional relevance to your students. It will motivate your students to recognize their own need for the difficult and esoteric skills you must also teach in your more advanced courses. For those of you who are already practicing quantitative, experimental, and quasi-experimental program-evaluation methods and are now called upon to apply your skills in an environment-behavior setting, this book provides both an entré into the specifics of that arena and a review in that setting of methodological maxims you already know. For those professionally practicing *qualitative* ethnographic evaluation, the book will likewise serve to remind you of the need for judgmental discussion of threats to validity and alternative explanations, which cannot be avoided by abandoning quantification and formal procedures. Teachers of applied social-science research methods for any setting will find that the concrete explicitness of the "treatment variables" and settings makes the examples in this book especially useful for conveying general methodological points.

The arenas of deliberate environmental change have a particular relevance for those of us in the field of program evaluation and those who would like our society to become able to learn more about the experiments it undertakes. In our wholesale application of our present techniques to "programs" of all types, an early self-confidence that we knew how to do it and could evaluate any program is being seriously undermined. The frustrations and ambiguities we encounter are chilling the motivation for reform by tempting many in our profession to abandon the goal of impact assessment and thus to abandon the image of an experimenting society. Two major aspects of the problem that have precipitated this loss of heart are the ambiguity and instability of our notions about what the "program" or "reform" consists of and the patent implausibility in many cases of the idea of a program package that could be identified as such for dissemination to other settings. "Community Mental Health Clinics," "Head-Start," "Follow Through," and "Decentralized Decision Making" have all proved to be elusive and unreplicable reforms. And these are among the more specifiable reforms. Governmental tendencies to label what is in actuality only topic-specific revenue sharing as though novel, specifiable alternatives to present practice were involved, and to accompany these with calls for immediate evaluations, have further confused the program-evaluation profession. These are not settings in which we can learn our trade.

In contrast, the innovative alternatives of the deliberate environmental-change professions provide experimental "treatments" that are concrete, often precisely replicable, and subject to precise reexamination as new theoretical understandings focus attention on different attributes. These are the sorts of reforms and programmatic alternatives through which we can improve our competence in the science of program evaluation and in the development of methodology for the experimenting society.

The slum-clearance and public-housing projects of the 1930s were striking social experiments for which we have no formal outcome records (although we have some insightful retrospective speculations). At that time, the architects, builders, and social planners thought they knew what they were doing; they were not aware that they were experimenting with one alternative among many possible ones. We missed that chance. Now we can only look with regret at the row after row of identical highrises, all repeating the same mistakes, and wish that there had been a deliberate variation in the alternatives generated by the planners and architects, plus outcome measures. When the great Model Cities programs came along in the 1950s and 1960s, Congress and the Washington administration, influenced by the ideology of social experimentation, set aside funds specifically for evaluation. But when the local Model Cities administrators went to colleges and universities for help in evaluation, the skills were not there. Nor did the Model Cities administrators understand how to implement their innovations so as to optimize impact assessment. No book that I know of will do more than this one to ensure that, when the political will to redesign our cities next returns, we will be ready to learn from our experiments.

PREFACE

This book is about using environment-behavior (E-B) research to make better design decisions and to develop knowledge. *Environment* refers to the physical, administrative, and social attributes of settings in which people live, work, and play. To a shopper, for example, a supermarket environment comprises aisles, shopping carts, and check-out counters; administrative rules, regulations, and prices; and other people—how friendly they are, how well they know one another, how they act.

Behavior refers to thing people do, including thinking, feeling, and seeing, as well as talking with others and moving around. This book focuses on how to find out how people behave in reaction to environments. Do people lie, sit, stand, or jump on park benches? When they move into a new home, do tenants tear down any walls? What do people feel when they see an all-glass, modern building in downtown Atlanta? How do tourists avoid getting lost when they try to find their way around an old city such as Amsterdam?

My topic, then, is E-B *research*—planning it, doing it, and using its results. The most effective way to study E-B problems is to employ several methods in parallel, the choice of methods depending on the specific problems and the research situation. I argue that applied E-B researchers need to participate in *design* decisions if they are going to help create natural environmental laboratories. Designers can contribute to a shared body of E-B knowledge if they make design decisions with an eye toward eventual evaluation.

I hope my readers will include members of at least the following groups:

- practicing *designers* and students of design, both graduate and undergraduate, who are interested in building a shared body of E-B knowledge;
- environment-behavior *researchers*, both students and practitioners, who want to understand and control the effects of the research tools they use;
- *instructors* of applied research methods at the graduate and undergraduate levels who want to see how social-science methods can be tailored to the study of problems in one particular field;
- policy and program *evaluators* in the experimenting society who want to carry out E-B evaluations of existing environments or who want to use such studies as examples of the useful information that committed, multidisciplinary efforts can yield.

The book has two parts. In Part One, I discuss design, research, and what researchers and designers can achieve if they work together. More specifically, I address such questions as: What can people do better by organizing their inquiry as research? What goes on in researchers' and designers' minds when they apply their skills? How can a model of these cognitive processes be used to improve the way research and design are carried out? How are research and design activities similar? How are they different? How can researchers and designers exploit their differences to get something out of working together? On what immediate problems can the two professions work better if they work together? What are some possible long-range benefits to people who collaborate?

I present a description of design that people can use to organize their own designing to achieve what they want (Chapter 1), and I stress the (often overlooked) creative and inventive attributes of research (Chapter 2). One reason researchers and designers may choose to work together is to better control the effects of their decisions, especially when the effects lie in the realm of the other discipline (Chapter 3). Another reason is that persons in one discipline, by learning the conceptual tools of the other, can define and approach their own problems in new ways (Chapter 4). I treat research as a set of activities designed to help solve problems in specific situations (Chapter 5). Research quality I describe as the degree to which the research can be shared, used, and improved upon by other people (Chapter 6).

In Part Two, I describe how to carry out E-B research to achieve specific purposes. I discuss five research methods: observing physical traces, such as paths across a lawn or decorations on a living-room wall, to see how people have affected their physical surroundings (Chapter 7); observing behavior in its environmental context to see how people use physical settings (Chapter 8); focused interviewing to probe how individuals define specific situations they have experienced (Chapters 9 and 11); using structured questionnaires to gather data about perceptions, attitudes, and aspirations that can be summarized across individuals to groups (Chapters 10 and 11); and using archival methods—for instance, analyzing documents such as newspapers and institutional records—to turn data recorded for other reasons into information useful in solving E-B problems (Chapter 12). I describe in somewhat greater detail a special E-B archival technique: analyzing the behavioral implications of architectural plans.

Each example in the book is drawn from an actual project in the emerging multidisciplinary field of E-B research; their sources are available in bookstores or libraries. The examples range from basic research like Altman, Nelson, and Lett's study of the behavioral ecology of homes (1972) to applied research like Howell and Epp's design guidelines for shared spaces suited to the needs of older people (1976). I discuss studies to plan environments, like Snyder and Ostrander's behavioral program for an older-veterans' residence in upstate New York (1974), and studies to evaluate environments, like Keller's research on a planned-unit housing development in New Jersey (1976). In explaining methods throughout the book, I draw on informal discussions several of these authors were gracious enough to have with me about the problems and opportunities their research provided them. I have chosen these examples to reinforce a major theme of this book: researchers and designers who want to use E-B research methods to solve important and interesting problems must know how to tailor their research to the particular questions and situations they are investigating.

Methodologists and designers who do not have a mental picture of the field of environment-behavior studies can develop one by reading the following books, which lie squarely inside this eclectic field. Some represent substantive and theoretical roots of E-B studies; others are more recent. Although other significant works are needed to give the full picture, this list provides an overview of the field:

Christopher Alexander, *Notes on the Synthesis of Form* (1964)
Irwin Altman, *The Environment and Social Behavior* (1975)
Roger Barker, *Ecological Psychology* (1968)
Paul Bell et al., *Environmental Psychology* (1978)
David Canter, *The Psychology of Place* (1977)
Clare Cooper, *Easter Hill Village* (1975)
Roger Downs and David Stea (Eds.), *Image and Environment* (1973)
Leon Festinger et al., *Social Pressures in Informal Groups* (1950)
Herbert Gans, *The Urban Villagers* (1962)
Erving Goffman, *The Presentation of Self in Everyday Life* (1959), and *Behavior in Public Places* (1963)
Robert Gutman (Ed.), *People and Buildings* (1972)
Edward Hall, *The Hidden Dimension* (1966)
Jane Jacobs, *The Death and Life of Great American Cities* (1961)
Christopher Jones, *Design Methods* (1970)
Jon Lang et al. (Eds.), *Designing for Human Behavior* (1974)
Kevin Lynch, *The Image of the City* (1960)
William Michelson, *Man and His Urban Environment* (1970)
Constance Perin, *With Man in Mind* (1970)
Harold Proshansky et al., *Environmental Psychology* (1970)
Amos Rapoport, *House Form and Culture* (1969)
Robert Sommer, *Personal Space* (1969)
Eugene Webb et al., *Unobtrusive Measures* (1966)
John Zeisel, *Sociology and Architectural Design* (1975)

Acknowledgments

There are three classes of people I would like to thank for contributing to this volume: those who directly contributed to its development through discussions, arguments, and editorial help; those who taught me what I know and who are therefore indirect contributors; and those authors from whose work I have learned and who are thus contributors twice removed.

Among people in the first class, Elizabeth Kline is responsible for clear writing in the book, especially when the reader can easily understand complex ideas. Gerard de Zeeuw is responsible for paradoxes. Thanks to many hours of argument I understand that problems provide opportunities to learn how to solve them and that simplicity is not necessarily clarity. Polly Welch organized the background material for examples and most of the methods. More important, Polly helped to establish the approach taken toward each method in Part Two. Barry Korobkin (1976) uncovered for himself—and, in turn, for me—the significance of "imaging" in design. Imaging remains a crucial tool in establishing links between research information and design decisions.

Irwin Altman, at an Environmental Design Research Association conference, told me to go away to a mountaintop and write this book. He has commented on it critically yet gently. He knows how to use his belief in others to get them to do what he wants them to do—and what they want to do, too. Stephen Demos gave me the chance to try out the ideas for Part One in a design studio. It was this teaching at Harvard's Graduate School of Design that gave me personal insights into how designers go about developing designs. Don Conway provided, in the Research Advisory Panel of the American Institute of Architects, a vehicle for discussing and learning about the needs of practicing architects. Eva Zeisel disputed all my ideas about design and thereby improved them incalculably. Don Campbell suggested I stop rewriting the manuscript.

Other people who have contributed ideas and critical readings to this volume include students, colleagues, family, and friends: Mary Griffen, Andy Seidel, Jan Reizenstein, David Strombom, Derk de Jonge, Bill Wilson, Katherine Murphy, David MacFayden, Gayle Epp, Gary Hack, Eric von Hippel, William Porter, Hans Zeisel, Rephah Berg, John Bergez, and my second and third editors, Dan Stokols and Larry Wrightsman.

People from whom I have learned include teachers, students, colleagues, and friends. Two persons stand out: Paul F. Lazarsfeld and Robert K. Merton. These two sociologists *were* the Columbia University Department of Sociology when I went to school there. Lazarsfeld taught me that it is irrelevant to know how to count things if you do not first know how to look. His jointly edited *Language of Social Research* (1965) showed me that research is a problem-solving tool, the use of which enriches both the tool and the user. Merton taught me that well thought-out concepts are useful for looking at the world in order to do to it what you want. The "glasses" sociologists put on when examining problems are as useful and unique as those of the doctor, lawyer, or physical scientist. His *Social Theory and Social Structure* (1957) is a model of clear and concise writing that I have used since I first picked it up.

Other people who have had an important influence on my writing and thinking about the uses of research include Kenneth J. Lenihan, Ann Ferebee, Alan Barton, Brent Bolin, and Ilse Zeisel.

A number of books and articles were important to my thinking as I wrote this book. In several cases I developed ideas along the lines they established. Although I have incorporated these arguments in discussions of my own and have referenced the sources, some deserve particular recognition: Barton and Lazarsfeld, "Some Functions of Qualitative Analysis in Social Research" (1969); Merton, Fiske, and Kendall, *The Focused Interview* (1956), which served as the model for Chapter 9; Webb et al., *Unobtrusive Measures* (1966); Payne, *The Art of Asking Questions* (1951); Hyman, *Survey Design and Analysis* (1955: 66–89); Galtung, *Theory and Methods of Social Research* (1967: 315–340).

These acknowledgments would not be complete without mention of two institutions that supported and sheltered me at different times while the ideas in this book were being nurtured and developed. The first is now defunct. It was the Bureau of Applied Social Research at Columbia University, directed by Alan Barton. The Bureau was a unique setting: it required that you work and that you think, but it looked the other way and let you sit in your office when you had other things to do, such as write a dissertation or study for doctoral exams.

The Netherlands Institute for Advanced Study in the Humanities and Social Sciences—a brainchild of the Dutch government—is equally unique. It brings together annually 25 Dutch and 15 international scholars to do their own work and to learn from one another. The majority of the writing and rewriting of this book was done from October 1977 to August 1978 at NIAS. Without the nurturing of NIAS—a more than suitable substitute for the mountaintop Irv Altman recommended—this book would not have been written.

John Zeisel

CONTENTS

CHAPTER   10   STANDARDIZED QUESTIONNAIRES   157

CHAPTER   11   ASKING QUESTIONS: TOPICS AND FORMAT   178

CHAPTER   12   ARCHIVES   197

RECAPITULATING THEMES   226

PART ONE

RESEARCH AND DESIGN

Chapter 1

DESIGN: IMAGES, PRESENTATIONS, TESTS

"Inquiry is the creation of knowledge or understanding; it is the reaching out of a human being beyond himself to a perception of what he may be or could be, or what the world could be or ought to be."

C. West Churchman
The Design of Inquiring Systems

During a physical design project, an individual or team generates ideas for changing the existing physical environment and presents them in a form to guide construction. Design begins when an individual or team first thinks about the project—for example, a building, an open-space plan, or an object. It includes a stage when detailed working drawings of a project are given to contractors instructing them how the designers expect the project to be built. It includes a stage when contractor and designer negotiate changes in design to respond to problems that arise during construction. The process formally ends when construction is completed. Designers conventionally break down this process into contractually binding stages: programming, preliminary design, final design, working drawings, construction supervision.

Design is difficult to describe because it includes so many intangible elements such as intuition, imagination, and creativity—which are essential to research as well. Nevertheless, several analysts have done a remarkable job of articulating parts of this process (Hillier & Leaman, 1974; Korobkin, 1976; and others). Their descriptions apply to a prototypical design process that, in an architect's office, might go something like this:

Posed with a design problem—let us say for a new elementary school—an architect gathers information about the specific site and about elementary schools generally. She does this by visiting the site, having discussions with clients and users, and studying books.

Through a series of trials, she generates a preliminary mental image of an "elementary school," responding to the information she has gathered, her personal experiences, and mental images of schools she knows and likes.

She draws general rough sketches or diagrams to begin to flesh out this image and reviews them with people in the office, with the client, and by herself. Possibly she even begins to present her concept by building rough working models.

3

Stepping back from her presentations, she asks herself whether they do justice to her concept and to the information she has. She might feel she needs to gather more data to adequately assess them. In this way the architect tests and refines her concept and her information.

She repeats this process several times within days, hours, or even minutes until she feels she has begun to generate a clearer mental image, one that corresponds both to her sketches and to the information.

Until now, each sketch might be different from previous ones, yet influenced by studies of previous sketches. She may even have developed several alternative but equally fruitful concepts.

Concept sketches and diagrams at this stage include ideas about overall building image, major spaces, and relationships among building components. These she shows to her clients and possibly to the building's eventual users. Both groups may have been consulted earlier in the process as well. Now they may suggest revisions, discuss alternatives, or request the designer to pursue a whole new direction.

After appropriate groups improve and approve concept sketches, the architect and her team think about and then draw schematic drawings—the first step in moving from concept to building. Schematic drawings begin to present specific room relationships, how big rooms are, where doors and windows are located, and where facilities will be.

As the architect designs schematic drawings, she repeatedly checks to make sure drawings are true to the agreed-upon concept, to government regulations, and to performance standards dictated by theory and empirical work.

She simultaneously develops and refines the overall design concept, paying attention to how its individual parts relate, how the whole building "hangs together," and how the building fits in context.

This process of design development results in "presentation drawings": plans, sections, elevations, perspective renderings that give clients an idea of what the final product will be. Such drawings specify what attributes the building will have, from dimensions to material to color.

When client groups review presentation drawings, they once again may respond with suggestions for improvement. At this point the designer again negotiates with clients in order to make decisions meet their needs.

After presentation drawings are approved, the architect and her team articulate their ideas in "working drawings." Working drawings detail for the contractor how each part of the building is to be built—from foundation to doorknobs.

While working drawings are being drafted, each decision is checked again to see that it meets legal regulations such as building and safety standards and that it reflects the initial design concept. Major conceptual design shifts made this late in the process can be costly.

When the design team feels that working drawings adequately present its ideas, when regulatory personnel have checked that working drawings meet legal standards, and when specialist consultants have reported that their criteria have been met, working drawings are complete. At this point a contractor is hired to construct the building.

The contractor constructs the building according to the drawings and written specifications in documents. If he does not understand a specification, has difficulty securing materials, or for some reason feels a change is necessary, he reports the problem to the architect. When both agree that a change is required, the architect issues an official change order. At this late stage, modifications in design are carried out with great care.

In most cases architects remain as construction supervisors on their projects until specifications have been officially fulfilled and the project is considered built.

Architects may return to their buildings after occupancy to learn more from what they have done. This information is useful for future design.

WHY DESCRIBE DESIGN?

Describing the design process may help designers and teachers of design understand their own behavior and thereby improve their design ability. Analysis may also be useful for researchers and designers who want to work together.

Although outsiders can directly observe behavioral and representational parts of designing, they cannot directly observe cognitive design processes taking place inside someone's head. Research evidence for describing what is going on when designers think is, therefore, necessarily indirect and inferential or intro-spective. Evidence includes personal experience (Jones, 1970; Korobkin, 1976), participant observation (Zeisel, 1975), stream-of-consciousness reports by design-ers designing (Foz, 1972), and analysis of successive design drawings (Foz, 1972). Some design theorists look to other disciplines to provide illuminating analogies: linguistics (Hillier & Leaman, 1974), artificial intelligence (Foz, 1972; Hillier & Leaman, 1974), biological evolution (Hillier & Leaman, 1974).

Design methodologists' theoretical, personal, and practical reasons for analyzing design result in their emphasizing different elements and using differ-ent analogies to describe how parts of the process fit together. In a particular situation one description may be more helpful than another to designers or researchers in achieving their ends. Comparing such descriptions is likely to provide both a useful, multifaceted picture of design and interesting problems for further study.

FIVE CHARACTERISTICS OF DESIGNING

Physical design inventively mixes together ideas, drawings, information, and a good many other ingredients to create something where nothing was before. Design can also be seen as an ordered process in which specific activities are loosely organized to make decisions about changing the physical world to achieve identifiable goals. However one thinks about design and for whatever purposes, five characteristics emerge as useful tools for understanding what designers do.

Five Design Characteristics

I. Three Elementary Activities

The complex activity called "designing" interconnects three constituent activities: imaging, presenting, and testing.

II. Two Types of Information

Information used in designing tends to be useful in two ways: as a heuristic catalyst for imaging and as a body of knowledge for testing.

III. Shifting Visions of Final Product

Designers continually modify predictions about their final result in response to new information and insight. The design process is thus a series of conceptual shifts or creative leaps.

IV. Toward a Domain of Acceptable Responses

Designers aim to reach one acceptable response within a range of possible solutions. This domain of acceptance is measured largely by how well a product is adapted to its environment and how coherent constituent parts of the product are with one another.

V. Development through Linked Cycles: A Spiral Metaphor

Conceptual shifts and product development in design occur as the result of repeated, iterative movement through the three elementary design activities.

I.   Three Elementary Activities

Designers working on an actual project do not just sit down and "design"; it is not a one-dimensional activity. Rather, like other developmental processes, such as writing a book or bringing up children, design is a complex activity more usefully thought of as including several analytically distinct elementary activities: imaging, presenting, and testing.

The first activity I will discuss is imaging (Korobkin, 1976). I might have said "The first activity in design is imaging," but this would have reinforced the false popular idea that using one's imagination is the most important element in creative action and that any design process must begin with an act of imagination. In reality, the starting point for any developmental process is among its least important aspects (Bruner, 1973: 160; Popper, 1972: 34, 72, 104).

Imaging. Imaging is the ability to "go beyond the information given," as Bruner (1973) calls the process of seeing something where nothing seems to have been before. This activity, often called "real creativity" by laypersons, might most accurately be called "imaging" after the verb *to image,* which the *Oxford English Dictionary* defines as

> to form a mental image of: to conceive (a) something to be executed: to devise a plan, and (b) an object of perception or thought: to imagine, to picture in the mind, to represent *to oneself,* as in Coleridge, 1818, "Whatever is admitted to be conceivable must be imageable," and in Browning, 1855, "Image the whole, then execute the parts". . .

Imaging means forming a general, sometimes only fuzzy, mental picture of a part of the world. In design as well as in other types of endeavors, images are often visual; they provide designers a larger framework within which to fit specific pieces of a problem as they are resolved.

How a designer's image is formed has been the topic of much discussion but little empirical research. The concept is well expressed in Jones' picture (1970: 46) of a "black-box designer," reflecting his interpretation of how Osborn (1963), Gordon (1961), Matchett (1968), and Broadbent (1966) describe design.

Designers can use their visions of eventual solutions to define better the design problem they are working on and to guide their search for answers. Comparing a design against a mental image makes visible where the design can be improved and perhaps where the image itself might be modified (Foz, 1972). One hypothesis about the nature of images is that they are deductive constructs akin to the "conjectures" that Popper (1963) describes as essential to scientific progress; that is, these visions of a "solution in principle" developed early in a design process parallel researchers' working hypotheses (Hillier, Musgrove, & O'Sullivan, 1972). Just as working hypotheses are refined during scientific exploration, images are developed during design activity.

Images, however, are more than just a person's internalized pictures. They represent subjective knowledge, used to develop and organize ideas in such areas

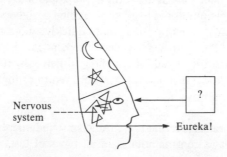

Black-box designer. From *Design Methods: Seeds of Human Futures*, by J. C. Jones. Copyright 1970 by John Wiley & Sons Ltd. Reprinted by permission.

as visual perception and learning (Bruner, 1973), language (Polanyi, 1958), child development (Piaget & Inhelder, 1969), and economics and politics (Boulding, 1956).

In understanding an internal process like imaging, we are unfortunately constrained to studying its external manifestations: (1) how designers present their images to others and to themselves and (2) how their observable behavior changes while developing internal images of situations.

Presenting. Designers sketch, draw plans, build models, take photographs, and in many other ways externalize and communicate their images. It takes skill not only to present an idea well but to choose the mode of presentation best suited to a particular time in the design process. Designers present ideas to make them visible so that they themselves and others can use and develop them. Presenting includes the very important characteristic that for each design one must choose and organize only some elements from a larger number. Presenting includes both variety reduction, in that "more and more specific drawings . . . exclude more and more detailed design possibilities" (Hillier, Musgrove, & O'Sullivan, 1972: page 29.3.9), and opportunity expansion, in that new problems for further design resolution are made explicit.

Of course, if images and their presentations were identical, it would not be possible to use one to clarify the other. Rather, designers present not images themselves but the implications of images (Simon, 1969: 15). The importance of "representation" may be stated in an extreme way by asserting that "solving a problem simply means representing it so as to make the solution transparent" (Simon, 1969: 77). Whether or not this conscious oversimplification is tenable, "a deeper understanding of how representations are created and how they contribute to the solution of problems will become an essential component in the future theory of design" (Simon, 1969: 77).

In a pilot study of how architects with different design experience solved a short two-hour sketch problem, the more experienced architects tended to be better able to make decisions in the form of presentations (Foz, 1972). They did not agonize over decisions as did beginners. Skilled designers used "three dimensional representation . . . more often, more quickly, more realistically" (1972: 72). In other words, the more experienced designers could quickly sketch out an idea, draw it, or build a model—even though that presentation may not have been perfect. They knew that soon they would return to the model with a fresh eye to evaluate and improve it.

Testing. Appraisals, refutations, criticisms, judgments, comparisons, reflections, reviews, and confrontations are all types of tests. After presenting a design idea in whatever form, designers step back with a critical eye and examine their products (Hillier et al., 1972; Korobkin, 1976), sometimes in groups and sometimes alone (Christopherson, 1963). Design testing means comparing tentative presentations against an array of information like the designer's and the clients' implicit images, explicit information about constraints or objectives, degrees of internal design consistency, and performance criteria—economic, technical, and sociological.

An interesting dimension of the design activity of testing is that designers look both backward and forward simultaneously: backward to determine how good a tentative product is, forward to refine the image being developed and to modify the next presentation. While reviewing, criticizing, and analyzing any presentation, designers are preparing the way for the next creative leap.

Although testing contributes to design innovation, it also makes a designer's task more manageable in the face of the potentially infinite number of alternative responses to any problem (Jones, 1970). Testing in design makes it "possible to replace blind searching of alternatives by an intelligent search that uses both external criteria and the results of partial search to find short cuts across the unknown territory" (Jones, 1970: 55).

Testing is a feed-back and feed-forward process, adjusting the relation between a design product as it develops and the many criteria and qualities the product is intended to meet.

In sum, imaging, presenting, and testing are elementary activities constituting a complex process called "design."

II. Two Types of Information

During a project, designers define problems that require them to add to what they know. Gaps in knowledge may be specific (what is the lightest readily available building material in Nigeria) or general (what about life in Nigerian universities is applicable to the university I have been asked to design there). Among the problems designers face are technological, chemical, economic, cultural, psychological, esthetic, social, and ecological ones. To cope with the great amount of information they need, some designers and researchers propose rationally organizing explicitly formulated architectural information to make it easily retrievable.

Many practicing designers and some design methodologists react by pointing out that proposals that fit discrete bits of scientific information into an artificially rationalized design process hinder design creativity and overlook more important information needs that designers have (Hillier et al., 1972; Rapoport, 1969a).

Korobkin (1976) elegantly resolves this debate, reasoning that having a clear idea of what different forms of information are useful to designers, and when, can stimulate design innovation. Korobkin groups information in the design process into two categories (1976: 20):

> *Image information* . . . provides a general understanding of important issues and of physical ideas pertinent to their resolution.

Test information . . . [is] directly pertinent to evaluating the good and bad points of a given hypothesis design.

This distinction is not necessarily one of information content. It primarily clarifies different purposes that the information serves.

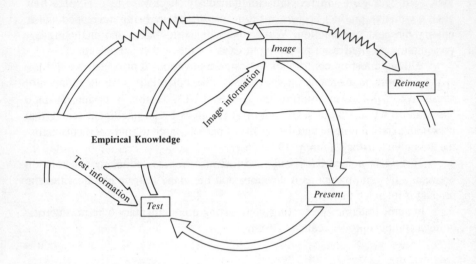

Designers use "image information" heuristically as an empirical source for basic cognitive design decisions: What is the meaning of a school in a child's life? What is life like for a handicapped person? What do teenagers see as their neighborhoods in suburban areas? Image information conveys a feeling or a mood of some environment. It cannot be used to evaluate isolated specifics of a design concept. Test information drawn from the same body of knowledge is useful to evaluate specific design alternatives. For example, is it easier for most elderly handicapped people to push themselves up with a horizontal grab bar next to a toilet or to pull themselves up on a slanting grab bar? (For most, a horizontal bar is easier.) (Steinfeld, 1975: 98).

Using the same information in this twofold way is remarkably efficient and contributes directly to design as a learning process. It also provides an important link to understand the relation between how research and design are carried out, in that "information which has been used heuristically [to help generate conjectures], can also be used to test the new conjectures" (Hillier, Musgrove, & O'Sullivan, 1972).

III. Shifting Visions of Final Product

What happens when designers test the responses they present? What do designers image? How do designs develop once conceived? Discussing questions like these may shed light on the dynamics of design.

As we have seen, designers form images of future products they intend to design. One reason designing is intriguing is that "the final outcome of design has to be assumed before the means of achieving it can be explored: designers have to work backwards in time from an assumed effect upon the world to the beginning of a chain of events that will bring the effect about" (Jones, 1970: 9–10). Designers must predict the future and then figure out how to get there! Of course, such predictions are not precise; they are approximate solutions that the design process is meant to make less approximate.

Images rarely appear fully formed in one cataclysmic blinding vision. Most images are developed and refined by means of a series of modest "creative leaps." The process by which such leaps are made has been called many things: variety reduction (Hillier & Leaman, 1974), reworking subobjectives (Archer, 1969), restoring balance (Sanoff, 1977), hypothesis refinement (O'Doherty, 1963), transformation (Schon, 1974). Creative leaping is triggered by testing the presentation of a tentative design response against quality criteria within the situation and its context to find out where the response is strong and where it is weak.

Making explicit tacit attributes of a design through testing helps designers reimage and re-present their designs with greater precision (Schon, 1974). Testing makes contradictions apparent (1) among elements of a design at a particular stage of development and (2) between the design and previously accepted requirements it was intended to meet. Designers can at any time generate and draw on additional information to refine their ideas and trigger further conceptual leaps.

Designers use the design process to learn, through testing, from themselves: "New [design] options are versions of earlier ones growing out of the thinking that went into the rejection of earlier ones" (Schon, 1974: 17–18). Critically analyzing tentative design responses and adding new information can progressively improve designs (Asimow, 1962; Guerra, 1969).

Designs develop cumulatively. Concepts originating in general form are developed to an acceptable level in a series of presentations, tests, and reimages. But what does "an acceptable level" mean? What is optimization (Markus, 1969) or fit (Alexander, 1964)? When do designers stop reducing variety? What is the goal of the design process?

IV. Toward a Domain of Acceptable Responses

Built buildings, manufactured objects, or enacted regulations may be looked at as preordained, perfect end points that people reach by designing. To improve the way we design, however, it may be more useful to see final design products as unique responses to particular problems. These theoretically fall within a set of alternatives controlled by things like our imagination, available technological knowledge, ethical values and personal skills, resources in the actual design situation, and our definition of quality.

We can influence available alternatives by adjusting any of these values— for example, by using our imagination, increasing our substantive knowledge, or finding additional time and money resources. Paradoxically, however, no matter what designers do to control it, there is an infinite array of equally good potential responses in any *domain of acceptable responses* (Archer, 1969: 83).

If we think of design as a process of choosing the best solution from among possible alternatives, we run into difficulties. First, among an infinite number of possible alternatives there will be an infinite number of best ones. Second, for complex problems there may be no such thing as a best solution—and any problem can be as complex as one wants to see it.

> When we come to the design of systems as complex as cities, or buildings, or economies, we must give up the aim of creating systems that will optimize some hypothesized utility function; and we must consider whether differences do not represent highly desirable variants in the design process rather than alternatives to be evaluated as "better" or "worse." Variety, within the limits of satisfactory constraints, may be a desirable end in itself, among other reasons, because it permits us to attach value to the search as well as its outcome—to regard the design process as itself a valued activity for those who participate in it [Simon, 1969: 75].[1]

After such a discussion one may well ask how designers decide what is acceptable. On what basis do they test and improve their designs? How do they decide on a final design to be built? In other words, what are their criteria for acceptability and quality?

Acceptability and quality criteria. These difficulties become clearer when we see designing as something going on in response to actual problems in actual situations. In such situations designers make decisions about practical, substantive attributes of the objects being designed. Such attributes might be, for example, material properties, like weight, elasticity, strength; properties of the physical setting of the object, like light, degree of urbanization, soil conditions; or administrative properties of the object, like cost, marketability, construction scheduling. Designers use such attributes, along with available real-world resources, to help test and improve their ideas and to help them decide when to end this process for any particular project.

Attributes of designed objects in actual settings can be grouped into two categories. The first is *contextual responsiveness,* or the degree to which objects respond to external conditions. In southern climates, for example, do buildings protect users from direct sun while allowing breezes to provide natural cross-ventilation? In different cultures do building forms respond to the cultural expectations of residents (Brolin, 1976)? The second is *internal coherence,* or the degree to which components of a design object are consistent with one another (Archer, 1969: 101; Jones, 1970: 30). For example, in a northern climate do material selection, room arrangement, and site orientation each contribute to

---

[1] From *The Sciences of the Artificial*, by H. A. Simon. Cambridge, Mass.: MIT Press, 1969.

protection from the cold, or does one decision—say, to plan open spaces—counteract the effects of others?

The use of responsiveness and coherence as criteria to evaluate designed objects constitutes a significant link between design and science, as Simon succinctly points out:

> Natural science impinges on an artifact through two . . . terms . . . : the structure of the artifact itself and the environment in which it performs; and symmetrically, an artifact can be thought of as a meeting point—an 'interface' in today's terms—between an 'inner' environment, the substance and organization of the artifact itself, and an 'outer' environment, the surroundings in which it operates [Simon, 1969: 6].

A complementary, two-sided approach to improving and evaluating the acceptability of a designed object underlies the work of the design methodologist Christopher Alexander (1964). Identifying the importance of design appraisal, he describes acceptable designs as those that achieve a degree of "fit" between a "form in question and its context." To him the artifact of design is form and context seen as one, not form alone.

This deceivingly simple idea has profoundly influenced design theory. The term *form* as Alexander (1964) uses it can be replaced by *internal coherence,* and *context* can be replaced by *external responsiveness:*

> *Form [Internal Coherence]:* Indeed, the form itself relies on its own inner organization and on the internal fitness between the pieces it is made of to control its fit as a whole to the context outside [p. 18].

> *Context [External Responsiveness]:* The context is that part of the world which puts demands on this form; anything in the world that makes demands of the form is context [p. 19].

> *Fitness [Acceptability]:* Fitness is a relation of mutual acceptability between these two. In a problem of design we want to satisfy the mutual demands which the two make on one another [p. 19].

A difficulty still remains, however. How do designers decide to stop developing a product? When do they accept it as ready to be built?

Stopping. Changing an environment has effects and side effects. Some may be visible beforehand, others not. Choosing to stop making one's product better means deciding one is willing to risk unintended side effects. What is an acceptable mix of knowing and risk taking in any actual situation reflects conditions like established professional norms, available resources, personal preferences, costs and rewards, and perceived competition.

Actual settings in which people design provide tools for making these decisions. The process of improving a design may stop, for example, when the allotted time and money have been spent and a design review team in the office judges that the product meets office standards. If the designer has an agreement with a client group that it has final say on the project, the group may be used to make the decision to stop.

There are innumerable ways designers can use their surroundings to help them decide when a project is acceptable enough. What is significant is that using quality criteria to improve a design keeps the process going. One cannot rely on the same criteria to set limits—to stop the process. Stopping is the result of someone's deciding that he or she is willing to live with potential, and as yet unseen, side effects of the decision.

V. Development through Linked Cycles: A Spiral Metaphor

The metaphor of design as a spiral process can be used to look at how the various elements in design fit together. A spiral process reflects the following characteristics of design: (1) designers seem to backtrack at certain times—to move away from, rather than toward, the goal of increasing problem resolution; (2) designers repeat a series of activities again and again, resolving new problems with each repetition; and (3) these apparently multidirectional movements together result in one movement directed toward a single action.

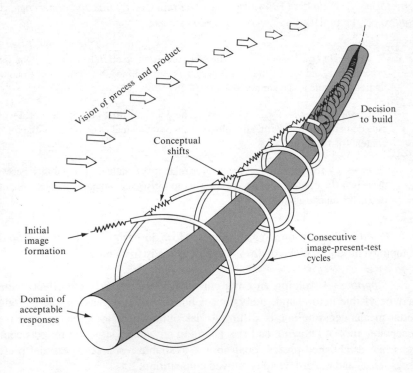

Design development spiral

Backtracking. Throughout a design project, designers return to problems already studied to revise or adjust earlier tentative decisions (Archer, 1969: 95). For example, a landscape architect designs a park assuming the final budget will support construction of both a wading pool for children and a decorative fountain. Later, finding that the larger playing field he wants costs more than expected, he combines the two water projects into one, which serves as both a fountain and a wading pool.

It might seem more efficient to choose problems to resolve early in the process that do not have to be reexamined later. But this is seldom possible. Each decision designers make, even if they think it is final, has consequences for future steps in the process and, as we have seen, for past ones as well. Problems arise which earlier decisions did not foresee and which cannot be resolved unless a previous decision is revised (Jones, 1970: 68). Backtracking is not only unavoidable, it is essential to improve design quality (Amarel, 1968). One can hope that later knowledge will not necessitate radical changes in earlier decisions, but of course this too occurs. Not surprisingly, a highly valued skill among designers is the ability to foresee consequences of later design decisions for earlier ones.

Testing can be seen as a form of backtracking. "Whenever the designer pauses to evaluate what he has done . . . [he occasions] . . . feedback loops, shuttle action, and other departures from linearity indicated in most models of the decision sequence. These are introspective and retrospective acts; for he looks back to earlier decisions" (Markus, 1969: 112). In sum, backtracking to adjust earlier decisions is an integral part of design, and a spiral metaphor indicates this activity.

Repeating activities with shifting focus. In separate cycles of a design project, designers present, test, and reimage responses to a set of related problems. Each repetition focuses on a different problem. For example, in one cycle a designer may focus on architectural style; in another, on kitchen hardware. A decision in one cycle may determine the context for a decision in the next (for example, a decision about architectural style may limit the range of choices for hardware), but this does not mean that foci are necessarily sequential by size. Designers may find it more efficient to examine very large, very small, and then very large questions than to progress linearly either from large to small or from small to large questions. Urban design decisions about street width may be followed by decisions about street hardware, which in turn are followed by decisions about the modes of transportation the streets will allow.

Design decisions in different cycles can vary also by subject: physical elements like materials or room sizes at one point; at another, systems like heating or plumbing; and at still other times, psychological and social issues like territory or privacy.

Imaging, presenting, and testing may not be equally important in each cycle. Designers may spend more time developing images in earlier cycles and more time presenting them in later ones. Testing can take place so quickly that designers appear to skip it entirely in a cycle; for example, when designers "think with their pen," testing can take place almost simultaneously with presenting and reimaging. In such cases neither actor nor observer may be able to differentiate the activities.

The time designers spend in image/present/test cycles varies. One cycle may last days or weeks before a conceptual leap and eventual reimaging take place. Another may last only seconds. And each activity in a cycle does not begin and end at a discrete point. Where one activity ends and another begins is not clear. Each contains remnants of the previous activity and roots of the next.

One way to envision re-cycling and repetition is to think of design as a conversation among three activities: imaging, presenting, and testing. The discussants remain the same, but the intensity and topics of the conversation change as time passes.

One movement in three. Designers are like good hunters and trackers. They appraise their goal not by rushing straight at it but by continually readjusting their position to gain new perspectives on their prey. Backward movement, repetitions at different levels, and progressively linked cycles combine into one movement leading designers through continual improvement toward the goal of an acceptable response.

Growth and learning are essential parts of design. It is a process that, once started, feeds itself both by drawing on outside information and by generating additional insight and information from within: "In the course of cycling the loop, the designer's perception of his real world problem, his concept of the design solution, grows" (Archer, 1969: 96).

The many adaptations, revisions, and conceptual shifts that take place during design are guided by a designer's vision of the design process leading to action. Something is built.

OVERVIEW

Farmers design when they figure out where and when to plant various crops. Lawyers design when they prepare a strategy for a client's defense. "Everyone designs who devises courses of action aimed at changing existing situations into preferred ones" (Simon, 1969: 55).

What architects, landscape architects, some planners, and other physical designers do can be seen as applying basic principles of action to solving a particular type of problem. Physical design as a formal set of disciplines presents opportunities for self-consciously analyzing design.

This chapter proposes that to organize our own design behavior to achieve the ends we want, it is helpful to see design as a loose ordering of three main activities: imaging, presenting, and testing. The chapter proposes that using a spiral metaphor to describe design enables people to identify some things they can do to use design as a way to grow and learn.

The next chapter describes research—its goals and uses, the way ideas develop, the role of an individual researcher in the process. Differences and similarities between design and research are not pointed out explicitly in every case; yet it should be clear that there is a close kinship between design images and research concepts, design presentations and research hypotheses, and tests in both disciplines.

Chapter 2

RESEARCH: CONCEPTS, HYPOTHESES, TESTS

"A cobblestone is more real than personal relationships, but personal relationships are felt to be more profound because we expect them yet to reveal themselves in unexpected ways, while cobblestones evoke no such expectation."

Michael Polanyi
Personal Knowledge

Research can provide deeper insight into a topic, better understanding of a problem, more clearly defined opportunities for and constraints on possible action, measurement of regularities, and ordered descriptions. Designers face many problems in which they can use environment-behavior (E-B) research to control effects of what they do. What street layout, sign system, and landmark location in a new town will make it easy for residents to feel at home? Why do teenagers vandalize isolated buildings in parks that they themselves could otherwise enjoy? Does high-density living make people friendlier or meaner? What does *density* actually mean?

What is research? It is more than just searching (which can be haphazard) or just solving problems (which can remain merely pragmatic). What researchers want to do is systematically use their experience to learn something to identify and help solve new problems. Presented with a problem, researchers draw on theory, training, accumulated knowledge, and experience to generate tentative ideas about how to solve it. Exploratory hypotheses serve as the basis first for observing and gathering data about the topic and then for describing and understanding it. Making visible the implications of the data leads to improved hypotheses, further data gathering, and so on until the problem is sufficiently redefined and a tenable solution is found.

In the course of their work, investigators develop concepts, formulate hypotheses, and test their ideas. During a research project, investigators carry out these activities in various sequences and combinations and in various ways. This complex activity is called "research."

Anyone can become a researcher by doing normal, everyday things in an orderly way and for interesting, generalizable purposes. The orderly way to do research can be learned rationally and impersonally. The ability to develop interesting concepts—to go beyond the information given—can also be learned. But it is a creative ability, to be learned as one learns a skill.

Doing Research
Developing Concepts

Characteristics
    Approaches
    Preconceptions

Formulating Hypotheses
Classifying hypotheses   Explanatory hypotheses
Empirical Testing
Observing   Sampling

DEVELOPING CONCEPTS

In a research project investigators want to define a concept with which to order information. A research concept does not pop out of the data; it is formed slowly. Investigators may have had a faint vision of it when their project began. They may have glimpsed it when they started to analyze a particular bit of data. They may have realized how to organize their study findings only when the last piece of information became clear.

In the beginning of a project, emerging concepts are visions defining what data to gather. In the middle, information clarifies the concepts. At the end of a successful research project, clearly stated concepts summarize increased insight and define areas where further research can increase precision.

Characteristics

Creative researchers invent and discover. Invention in E-B studies has given us new concepts to order what we see: Sommer gave us personal space (1969), Hall the hidden (spatial) dimension (1966), Gans urban villages (1962), and Lynch the image of the city (1960). Sommer, Hall, Gans, and Lynch carried out research to its full creative potential, giving others new images with which to illuminate part of the world.

The concept "personal space" helps us to see why low lighting levels in bars bring couples closer together, why others get upset when we read over their shoulders, why psychiatric clients feel that counselors who sit far away are not receptive, and why passengers waiting in airports feel uncomfortable when seats bolted to the floor prohibit adjusting their seating arrangements. The concept "city images" helps us understand why most of us see cities in terms of elements like the Eiffel Tower and Times Square (which Lynch calls "nodes"), the Charles River and Lake Michigan (which he calls "edges"), the Los Angeles freeways and the Amsterdam canals ("paths"), and Greenwich Village and Chinatown ("districts").

Polanyi concisely defines the intangible activity of discovery by which an investigator describes something he cannot see:

> How can we concentrate our attention on something we don't know? Yet this is precisely what we are told to do: 'Look at the unknown!'—says Polya [1945]— 'Look at the ends . . . *Look at the unknown*. Look at the conclusion!' No advice could be more emphatic. The seeming paradox is resolved by the fact that even though we have never met the solution, we have a conception of it in the same sense as we have a conception of a forgotten name . . . *we should look at the known data, but not in themselves, rather as clues to the unknown, as pointers to it and parts of it*. We should strive persistently to feel our way towards an understanding of the manner in which these known particulars hang together, both mutually and with the unknown [1958: 127–128].[1]

Explanatory concepts tend to be *holistic;* that is, they describe entities that cannot be analyzed into the sum of their parts without residue. Personal space is not merely the sum of body movements, cultural habits, and attitudes toward one's own body. A designer's office cannot be fully defined by describing the people there, the settings, the rules, the services, and the output. The holistic character of concepts is like that of a chord in music: "The musical chord . . . as long as it is a chord, is utterly different from its component tones. It does not even have tones until it is analyzed. Indeed, one cannot say that it is a synthesized whole until this is done; otherwise it is an elementary phenomenon" (Barnett, 1953: 193).

By reasonably extending creative research concepts, investigators generate new problems to study and new hypotheses. For this reason such a concept is sometimes called a *generating formula:* "a formula capable of summing up in a single descriptive concept a great wealth of particular observations" (Barton & Lazarsfeld, 1969, p. 192). Gans' "urban village" concept is just such a formula. In describing the group of people living in Boston's primarily Italian West End neighborhood during the 1960s, Gans points out an essential contradiction in their lives. Social relations among residents are almost like those in a rural village: people know one another well, they get their news from friends at local bars, and they know who does and does not "belong." But economic and political life are embedded in an urban context: residents work in the city, they elect representatives to the city council, and university students from the city come to the West End to live.

Summing up this neighborhood in the term *urban village* raises a host of

---

[1] From *Personal Knowledge: Towards a Post-Critical Philosophy,* by M. Polanyi. Chicago: University of Chicago Press, 1958.

questions: If village residents hold mainly local values, how do they react to the constant influx of outsiders? Does the village nature of the neighborhood result in tighter social control over crime? What pressures does the urban context exert on family life? With this generating formula in mind, one can identify urban villages in other cities as well. Before Gans' invention these districts were not clearly seen.

Approaches

If research aims at developing concepts, how do researchers do this? One way to go about this murky task is to become as intimate as possible with data and also as distant as possible from them.

Intimacy for one researcher may mean stewing over a particular photograph or staring at a map a respondent has drawn to find what sense can be made of it. Another investigator may look over one computer printout a dozen times or read through a large number of completed questionnaires from beginning to end, getting a feel for what to ask the data. These methods enable an investigator to focus her attention on particulars of diverse phenomena until she begins to see them as a coherent whole, just as a musician practices a piece until it comes together for him. The term *indwelling* is used to refer to these methods, to make clear that they are attempts to become as close as possible to the data—to dwell in them (Polanyi, 1967: 16).

When researchers achieve such internal awareness, they cannot necessarily articulate it—either verbally or diagrammatically. Another step is required to articulate the tacit knowing that indwelling can bring.

Using *analogies* as organizing principles can be this step. Doing so enables researchers to articulate how they envision fitting data together, because analogies help them to use related past experience. In analogies "there is a sameness of relationship—but a substitution of its parts. These parts may be things, or they may be behaviors or ideas. In any event, there is a change of the content . . . but a retention of its shape or form because of the retention of relationships" (Barnett, 1953: 267).

Thinking of analogies to summarize a large body of information enables investigators to temporarily picture and use what they do not know by substituting known elements for gaps in their knowledge. For example, the idea of map reading may help someone describe the way people envision the future, and the idea of a theater lobby may help someone else describe the channeling operations carried out in a hospital emergency room. Analogies provide holistic mental models that can be used to loosely organize data, although these models may not be derivable from the data.

Discovering scientific images and generating scientific concepts demand inspirational, imaginative, and intuitive skills:

> True discovery is not a strictly logical performance, and accordingly, we may describe the obstacle to be overcome in solving a problem as a 'logical gap,' and

speak of the width of the logical gap as the measure of the ingenuity required for solving the problem. 'Illumination' is then the leap by which the logical gap is crossed. It is the plunge by which we gain a foothold at another shore of reality. On such plunges the scientist has to stake bit by bit his entire professional life. . . .

Established rules of inference offer public paths for drawing intelligent conclusions from existing knowledge. The pioneer mind which reaches its own distinctive conclusions by crossing a logical gap deviates from the commonly accepted process of reasoning, to achieve surprising results [Polanyi, 1958: 123].

Preconceptions

Researchers do not approach problems with empty minds. Each researcher knows something about his problem from related empirical work and theories. We have all had personal experiences that influence how we look at the world: early family life, school, trips, friends, professional training, books. As we think and talk, we draw on a mental picture of our topic, either vague or clear, held either consciously or subconsciously (Korobkin, 1976). When our topic is a physical environment, we call our mental picture a "cognitive map"; when our topic is less tangible and more conceptual, a related term—*cognitive image*—can be used (Boulding, 1973). The more we think we know about a topic, the more detailed is our cognitive image of it. The preconceived images that investigators begin research projects with can distort what researchers see, bias explanations, and limit how concepts develop. But they do not have to.

Preconceptions can be helpful if they are made explicit as a first step in research projects. For example, in a study of how people work and feel in open-plan offices—offices without walls—one researcher might begin with a preconception that everyone will be miserable because there is no privacy. Another investigator expects everyone to be smiling and happy because the lack of walls brings people together. These preconceptions, or advance guesses, no matter where they come from, can be used as reference points for future observations.

Explicit preconceptions like these can sensitize researchers to see and to be surprised by what they see. In our hypothetical open-plan office, because both researchers thought about workers' happiness, both will look for indicators of attitudes: smiles or frowns, backslapping, chatting, angry looks, fights. Both researchers will be able to improve their pictures of the situation. Each preconception made explicit at the beginning of an investigation serves as a useful sensitizing tool and as a beacon pointing out realms for fruitful data gathering.

FORMULATING HYPOTHESES

To improve concepts and preconceptions, investigators confront them with empirical evidence and other concepts. This is possible if concepts are presented tangibly and testably—whether they be statements about possible resolutions to an investigator's problem, diagrams, drawings, or even buildings.

Investigators first formulate hypotheses in an exploratory way based on theory and previous empirical data; then they use preliminary, unfocused investigation to decide with what specific data to confront these hypotheses. As data are gathered and made more visible, exploratory hypotheses are developed into descriptive ones with which investigators seem to say "This is what I think I see." More-detailed information determines the tenability of such hypotheses. The more-tenable ones tend to help investigators organize, simplify, and explain ever greater amounts of related information. Testing these explanatory hypotheses in turn enables investigators to make explicit the holistic conceptual framework they have been developing.

Complex and sophisticated possible solutions to a problem—that is, hypotheses—can be thought of as conceptual models analogous to the physical models that designers use. Designers' models, often constructed of lightweight wood, clay, fiberboard, or colored paper, are systematically built as scaled reductions of the intended final product. Physical models represent abstract attributes of a concept: massing of buildings, openness of space, clustering of elements. Sometimes they represent what the actual final building might look like. Designers' models constructed early in the process are usually inexpensive and easily dismantled. Such working models change rapidly as designs develop, just as hypotheses change under the impact of newly gathered information when a research project develops.

Models represent the intended resolution of problems in mathematical, symbolic, physical, or some other form. Investigators and designers can therefore learn from models by observing what happens to them under different conditions, as if they were the final research or design concept. Developing and testing working hypotheses and working models allows researchers to make major adjustments in approach before it is too late—before such changes would mean destroying the whole project and starting from scratch.

The following discussion points out some important types of hypotheses, moving from simpler to more sophisticated ones.

Classifying Hypotheses

Classifying hypotheses order available information so that researchers can more clearly define their problem and can decide how to study it further. Explanatory hypotheses try to get at the roots of a problem and identify possible solutions.

List of types. A simple way to order information is to classify it into a list of types. When Weiss and Bouterline (1962) wanted to understand why exhibits at the 1962 Seattle World's Fair differentially interested visitors, they started by noting how much time visitors spent at each of 33 exhibits in five pavilions. They felt, however, that describing each exhibit separately would not lead to better general rules of thumb about how to design interesting exhibits.

They therefore grouped the exhibits into seven major types: (1) participation exhibits, with which visitors somehow interact; (2) demonstration exhibits, where a person acts as a guide or teacher; (3) models of objects or complex phenomena (subdivided into full-scale, small-scale, and complex teaching models); (4) panel exhibits with still or moving lights; (5) filmstrips that include a voice narration and tell a story; (6) totally housed exhibits that separate visitors from outside distractions; and (7) animal exhibits. These rough exhibit types at times overlap; nevertheless, the list enabled the researchers to identify demonstrations, filmstrips with story lines, and animal exhibits as the ones that held visitors' interest the longest. Further explanation of why these "types" work the way they do can be useful in deciding how to convey public information effectively.

Substructures. Investigators can also organize information by structuring it within a descriptive ordering system.

This organizing system may be constructed by juxtaposing several attributes that describe the research problem. For example, degree of legibility and impact on behavior might describe how a sign system works. Or the organizing principle may be a combination of ordered physical parts; for a hospital the parts might be beds, rooms, nursing stations, wards, floors, and buildings. When one juxtaposes attributes or parts, one forms a multicelled table, or matrix, within which each cell represents one of a total set of possible combinations of variable values (Barton & Lazarsfeld, 1969).

Such a table can be used to identify dimensions of a problem for further study. For example, Zeisel (1976a) redefined the term *vandalism* and identified fruitful research avenues by substructuring the problem of school property damage. Interviews and a literature review showed the research team that the broad term *vandalism* means different things to different people. The team realized that

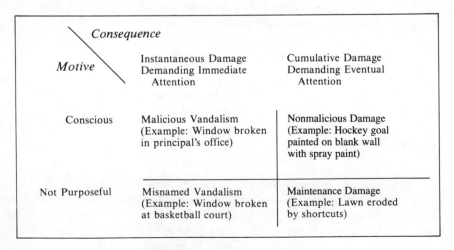

Substructure of property damage

to remedy discrete and manageable problems, they first had to introduce more-precise terms. They began by listing the ways in which people used the term: all property damage; vicious kids attacking a building because they hate it; graffiti; desecration of religious buildings.

Further analysis was organized according to two attributes: whether "vandals" are conscious of the damage they do and whether the damage requires immediate repair if the school is to continue working adequately. Combining these two dimensions generated a substructure clarifying different kinds of vandalism and providing direction for the rest of the study.

Explanatory Hypotheses

Investigators, by looking at the implications of their problem organization and at the data they gather, can develop tentative answers to the question "How did something occur? Why did someone do something?" Some answers will be provided by subjects participating in the research who describe why they think they did something: their motives and the consequences of actions they are conscious of. For instance, a designer may give a reason for making a certain decision.

In designing a housing project in South Carolina, Brolin provided adjacent driveways for neighboring houses instead of a driveway on the same side of every house (Zeisel, 1971). Brolin intended with his design to increase the chances that neighbors would run into each other and possibly become friendly and to make a street that residents would find less regular and more attractive. Each of these conscious intentions can be turned into a hypothesis and tested. Do neighbors with adjacent driveways meet more than other neighbors? Are they more friendly? Are streets perceived as irregular? Tests of conscious intentions explain part of the story. Building on them, researchers can generate hypotheses of which subjects may be unaware—hypotheses having to do with unforeseen consequences of actions. Explanations of actions that refer to an actor's intent can be called *manifest* explanations; explanations that refer to unforeseen effects can be called *latent* explanations (Merton, 1957).

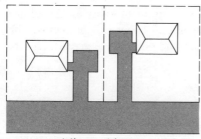
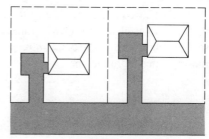

Adjacent driveways   Parallel driveways

Layout of driveways in Spartanburg, South Carolina, housing project. Site design by Brent C. Brolin.

Latent explanations, once formulated, are also testable. But they are harder to formulate because they are unexpected by participants and often are based initially on a researcher's theoretical expectations rather than empirical observation (Zeisel, 1978).

Gans' *Levittowners* (1967) provides a basis for hypotheses about the possible latent effects of adjacent driveways. Gans found that neighbors next door or across the street do tend to meet often. But he also found unexpected consequences of contact between neighbors at Levittown: It is not always as friendly as planners might predict. When neighboring children ride bikes, roller-skate, and play together on driveways, they sometimes fight. Children soon forget fights and go back to playing; parents do not. Parents expect the aggressor—usually the neighbor's child—to be punished, and punished in the same way they would punish their own child.

Levittown neighbors—although earning roughly equivalent salaries—came from different cultural backgrounds with different attitudes toward child rearing and punishment. Some parents believed more in hitting children, others more in giving the children a stern talking-to. Gans found neighbors fighting because they were not satisfied that a child had been sufficiently punished or were unhappy that the punishment was too severe. Brolin's shared driveways, by bringing neighbors together, might drive them apart.

Research that generates and tests both manifest and latent explanations is likely to provide new insights into a problem.

EMPIRICAL TESTING

You may test hypotheses by confronting them with empirical data and other hypotheses. If no data have yet been gathered, you might do so by carrying out empirical research. If all data in a study have been collected, however, hypotheses are tested by reassessing those data from another point of view—by analyzing and ordering them in new ways. Testing hypotheses leads to their replacement, improvement, and refinement and to reformulating them for further testing.

Part Two of this book will describe observation and interview techniques that can be used to help develop and test hypotheses about E-B problems. This section, therefore, will focus on reasoning useful to organize such research—no matter which technique one uses.

Observing

The term *observation* as used here means looking at phenomena connected to a problem by whatever means necessary: looking with one's eyes, asking questions, using mechanical measurement devices, and so on. We use the term in the same way as when we say that a patient goes into a hospital for "observation." Doctors and nurses do more than just look: they measure temperature and blood pressure; they take X rays; they make specimen analyses.

Single observations. One observation may be thought of as the simplest research datum: a smile, Central Park, a movement, an answer to a question, an event. Single observations that surprise the observer tend to indicate interesting research avenues because such observations conflict with exploratory hypotheses formulated from theory, from other empirical research, or from common sense.

As a researcher it is useful to keep your mind open to things you do not see—to be surprised by what does not happen. Given some direction, commonplace observations of things most people do not notice become strange and problematic. "The ability to take a commonplace fact and see it as raising problems is important because it can lead to . . . enlightenment" (Barton & Lazarsfeld, 1969: 168).

Whyte's research on how people use open spaces, plazas, and streets in New York City (1980) provides an illuminating example. Whyte wanted to provide city planners with information to help them design pedestrian zones that would accommodate the large diversity of needs of users, like pedestrians, window-shoppers, people watchers, and peddlers. During preliminary research on busy sidewalks, he noticed that pedestrians chose to converse in places where they most disrupted other pedestrian traffic—in the middle of traffic and near crosswalks.

This seemingly common observation raised problems: Was it a freak occurrence or part of a recurring pattern? What type of conversation was going on? Why were conversants apparently so unreasonable as not to get out of the way? Further research led to the hypothesis that finding a more convenient place to stand would commit the talkers to continue for a long time. Standing precariously in traffic made it easy for either person to break off the conversation at any moment.

Regularities. One way to test a hypothesis developed from a single observation is to look for other observations like it—for example, other people conversing in traffic. This is particularly relevant if the problem you are studying aims toward doing something to affect such a pattern: designing sidewalks to accommodate regular uses or designing schools to avoid major types of nonmalicious property damage.

Looking for a regularity and not finding it makes visible another regularity—its absence. If, for example, Whyte had first observed one couple speaking near a wall and looked for this as a pattern, he would have naturally been led to notice the recurrence of in-traffic conversations.

When investigators find no other observations like the first, this too may be useful. For example, a planner may find no park as large as New York's Central

Park in other U.S. cities. If she is studying problems associated with designing urban environmental legislation, it may be helpful to know why no other landscape architect since Olmsted achieved this unique feat.

A surprising regularity or unique event raises questions: Why does it occur? What effect does it have? What does each one mean? How can it be used by others? What can be done to change or accommodate it? To improve one's answers to such questions, it is often helpful to look not for more of the same but at other things connected to it—namely, its context.

Contexts. To test an explanatory hypothesis of an observed event, researchers use its context—how the event is linked to it and how isolated from it. The context of Whyte's sidewalk talkers included at least others around them, their motives and attitudes, their destination, time of day, and location. Although not everything in the context of an event is significant to solving a researcher's problem, some things are likely to be.

For example, a team of researchers in Baltimore studied an urban rowhouse neighborhood with small playgrounds behind the backyards and stoops in front of the houses. They wanted to know whether these playgrounds were used, and if not, why not. They observed more people using the front stoops than the playgrounds in back (Brower, 1977). To understand why, the research team looked to the context. Brower noticed that when residents sat on the stoops, they talked together, visited each other, watched strangers passing by, and supervised children playing on the sidewalk. On the basis of these findings, he developed, tested, and refined the hypothesis that residents felt that their neighborhood network included people who lived on the vehicular and pedestrian street in front rather than the people on the physical block whose backyards were adjacent to the common playground areas.

In sum, testing your hypotheses against empirical data requires that someone first make interesting observations that shed light on your problem. To do this, no matter what observation techniques and methods you use, it is essential to see significant single events, to perceive regularities over events, and to take into account the context of your problem. This approach will help you use the real world to improve the way you look at it, what you know about it, and the actions you take in it.

Sampling

When you test an idea by gathering empirical evidence, you *may* be able to examine every instance in which the idea is relevant. For example, when studying the 212-unit Charlesview housing development, Zeisel and Griffin (1975) used this "census technique" to test the hypothesis that residents were more likely to decorate and personalize enclosed front yards than nonenclosed backyards. They found that, of the 49 residents with enclosed front yards, over 80% planted grass and flowers or kept furniture there, whereas fewer than 10% decorated their backyards.

It is not always possible, however, to observe every instance in which your hypothesis might apply. You may not have the resources to find all the people or situations that have a certain characteristic. The group you want to study may be too undefined, as were the crowds of New Yorkers Whyte (1980) observed on sidewalks. Or you may want to say something about the likelihood of future events that are clearly impossible to observe.

Because of limitations such as these, researchers who have to generalize take a sample of people, places, or events to say something about a larger group. Generalizing always entails some error, however. Researchers may generalize too much, too little, or in the wrong way.

Festinger, Schachter and Back (1950) probably generalized too much. They observed that MIT married students living in apartments or houses whose location forced them to cross paths with certain neighbors tended to choose those neighbors as friends more often than neighbors living the same physical distance away whose paths they did not have to cross. These researchers and others used these observations to develop a more general principle—that physical distance, together with "functional distance" (the likelihood of daily chance encounters), leads to increased liking among residential neighbors. It took Gans (1967) to point out that the generalization probably holds only when housing residents are homogeneous in background and interests—as were most of the MIT married students Festinger and his team studied. Gans found that neighbors in the New Jersey planned community of Levittown tended to choose as their friends those neighbors they considered most compatible, whether they lived adjacent to them or across the street.

Certain *sampling procedures* can help to reduce errors that you know you will have when you test hypotheses and generalize the results. *Randomizing* procedures help control error from sources you do not anticipate. *Matching* or *stratifying* procedures are used to reduce the chance of errors from conditions that previous knowledge says are likely to influence your results. Randomizing and matching procedures can be combined to reduce overall generalization error in a particular situation.

Randomizing. E-B researchers often study diverse groups of people, places, and environments they know little about relative to the hypothesis being tested. For example, if you wanted to study people buying tickets at an airport in order to plan an airline terminal, you probably would not know in advance what about them influences their ticket-buying behavior: their age, cultural background, how they feel that day. Randomizing procedures are used to disperse such characteristics in the sample as they are dispersed in the population, so that the generalization error they cause is reduced. Interestingly, you don't have to trace how a characteristic is dispersed to control its effects.

Randomizing is not only a useful idea but a surprising one. If you draw a random sample from a large group, you can generalize or project results from the sample to the group within statistically definable limits. For example, from a randomly selected sample of 1500 people, political pollsters can predict within an accuracy of 3% how 70 million people will vote. Another surprising attribute of randomizing is that the accuracy with which you can project from randomly chosen sample data to a population depends mostly on the absolute size of the sample, not on the ratio of the sample size to the size of the population. In other words, generalization error from a suitable sample of 1500 will be the same whether you project your results to a town with a population of 50,000 or to a city with a population of 5,000,000.

"Random" in this context does not mean haphazard, helter-skelter, or unsystematic, as it does in everyday usage. Its meaning is actually closer to "unpredictable" or "by chance." Specifically, the word "random" as used in statistics is a technical term describing the process by which a sample is chosen. The principle of random sampling is simple: selection of the sample group must be left to chance, so that every member of the population and every combination of members have the same opportunity of being selected.

A common-sense way to select a random sample is to put names or numbers of elements on pieces of paper, throw them into a hat, and have someone choose a few with eyes closed. But this procedure can be inexact: if some pieces of paper stick together, that group of elements has a higher chance of being selected than any other group; if the hat is not thoroughly shaken, numbers or names put in last have a higher chance of being chosen. We could go on thinking of things that can and do go wrong when sampling is carried out manually.

Researchers who want to select random samples for actual projects can use a "Table of Random Numbers" generated by a computer. In E-B research, the simple device of taking every nth name from a list will often suffice as a "systematic" random sampling procedure, assuming that the interval n is unconnected to what you want to test. If there is no list, you can make one somehow —for instance, by observing every tenth person in line at a ticket agent's counter.

Matching. When you want to observe a sample from a larger population with which you are familiar, and you think that a characteristic of the larger group will affect what you observe, you can match the sample to the larger group on that characteristic. For example, suppose you are interested in what the residents of a neighborhood feel about having a playground located near where they live. You are likely to get different answers when interviewing women, especially women with children, than when interviewing men. Stratifying the proportion of men and women you include in the sample to reflect the proportion of men and women actually living in the neighborhood will reduce error when you project from your sample to the whole neighborhood.

The same principle applies when observing behavior over time. You would get a very unusual picture if you observed airline ticket counters only on Friday afternoons and Monday mornings, the peak traffic hours. Because experience says that air traffic varies with the cycles of the day, week, and year, you want to be certain to include all periods of the day, days of the week, and possibly months of the year in the random sample of times you choose to observe.

Researchers carrying out experiments match groups before observing them, constructing experimental groups in which an experimental change is introduced, and control groups, in which no planned change is made. For example, an experiment might be designed to test the hypothesis that people's reactions to interviews vary with an increase in the size of the room. If the researchers think that age and professional experience with interviews could affect the results, they would match the two groups to make certain that the experimental group did not have mainly older doctors and lawyers, while the control group contained mostly college freshmen. Otherwise, should the researchers find a difference between the groups, they would not know how to generalize the results: is the observed difference due to the experimental manipulation or to the different makeup of the groups?

Combining randomizing and matching procedures. When researchers want to reduce generalization error from both known and unknown causes, they use a mixture of randomizing and matching (or stratifying) procedures to select their sample. For example, suppose the population you want to find out about contains five important subgroups. After dividing the population into these subgroups, you would randomly select individuals from each subgroup for your sample. Similarly, after grouping the times of day, week, and year, you would use randomizing procedures to decide what particular times you were going to observe.

When researchers test a hypothesis by confronting it with empirical data, they will want to generalize these results to new situations. Using randomizing and matching procedures to organize empirical tests enables them to reduce, estimate, and control the errors inherent in making generalizations.

OVERVIEW

Research is essentially a creative endeavor requiring a subtle blend of personal skill and impersonal order. Relying only on order in research minimizes individual responsibility and risk, although it shows that you know how to play the game. It also limits the contribution research can make to new knowledge.

This chapter stresses the importance of personal knowledge (Polanyi, 1958) and skill in developing concepts, formulating hypotheses, and testing them. The chapter proposes that researchers can achieve the results they want by systematically presenting and testing concepts as they are developed.

The principles presented for organizing research are intended to enable the investigator to control his or her own research activities and their consequences.

The next chapter discusses reasons designers and researchers work together, occasions they have for cooperation, and problems they resolve by doing so.

Chapter 3

RESEARCH AND DESIGN COOPERATION

"And the Lord said, Behold, the people is one, and they have all one language; and this they begin to do: and now nothing will be restrained from them, which they have imagined to do."

Genesis 11:6

People look to cooperate with others when they want to do more than they can do alone.

An architect is commissioned to design an open-plan office building that the clients can periodically reevaluate and redesign as their needs change. The designer has no problem designing a quality office building. But he has no tools in his arsenal to assess the effects periodic redesign might have on the clients' organization.

An environment-behavior researcher is funded to study impacts of physical environment on hospital patients' self-confidence. She has no problem documenting the state of knowledge about this issue, studying people in existing settings, and developing research hypotheses to test. But she has no tools in her arsenal to predict how using her information will change designs.

Research and design cooperation grows out of the variability of social reality: boundaries of problems change, situations differ, viewpoints are flexible, and people grow. The solutions that designers or researchers provide to their own problems have side effects in the other discipline. Cooperation is fostered when designers or researchers decide they want to use the other discipline as a tool to improve their control over side effects—that is, to solve more broadly defined problems than they can solve alone.

PURPOSES OF COOPERATION

Researchers' Purposes

One reason researchers work with designers is to increase the control they have over testing hypotheses. Researchers who want not only to generate but also to improve knowledge want to test it. When applied environment-behavior re-

Research and Design Cooperation
Purposes of Cooperation   Researchers' purposes   Designers' purposes
Occasions for Cooperation   Programming   Design review   Evaluation research

searchers happen to find actual physical settings well suited to testing their ideas, they usually adjust their hypotheses and research goals to learn what these available settings allow them to learn. The more involved researchers are in making decisions about the setting in which ideas will be tested, the more they can learn.

Researchers who want their information to be used and useful want to know the types of problems designers have that E-B studies can help solve. What types of E-B design problems do landscape architects face most often? What unsolved design problems have the most critical behavioral side effects for designers? Do clients ask designers questions about the impact of rules on behavior in physical settings? What common-sense and generally accepted perspectives about people have the greatest chance of being revised on the basis of research? When researchers choose to study E-B problems and eventually present problems and their solutions to designers, one measure of success is the degree to which designers find the problems relevant to their concerns. Researchers work with designers to find out what these concerns are—that is, to identify problems that designers may not see themselves but will see immediately when made apparent through research.

Researchers who want to share their information with designers want to know how designers work. Understanding how architects make decisions enables researchers to present research information in a form that meets decision makers' schedules. The clearer the process of using information in design, the easier it will be to modify that process so it can better accommodate new types of information. The boundaries between decision making and information development can be examined and, for certain purposes, improved. When meshing like this takes place, there is also a greater chance that research information will be tested in practice.

There is precedent for applied research activity: Non-environmentally oriented behavioral scientists at present make decisions or advise others who make decisions in hospitals, schools, social-work agencies, policy-making offices, and many other settings where people think that behavioral research information and perspectives are useful. Investigators learn from such situations partly by making hypothetical predictions, evaluating outcomes, and modifying their hypotheses. They also are able to identify interesting problems and research issues in such settings. And by working with decision makers they learn how to organize their information to respond to the needs of those who use it. Methodological and substantive advances in science are significantly helped by the exchange and use of information between basic and applied scientific settings (Lazarsfeld, Sewell, & Wilensky, 1967).

Designers' Purposes

Designers have a different problem: Although their main objective is to change physical settings, they want to control the behavioral effects of the design decisions they make. They want their buildings, open spaces, and objects to meet the social and psychological needs of those who use them. This is not easy in our increasingly complex society, where designers often build for strangers and strange groups. The gap between decision maker and user is too great to be overcome by designers using only a personal perspective. If government regulations or the free market would ensure that users' needs were taken into account, there would be no problem. But this does not appear to be the case.

The gap that designers face between themselves and those who use what they design has developed historically. In primitive societies everyone could and did build his own house, designing—if it could even be called that then—according to one model of a building. This model was developed and adjusted over generations to satisfy cultural, climatic, physical, and maintenance requirements (Rapoport, 1969b: 1–8).

As trades became increasingly specified, what Rapoport calls vernacular design traditions emerged. Everyone still knew the traditional rules of construction, organization, and style, but craftspeople knew them in greater detail. Because craftspeople and clients shared an "image of life" (Rapoport, 1969b: 6), they could work together to introduce individual variation into accepted residential and ceremonial building models while still respecting the traditions the models embodied.

Since the Industrial Revolution several new ways have developed in which buildings are designed and built. In the marketplace, users affect decisions through selective buying. The gap between designer and user has grown, but market research and the sensitivity of builders to market conditions help to narrow it, resulting in open-market buildings that embody commonly held values even though users did not participate directly in their design. One example is the Levittown development tract (Gans, 1967), which included such design elements as pitched roofs, picture windows, and large front lawns.

In another tradition, designers contract with individual clients who request styled, one-of-a-kind buildings. Clients pay for the building, criticize it during design, and eventually use it personally. To determine clients' needs, designers negotiate with them, reaching agreement on design. In such settings clients may delegate considerable authority to the professionals they pay, because they want to benefit from the special expertise these professionals have: expertise about such things as style, methods, and materials.

The most dramatic postindustrial development in environmental design began when people concentrated around factories in cities and when new technology enabled construction of large buildings. Governments, factory owners, corporations, and other often well-intentioned groups of people contracted with designers to construct settings and objects for masses of people to use daily: parks, furniture, schools, hospitals, appliances, playgrounds, offices, dormitories. In mass design like this, designers have two clients: clients who pay for what is built and clients who use it (Madge, 1968). The user client has no choice and no control. This situation presents designers with a problem: no matter how much they negotiate with paying clients, it is difficult to plan for needs of user clients who are neither well known nor readily available to plan with.

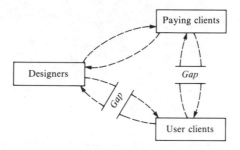

The user-needs gap

To solve or at least improve the user-needs problem, designers, administrators, researchers, users, and others have developed mechanisms that change the boundary between designers and user clients. For example, citizen-participation techniques include user clients as partial members of design teams and give them control traditionally reserved for paying clients. Flexible building frameworks, with partitions and even alternative façades (Habraken, 1972; Wampler, 1968), provide user clients with more direct control over their surroundings by enabling them to adapt a structure themselves. E-B research changes the boundary by making more visible to designers the needs, desires, and reactions of users to their surroundings, thus enabling designers to better negotiate with users and understand the effects of decisions on them. Solving the user-needs problem offers both researchers and designers opportunities to learn from users and from each other.

OCCASIONS FOR COOPERATION

The day-to-day practice of design offers at least three occasions for research and design cooperation: (1) user-needs *programming* research for designing a particular project; (2) *design review* to assess the degree to which designs reflect existing E-B research knowledge; (3) *evaluation* of built projects in use. Each occasion can contribute to the fund of *basic E-B knowledge,* improving our general ability to solve design and research problems (Conway, 1973; Zeisel, 1975: 20).

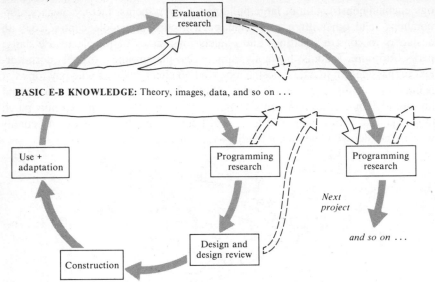

Occasions for research/design cooperation in the design-process cycle

Programming

A design contract may specify that the client or the client together with the designer is responsible for stating clearly what the building (or other setting) is expected to do. This document is called the "program" and the process of preparing it "programming."

Programs reflect a broad array of concerns affecting design decisions. Economic, cultural, stylistic, ecological, structural, sociological, and psychological concerns are just a few. Some programs quantify design goals and requirements: amount of floor space, minimum room dimensions for certain uses, types of spaces, specific materials and hardware, maximum cost estimates, minimum window area in proportion to floor area. In programs such as these, the level of performance for design concerns generally remains implicit. For example, particular park benches that a landscape architect's program might specify will have a certain durability, ease of maintenance, and economy not necessarily detailed in the program.

"Performance" programs make explicit what conditions a design decision is intended to meet—its performance—allowing designers to decide on particular responses (National Bureau of Standards, 1968). For example, a behavioral performance program developed for the cancer radiation clinic at the National

Institutes of Health (NIH) included the criterion that patients and their companions be easily able to handle other aspects of their lives, such as work and family, while they wait to be treated. But the program did not tell designers how to accomplish this (Conway, Zeisel, & Welch, 1977). Performance programs are intended to make user needs visible rather than to delimit designers' options. E-B research is particularly helpful to designers in determining cultural, social, and psychological performance criteria.

User-needs programming research is not limited to the contractual stage of a design project called programming. Such cooperation continues to be useful in solving E-B problems raised when designers sketch, draw, and draft, especially when they are faced with making tradeoffs—deciding the relative importance of the effects of decisions.

Although it is often uncertain who the users of a particular physical setting will be, people design particular settings for particular residents with particular problems. Designers and researchers at Oxford, New York, for example, prepared a behavioral program and designed a residence for present and future older veterans, many of whom are ill or handicapped (Nahemow & Downes, 1979; Snyder & Ostrander, 1974). Yet, if the present residents who participated in the research change or are replaced by new and different residents, results may eventually become irrelevant. And if a planned setting is new, as many are, you do not even have the questionable benefit of present users to work with.

One way to resolve this seeming paradox is to locate and study settings, users, and problems representative of future ones, generalizing from these to the probable future setting and its users. There are two types of representative groups: those who will immediately use the new setting (commonly called "users") and those who merely represent the type of persons actual users are likely to be.

When designers and investigators know the people who will inhabit a setting, as at Oxford, they assume that although present users will eventually move out, the second and third waves of inhabitants will resemble them. In programming a school, for example, designers assume that although particular administrators, teachers, students, maintenance workers, and parents will change, the patterns of reactions and needs of such groups change relatively slowly. They also assume that changes that certainly will occur in the situation will in some way include the initial users of the setting: as the starting point for change, as catalysts, as limits, as some part of the context for change. In this way, by identifying tendencies for change among users—for example, trends in methods of teaching or new types of care administered to mental patients—designers and investigators can plan for change. Predictions are more accurate when they reflect knowledge of the present.

Designers sometimes do not have a group of actual residents to plan with and study. They may know only the project site (urban/rural, north/south), the type of setting (park, school, plaza), and general characteristics of future users (incomes, ages, culture, health needs, life-style stages). They can then choose a representative substitute user group to work with from people with similar problems in similar settings.

For example, when investigators programmed a cancer clinic, they carried out case studies in four large urban cancer-therapy clinics, interviewed users, observed their behavior, and documented physical traces (Conway et al., 1977). They observed at each location during different days and at different times of day. They assumed that the people, settings, and situations there represented the types of people, settings, and situations for which the clinic was being designed—that the information they gathered was generalizable to the larger group from which future users would be drawn.

Design Review

In a design project designers use existing information from their program and from available research to generate and test design ideas. The process of testing ideas, design review, provides another occasion to link design and research.

Design review problem: how to present information. As many practicing designers and others involved in design attest, it is not always apparent how basic research findings are helpful to solve design problems (Reizenstein, 1975). Consequently, much basic research goes unused, untested, and unimproved in applied design situations. A fundamental problem E-B researchers face is to make apparent how basic research information can be helpful to design decision makers: user clients, paying clients, design professionals, administrators. The way this research task is done affects how various design-team members can help change design decisions, and it affects the likelihood that useful knowledge can increase and be developed further.

Researchers who want their information to be helpful to designers and to be improved by its use in design projects present information so that (1) people who affect decisions can share it, (2) design-team members can use it in their interaction during the design process, and (3) users of the information can question and confront it (Argyris, 1977). At least as important is that E-B information be presented so that it draws out the knowledge about a particular problem that participants bring to design and design review. The more they can combine research information with what they know about themselves, other participants, the setting, and its context, the more they can tailor information to do what they want it to do.

A helpful way to approach solving these problems is to ask where research information fits in the designer's cognitive process. Design, according to the formulation in Chapter 1, comprises at least three primary activities—imaging, presenting, and testing. Research information can influence design through these activities. When people participating in design meet at the beginning of a project, they can use research information to help develop shared images. When presenting ideas about settings and behavior, people can use research to show how they expect decisions about physical things to influence behavior. And to test their design decisions and the information used to make decisions, people need to have questions that encourage them to confront what is presented with outside information. The following techniques are aimed at achieving these ends.

Presentation technique: shared E-B images. Designers try to formulate problems so that better design responses can be developed without expending more resources. Images suited to a problem can be used to decide which resources are useful to solve it and which are not. For example, seeing housing for older people on an urban site mainly as a building-design problem has different consequences than seeing it as a problem of designing part of an urban context. The first image of the problem would indicate that information about available services and nearby facilities is not so useful. If eventual users of the building do not use the surrounding area heavily, there is no new problem. If they do use it, however, this image turns out to have unwisely excluded useful information from consideration, and eventually more resources will have to be expended to improve the now problematic solution.

Choosing "a 'point of view' of the problem that maximally simplifies the process of finding a solution" is essential for researchers as well as designers (Amarel, 1968: 131). This is one impetus researchers have to formulate information in such a way that it helps designers when they develop an image for their problem. The words that researchers use to describe problems, concepts, and analyses can easily be interpreted differently by different people. What do you think of when you hear the words *privacy, territory, invasion of personal space?* Mathematics provides opportunities for greater precision and less misinterpretation. But mathematical expression is not always useful in making decisions. A numerically expressed measure of annoyance at having one's privacy invaded does not necessarily help designers design an open-plan office.

Research presented so that it "paints a picture" of an idea for design-team members begins to help them go beyond the information—build on it, develop it,

Negotiating a shared image (from Zeisel, 1976b)

and transform it so that it applies to the particular decision being made (Korob-kin, 1976). Pictures of familiar settings, drawings, verbal scenarios of typical situations, cartoons, diagrams, films—all not only express information; they encourage groups of people to discuss what they see. Such discussions in turn can enable participants to negotiate shared group images useful to their problem (Zeisel, 1976b). If designers are planning a school with citizens, for example, it is essential that each understands what the other means if they are to be able to design together. Research presented holistically as well as analytically can be used to develop shared images of people's behavior and of physical settings.

Presentation technique: behaviorally annotated plans. Designers who want to provide places for people and behavioral scientists who want to under-stand how physical environments relate to people are interested in the same topic

Visual images used to communicate E-B concepts—cartoons, photographs, perspectives.

Personal space: Social distance—a zone used widely in public settings. Photo © Jim Pinckney. (From Altman, 1975)

Territorial behavior: Janitors have jurisdictional rights in others' territories and often ignore the occupant as they go about their work. Drawing by Chas. Addams, © 1942, 1970, The New Yorker Magazine, Inc. Reprinted by permission. (From Altman, 1975)

"Window to the world": Older people need a place to view life around them. (From Zeisel et al., 1978)

(though in different dimensions of it), whether it is called "behavior settings" (Barker, 1968; Bechtel, 1977; Wicker, 1979), "man-environment systems" (Archea & Esser, 1970), or simply "places" (Canter, 1977; Moore, Allen, & Lyndon, 1974; Zeisel, 1975). This often overlooked identity of interests provides researchers and designers an obvious common ground on which to share information.

Behavioral plan annotation is a technique for presenting behavior information together with traditional symbolic design information: diagrammatic and schematic plans. Annotated plans are design drawings on which, written in words and other easily understood symbols, is information about the relation between the planned environment and behavior. This information includes data used as background for making the design decision; behavioral expectations held by the designer; and, for future testing, hypotheses about behavioral responses. As an example, a team of architects and researchers designing a cancer-treatment center for the U.S. National Institutes of Health used annotated plans to present explicit predictions about what they supposed the eventual relation between setting and behavior would be (Conway et al., 1977). One E-B prediction that the annotated plan shows they made was that if the receptionist can see and be seen by patients in corridors, all users will feel comfortable with letting patients walk around more freely.

Plan annotation encourages people to look closely at the behavioral rationale behind each decision: to confront and question both their decisions and the information on which they are based. As you annotate plans, you not only present, you begin to test what you know. You become engaged in linking research information to particular design decisions (Epp, Georgopulos, & Howell, 1979). You find out both what you know and what you do not know, in a structured way.

Presentation technique: design review questions. Throughout any design process, some decisions are made so rapidly that designers are unable to look up relevant research data to justify or question the decision. This would not be a problem if intuitive decisions had no unintended negative side effects—but most do.

Even when research data are arrayed systematically and extensively, it may not be easy to locate appropriate data to test a particular design decision. Designers may have to wait until they are faced with unresolvable technical dilemmas or with users who react in contradictory ways before they realize that somewhere information had been available to test and inform a much earlier decision.

Information-utilization problems are confounded still further when, at various stages of design, users and paying clients participate as design reviewers: community school-board or housing-board members, corporate officials, or just citizens concerned about their community. If professional designers do not know what questions to ask, how should user clients be expected to? User clients have an additional problem. Before testing designs with research information, they must test the information by comparing it with their own lives, answering the question "Do these issues actually describe needs of people like me?"

Korobkin (1976) ingeniously suggests that one form of research presentation for environmental design be a series of questions to be used during reviews of designs as they are being developed. This technique helps to involve every member of a design process in testing and improving design ideas. In the early stages of a design project, questions aim to make sure designers address issues that research has shown to be salient to the problem being worked on. For a dormitory, questions might raise issues of privacy, quietness, independence, and supervision; for a school playground, issues of teenagers hanging out and potential property damage. "Accountability questions" like these (Korobkin, 1976) are formulated in general terms: "How has the design addressed teenage hanging-out behavior (or students' needs for privacy or the potential problem of property damage to nearby facilities)?"

When designers want to identify data, problems, and issues that bear on making detailed design decisions, more-specific design review questions are appropriate. For example, in their behavioral guidelines for design of low-rise housing for older people, Zeisel, Epp, and Demos (1978) first summarized existing published research by describing a series of E-B problems that older people face when they live in and move around housing projects. For the issue "pathfinding" they developed the following description:

> Finding one's way around a housing site can be difficult for both residents and visitors when pathways are not clear, when there are no identifiable landmarks, and where entrances are not marked. As a result, careful consideration must be given to site "legibility" so that the giving and following of directions from one place to another on site can occur with ease. People must know where they are on the site and where they are going at all times. Pathfinding confusion also arises when streets or paths which are at the back of one unit are at the front of another unit; when there is no distinction made between areas for resident use and areas open to the general public; and when buildings seem to have two "front" sides. It is important to resolve these issues because clear pathfinding opportunities add to older residents' sense of security [86].

Following each description of an issue is a series of design review questions to identify behavioral problems related to the issue. For "pathfinding":

> Is the site organized to provide clear unit addresses within the conventional address system of streets, entries and units?
> Is it easy for residents to describe to friends how to find where they live?
> Are units and clusters designed and located so that it is easy for residents and visitors to orient themselves?
> Is there a clear and consistent distinction between front door and back door of units?
> Are natural and built landmarks utilized to help give individual identity to different clusters and different parts of large sites? [88]

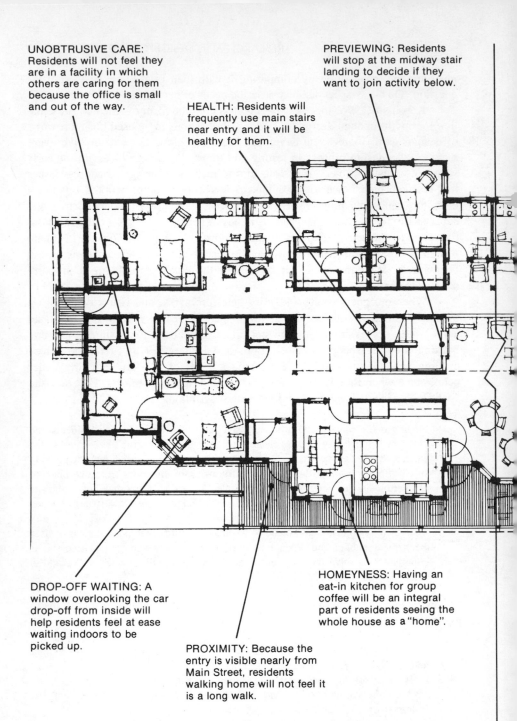

UNOBTRUSIVE CARE: Residents will not feel they are in a facility in which others are caring for them because the office is small and out of the way.

HEALTH: Residents will frequently use main stairs near entry and it will be healthy for them.

PREVIEWING: Residents will stop at the midway stair landing to decide if they want to join activity below.

DROP-OFF WAITING: A window overlooking the car drop-off from inside will help residents feel at ease waiting indoors to be picked up.

PROXIMITY: Because the entry is visible nearly from Main Street, residents walking home will not feel it is a long walk.

HOMEYNESS: Having an eat-in kitchen for group coffee will be an integral part of residents seeing the whole house as a "home".

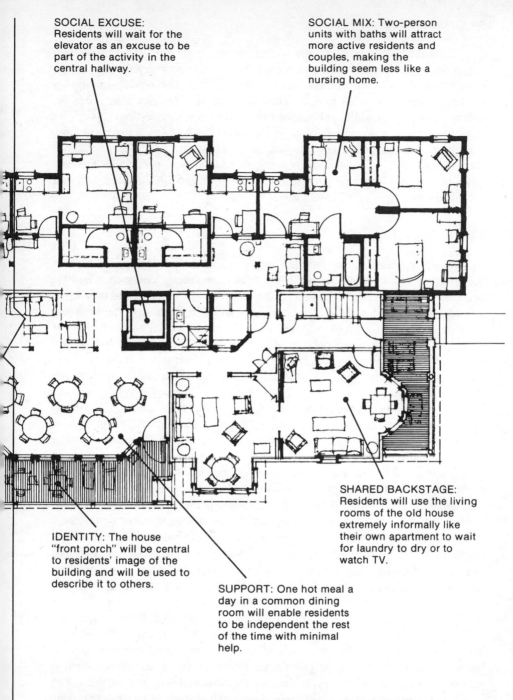

SOCIAL EXCUSE: Residents will wait for the elevator as an excuse to be part of the activity in the central hallway.

SOCIAL MIX: Two-person units with baths will attract more active residents and couples, making the building seem less like a nursing home.

SHARED BACKSTAGE: Residents will use the living rooms of the old house extremely informally like their own apartment to wait for laundry to dry or to watch TV.

IDENTITY: The house "front porch" will be central to residents' image of the building and will be used to describe it to others.

SUPPORT: One hot meal a day in a common dining room will enable residents to be independent the rest of the time with minimal help.

Annotated plan stating environment-behavior hypotheses to be evaluated when building is in use. Captain Clarence Eldridge Congregate House for Older People, Hyannis, Massachusetts. Design-research team: Barry Korobkin, John Zeisel, and Eric Jahan. Donham & Sweeney, associated architects.

Design review questions have no right or wrong answers; they simply raise issues for discussion. By trying to answer the questions, every member of the design team gains greater control over design decisions. This holds for designers as well as users and other clients. They all contribute to improving a design. Users gain a special additional benefit from design review questions. Assessing how well each question corresponds to their own lives makes apparent to them knowledge and experience they have but do not know they have. They are put in the position not of individual clients being asked to express personal desires and tastes but of knowledgeable participants whose ability to tailor the research to a particular situation is valuable to design.

Evaluation Research

Another occasion for designers and researchers to cooperate is when a building or other setting is in use. Such evaluation research answers questions like these: What were the designers' original intentions, and how did they try to implement them? What is there in the design that influenced use of the setting in ways the designers did not intend? How did position, expertise, and know-how of design-team members affect decisions during design? Answers to such questions can be used to reorganize design teams, improve designers' control over the effects of future design decisions, and test theories on which design decisions are based.

A problem in evaluation research is how to reconstruct design decisions. Investigators can better use evaluation research results to improve the process of making design decisions in the future if they can identify and make visible the design decisions that led up to the setting being evaluated. If designers and researchers collaborated throughout the design process—programming, design, construction—making the process visible is less of a problem; it is more of a problem if behavioral information was not made explicit during design.

A behavioral performance program and drawings on which designers have presented behavioral expectations provide a solid footing for evaluation researchers to reconstruct the behavioral components of a design process. For example, in the NIH cancer-treatment center designed with research, the program and annotated plans could be translated into testable hypotheses, as in Table 3-1 (Conway et al., 1977).

The more inventive evaluators are, the more hypotheses they will generate from any stated intention, and the more they will profit from their study.

In evaluating a setting for which no behavioral program or written explanation of design decisions was prepared at the time decisions were made, investigators have greater difficulty reconstructing the how and why of decisions. The problem is further compounded when decisions were made by designers who no longer work for the firm, or by one of several unidentifiable draftspeople instructed to solve a design problem as they saw fit. Often so much time elapses during a design and so many people work on a design project that asking decision

Table 3-1. Behavioral hypotheses derived from annotated design features of a cancer center

Design Decision	Annotated Intention	Testable Hypothesis
Stairs and elevators are adjacent, making available only one possible path for patients.	That patients clearly understand how to get into and out of the setting.	Environments offering only one option for direction are more easily comprehended than those providing several options.
Receptionist desk overlooks and is visible from all patient areas and corridors.	That patients are not afraid of being lost when they walk down corridors to treatment. That staff is not worried about patients getting hurt or upset, consequently limiting patient movement.	Environments enabling patients and staff to see each other will be more reassuring to both groups than settings in which this is not possible.

makers what they intended creates a *Rashomon* problem of recall (Keller, 1978). To determine behavioral intentions of design decisions in a Planned Unit Residential Development in New Jersey, Keller (1978) faced problems such as these and therefore turned to maps, models, official statements, and commercial advertisements in addition to interviewing designers and planners.

Analysis of physical plans can be used to identify a design team's implicit assumptions about behavior, and knowing the assumptions helps to structure a focused interview with a designer on the subject of his intentions. For example, in St. Francis Square, Cooper and Hackett (1968), noting specific design features, inferred the assumptions stated in Table 3-2.

Table 3-2. Behavioral hypotheses derived from design features of the St. Francis Square housing development

Design Feature	Assumption about Behavior
Fenced patio or balcony attached to each unit—with access to most patios from the living room of apartment only.	Mothers of small children will not object to them entering the apartment via the living room after they have been playing in the patio.
Service facilities like common drying yards are provided in each court—visible in two courts from every apartment.	Residents in these two courts will use the common drying yards, since they are within view of all the apartments.

From *Sociology and Architectural Design,* by John Zeisel. Copyright 1975 Russell Sage Foundation, New York. Reprinted by permission.

When Cooper later investigated these behavioral predictions, she found that drying yards, underused by residents, were turned into handball courts. She assumed this was due to nearby drying machines and "the fact that people felt their clothes might be damaged or stolen if they left them unattended in a communal yard" (1970: 20)—even though the yards were visible from the apartments.

If you want to be sure not to miss significant design decisions, you will analyze plans at small and large scales of design decision making. In housing, you will look at the range of decisions from hardware and apartment unit to site plan (Cook, 1971, 1973; Cooper, 1970); in town planning, from building and street layout to location of the town center (Brolin, 1972); in institutional buildings, you might include hardware, offices, and internal services as well as site location (Zeisel & Rhodeside, 1975). Research organized on the basis of systematic plan analysis is likely to include essential design questions—especially small-scale ones—that might otherwise be overlooked.

Other useful sources for understanding designers' behavioral implications are presentation drawings on which designers label places and insert sample furniture layouts or equipment and renderings that present places in perspective drawings as designers see them, often including people. Visual documents like these are particularly fruitful because they represent a designer's overall image of life in the future setting (Montgomery, 1966; Zeisel & Griffin, 1975).

Architect's rendering of interior street in the Charlesview housing development. Courtesy of Sy Mintz, Mintz Associates Architects/Planners, Inc.

When you have made design decisions and intentions explicit and have translated them into testable hypotheses, an evaluation study can be extremely instructive. In her Twin Rivers study, for example, Keller (1976, 1978) evaluated planning decisions for a Planned Unit Residential Development intended (1) to create microcommunities within the overall development, (2) to make the community self-sufficient, and (3) to induce residents to take up walking as a major mode of locomotion.

Planners there tried to create microcommunities by dividing the development into four roughly equal areas, two on one side of a highway and two on the other. Keller found, however, that residents did not identify with the four intended subdivisions; instead two larger identification areas developed, divided by the highway. Meanwhile, loyalty and local pride centered in smaller areas around people's homes. To help engender community feelings, Keller concludes, the size of formal subdivisions must reflect a better understanding of how people develop community feelings and how different types of communities interact.

To create a self-sufficient community, planners wanted to provide within Twin Rivers all services necessary to support residents. At the same time, they could not provide services before enough residents were living there to support the services economically. This internal contradiction resulted in a sparseness of available facilities for earlier residents, forcing them to leave Twin Rivers for church services, health care, movies, and concerts. Community feelings, of course, developed slowly because residents depended so much on support from surrounding towns. Planners can avoid such Catch-22 situations only by identifying secondary consequences like these and modifying their objectives before it is too late.

Finally, Twin Rivers planners believed that if houses, shops, and schools were accessible to residents on foot, walking would become a "major mode of locomotion." Research pointed out, however, that residents were part of a car culture and drove even to nearby locations, citing as reasons bad weather, no time, and the lack of anything interesting to look at on pedestrian paths. Perhaps the most obvious reason for car use was that whenever residents had multiple destinations (which was most of the time), a car was clearly more efficient. One lesson Keller draws from these findings is that rather than thinking they could banish the car and car culture by providing pathways, Twin Rivers planners should have developed with residents a shared image of their life-style.

Evaluation research, as this example shows, holds special potential for building a body of tested E-B knowledge.

OVERVIEW

People from different disciplines work together because they want to, not because they have to. When researchers and designers cooperate, each uses the other to do more than either can do alone: researchers to have designers use and improve their information; designers to have E-B researchers help close the gap between them and their anonymous user clients.

The practical side to multidisciplinary professional cooperation is that designers make decisions about real environments for real clients and expect that applied E-B research can mesh with design—on a day-to-day operational basis. Occasions for cooperation in design include (1) user-needs programming research, in which investigators work with and study representative groups of potential users to arrive at a behavioral program; (2) design review during the design process, when researchers and designers test and modify their ideas in the light of available E-B knowledge; and (3) evaluation research of built projects in use in order to improve future designs and design processes.

Applied design research poses problems: How do you find out about users of an as yet unbuilt setting? How do you present research information so that designers can use it? How do you reconstruct a past design process? How do designers present their decisions so that researchers can use them to improve a body of knowledge? Techniques invented to answer these questions represent practical ways to link applied E-B research to professional environmental design.

Cooperation enables people who work together to achieve more than the sum of each working separately. Even when people are through working together to solve shared problems, something remains: a knowledge of the other's discipline and point of view; new ways to define problems; an improved knowledge of how to cooperate with others. These and other side effects of cooperation are the topic of the next chapter.

Chapter 4

SIDE EFFECTS OF COOPERATION

"I see in science one of the greatest creations of the human mind. . . . It is a step at which our explanatory myths become open to conscious and consistent criticism and at which we are challenged to invent new myths."

Karl R. Popper
Objective Knowledge

Designers and researchers working together to make places to live, work, and play better suited to people's needs also enrich and improve themselves. Through cooperation they take advantage of the other person's difference to order what they do in a new way, extend their skills to do new things, and replace old ways with new options. Each uses the other person to improve his or her own ability to contribute.

People use research and design skills jointly whenever they identify problems, observe the world around them, develop concepts, decide to act, develop plans for what to do, and do it. Disciplinary boundaries were erected to help us isolate and develop one or another of these activities in order to better achieve particular ends. For example, designers who want to control how others—such as contractors—carry out their instructions have highly developed methods for presenting plans. Researchers who want to be able to share with others their observations about the world have highly developed methods for observing.

Differences between the structure of research and design, their content, their emphases, and their values provide a basis for the two fields to borrow from each other, to incorporate new elements, to rely on each other, to invent shared methods, and generally to broaden themselves. Particularly rich chances for mutual improvement can be found in the following differences: (1) Designers, more than researchers, work on problems requiring them to make *high risk* decisions. (2) Researchers have a longer tradition of rigorously and critically *testing* their knowledge in order to improve it. (3) Researchers tend to emphasize *explicit* knowing, while designers tend more to accept *tacit* knowing.

Opportunities for Researcher and Designer Growth

Risk Taking

    Intradisciplinary
    Interdisciplinary
    Transdisciplinary

Critical Testing

    Appropriateness
    Testable designs
    Reactions

Tacit and Explicit Knowing

    Theories
    Hypotheses
    Exemplars
    Models

RISK TAKING

Throughout a design project, decisions are made—for example, when to present drawings to a client or how to specify a particular construction detail. Researchers make similar decisions—what research design to choose, when to publish an empirical report. In making a decision, people weigh what they think are the possible effects of the decision against the risks of unintended consequences they are willing to take.

Designers and researchers weigh knowing against risking under different conditions: different professional norms, degrees of visibility, costs and rewards, and so on. It is hard enough within one disciplinary framework to determine what is tenable knowledge and what action the problem at hand demands. When two or more disciplines are involved, the potential for problems is even greater. There are difficulties of communication. There are difficulties of deciding who has the power and responsibility. There is an inherent difficulty that pressures to take action in one discipline may be inconsistent with the pressures in another, creating a tug-of-war for control between participants. In designing the Oxford veterans' residence, for example, when the architects felt under pressure to begin developing concept sketches, they asked the researchers to tell them what they had found so far. The researchers complained that their findings were merely exploratory. The designers argued that any findings they had would be acceptable because those were the best knowledge about the problem available at that time (Ostrander & Groom, 1975).

Decisions made in actual multidisciplinary situations are determined by the procedures that participants have expressly or implicitly agreed on for resolving disagreements. When researchers work for designers or designers for researchers in a traditional consultant relationship, for example, *intradisciplinary* procedures are used. One person works within the discipline of the other. The member of the primary discipline retains responsibility for the outcome of the process and has final authority in making decisions—for example, whether to spend resources to carry out further research on a problem. A researcher working for a designer in such a situation might say "Although my scientific norms say I ought to study the problem longer, I will stop because the designers in charge decided that I have provided them with enough information on which to base their decision." In intradisciplinary settings, consultants learn how other people solve problems, and consultants influence the solution to the degree that they visibly contribute to the decision maker's definition of the problem. The better suited the contribution is to the accepted problem definition, the more the consultants control the effects of their input.

Some problems can be solved by dividing them into subproblems to which team members from different disciplines can separately apply their own professional standards. For example, if a client wants a building both built and evaluated, a design and research team might decide to carry out the two sets of tasks separately but in parallel. Investigators decide when research is needed and when findings may be published; designers decide when design concepts are sufficiently informed and when buildings go into construction. These procedures can be called *interdisciplinary* because they rely for their success on how well participants construct links between two or more separate disciplines. Responsibility for each part remains separate, but team members have joint responsibility for the quality of links.

Possibly the most rewarding procedures to use are ones by which team members jointly decide what to do throughout a project. Such procedures might be called *transdisciplinary* because the criteria the team uses neither wholly reflect any one discipline nor join different disciplines. They are new procedures developed by team members who respect each other's disciplinary norms, rewards, and sanctions and who are willing and able to reevaluate their own norms in the light of the team's common goals.

The flexibility a team has to institute transdisciplinary decision-making procedures is controlled by the real setting in which the team works, by clients, and by members' energies. If they are instituted, however, team members benefit by taking part in tasks not part of their normal work; for instance, designers assess the validity of research methods and researchers generate design images. They benefit by doing entirely new tasks: designers may analyze their own completed plans to identify implications for behavior of which they were not aware while designing and from these formulate research hypotheses. Each team member benefits by inventing new types of shared presentation methods and by increasing the number and types of tools he or she can use separately, such as behaviorally annotated plans and behavioral design performance programs.

To researchers one of the greatest benefits is that they are able to share in making, and taking responsibility for, risky decisions. Such training is invaluable, especially if it leads to the ability to be a bit more daring in carrying out research projects. This skill is not always nurtured in scientists' training, but it is an important one to develop:

> We must commit ourselves to the risk of talking complete nonsense, if we are to say anything at all within any [deductive] system [Polanyi, 1958: 94].

> Give me a fruitful error any time, full of seeds, bursting with its own corrections. You can keep your sterile truth for yourself [Pareto, cited in Gould, 1978: 22].

> The 'better' or 'preferable' hypothesis will, more often than not, be the *more improbable* one [Popper, 1972: 17].

By learning how to choose "bold" hypotheses (Popper, 1972: 53), researchers may be able to increase their chances of eventually making significant contributions to scientific knowledge.

CRITICAL TESTING

Science may be thought of as continual criticism of necessarily incomplete knowledge (Popper, 1972). Scientific researchers rely mainly on explicit test procedures to decide whether an assertion is tenable enough to be included in a growing body of shared knowledge. They are not unfamiliar, however, with using tacit criteria to assess, for example, the elegance of an argument.

Designers who use tests to improve their knowledge rely mainly on tacitly understood criteria, having only a weak tradition of explicit shared tests. In itself this is not a problem. It is a problem only for designers who want to make empirically testable assertions and then have no way to test them: "Designs which are unevaluated are just assertions no matter how they are derived. Testing and evaluation are the only way of deciding whether a design is a success and of building up a *body of knowledge*" (Rapoport, 1969a: 146). This statement could easily be adopted as the keystone for all research and design endeavors. Rapoport rightly assumes that design is potentially a developing body of knowledge. Designers who want to contribute to it can use collaboration with researchers to develop new test procedures and to improve the testability of designed objects.

Effective environment-behavior tests (1) are appropriate to their subject matter, (2) are used on testable presentations, and (3) provide results that participants do not disregard.

Appropriateness

Designers and researchers sometimes mistakenly think they add to knowledge by making assertions (a building; a hypothesis) that they justify by referring to the past rather than by testing. Justifications take different forms (de Zeeuw,

1978). One is *personal* judgment: "I say this building works or this hypothesis is sound because So-and-So says so." Le Corbusier, Parsons, Lewin, Ada Louise Huxtable, and Freud are often-used "so-and-so's" in E-B debates. *Intersubjective* justifications assert that a group of people agrees with one's point of view: important designers, scientific peers, the public. Such authorities may be appropriate for judging how beautiful a group considers a design to be, for example, or how well it fits certain Modern Design beliefs.

Personal judgment and intersubjectivity, however, are inappropriate when used to test whether a building leaks or whether it satisfies psychological and social needs. These situations offer designers a chance to take advantage of developed research procedures.

Testable Design Presentations

The less testable hypotheses are, the less meaningful they are for researchers who want to solve a problem. If drawings, plans, and even buildings are presented in such a way that assertions can be empirically tested, knowledge and action can be improved. For E-B questions this implies that designers and researchers can develop a body of shared knowledge by making explicit some of the behavioral expectations they hold for planned buildings, the operational procedures they see being used to test their expectations, and the theories on which their expectations are based.

Two pitfalls peculiar to design can make buildings untestable. The first is that designs are often presented *ceteris paribus* ("all things remaining equal"): "As designed, this building will be a success using the following criteria . . . all things remaining equal." Presenters using a *ceteris paribus* clause take responsibility for the success of a building under a range of conditions; but, conversely, when conditions vary at all, they can insulate themselves from test results by saying "All things did not remain equal."

Buildings may also be presented *fait accompli*—after all chances are past for effective criticism, testing, or sanctions. Although testing can theoretically still take place, in reality the presentation goes unchallenged.

Reactions to Test Results

A reasonable degree of "methodological tolerance" (Lakatos, 1970: 157) helps maintain fresh ideas in a developing body of knowledge. Tests applied too harshly run the risk of nipping in the bud young ideas that with hindsight may prove to have been the beginning of important shoots. However, the suspended judgment necessary in such situations does not give either researchers or designers license to submit fuzzy and incoherent ideas. Rather, it provides temporary license to present and develop tacit aspects of their work without fearing ruthless criticism because certain parts of the whole are still unclear.

Methodological tolerance is an attitude toward constructing and applying tests to nurture new ideas. It is not an appropriate response to agreed-on test results after receiving them. In multidisciplinary work both researchers and designers have a natural tendency to retreat into their own disciplinary shells and say *"Your* test results are not relevant for me." Severe arguments are avoided when designers and researchers working together both understand that if they want to improve what they know, they must see problems made visible by test results as opportunities for further learning.

TACIT AND EXPLICIT KNOWING

Scientific procedures are expected to be formulated in such a way that they can be shared in a broader community. Many people interpret this to mean that scientific knowledge is explicitly held. In fact, among philosophers of science there is an ongoing debate about the role of objective knowing and tacit knowing in science (Kuhn, 1970; Polanyi, 1958). There is a similar debate among designers and design researchers about the need for "objective," systematized design knowledge.

When scientists and designers work together, they learn about different types of knowing useful in both fields. Scientists can test the usefulness of such expressions of tacit knowing as exemplars and models. Designers can see what they might gain from testable theories and hypotheses.

Explicit Knowledge

Theories about a subject summarize past experience in a set of statements, using quality criteria to ensure that the statements are internally coherent, that they are explicitly transferable to other people, that they can be connected to new experience by testing, and that from them one can derive new testable statements about unknown experience.

Theories in social science form the basis of research programs carried out by generations of investigators, such as Parsons' theory of action (Parsons & Shils, 1951) and Lewin's field theory (Lewin, 1951). Environment-behavior researchers have few formal macrotheories to develop; Barker's ecological psychology (Barker, 1968) is unique in its theoretical completeness. There are, however, important middle-range theories (Merton, 1957) summarizing empirical evidence in E-B research—for example, Hall's proxemics (Hall, 1966). Altman (1975) astutely responds to the need for formal theory in environmental design by proposing a "boundary-regulating" theory to combine previous research on privacy, personal space, territory, and crowding. Although design disciplines have not traditionally emphasized formal theory, cooperation between designers and researchers serves as an opportunity to develop E-B theory.

Hypotheses are explicit provisional suppositions or conjectures explaining empirical research which serve as starting points for further investigation and can be made more or less tenable by this research. In other words, hypotheses, like theories, are explicit and testable guesses about the world.

Theories comprise hypothetical statements. Some hypotheses refer to directly observable phenomena (like the height of a door or the percentage of teenagers using a park). Some refer to indirectly observable, deduced phenomena (like the relation between the weight of chairs in a room and inhabitants' feeling of control over their environment). Designs, sketches, and even buildings may be seen as hypotheses adding to a body of knowledge if they serve as starting points for further research and if the conjectures they make are testable.

Tacit Knowledge

Tacit knowledge is knowledge we use that we cannot make explicit, as when we recognize that someone is angry or is feeling pity without being able to describe just what it is about the person's face that expresses the mood (Polanyi, 1967). It is therefore not codified in explicit "rules, laws, and criteria for identification" and is "learned by doing . . . rather than by acquiring rules for doing" (Kuhn, 1970: 191–192). Often tacit knowing is relegated to the back of the bus in research, as intellectually inferior to other types of knowing. One reason is perhaps that forms of expressing tacit knowledge are so poorly understood, among them exemplars and models.

Exemplars are typical examples that members of a group agree exhibit certain qualities common to a class of objects, processes, or ideas. Students study exemplars to gain new knowledge—to "grasp the analogy between two or more distinct" situations and thus assimilate "a time-tested and group licensed way of seeing" (Kuhn, 1970: 189), learning to apply the analogy to new, similar situations when they arise.

> One of the fundamental techniques by which the members of a group, whether an entire culture or a specialists' sub-committee within it, learn to see the same things when confronted with the same stimuli is by being shown examples of situations that their predecessors in the group have already learned to see as like each other and as different from other sorts of situations [Kuhn, 1970: 193–194].

In science, laboratory experiments carried out to demonstrate methodological principles are exemplars of a way of doing things. In an E-B seminar, students may be asked to analyze in detail Cooper's *Easter Hill Village* (1975) as an exemplar of the principles necessary to carry out a competent evaluation study. Professors teach architecture and art-history students to recognize styles by showing them examples of buildings representing a style while describing certain of the style's characteristics. And in some business and law schools, established wisdom is conveyed by the "case study" method: descriptions of situations are read and discussed by students under the direction of a leader who points out exemplary methods of resolving problems in the cases. Exemplars like these are frequently used in the sciences, arts, and professions.

Models for a subject are representations—sometimes analytic, sometimes more poetic—that imply that one can learn how the subject acts by treating the model "as if" it were the subject itself. Models express primarily tacit knowledge. In science models include such statements as "The molecules of a gas behave like tiny elastic billiard balls in random motion" (Kuhn, 1970: 184). In modern architecture, models run rampant, the most famous probably being Le Corbusier's dictum that "the house is a machine for living in" (1965: 100).

Models differ from analogies in that a model, in addition to communicating similarities of whole shapes and ratios among some parts, implies that doing something to the model will have the same consequences for it as doing something to what it represents. Models provide designers with ways to learn about things they do not know by providing the chance to generate questions and try out answers on things they do know. If gas molecules behave like elastic billiard balls, what happens if the billiard table is made smaller? What happens if pairs of elastic billiard balls are glued together? In a machine for living, what are measures for operational efficiency? What happens if the energy source for the machine is stopped? And so on.

OVERVIEW

Collaboration among disciplines is rewarding to participants when it helps them improve their results: more useful information, better products, greater payment. But collaboration can also be rewarding for its own sake when it improves participants themselves—when they come out of it with more skills than when they went in.

This chapter proposes that among the skills researchers and designers working together can learn are how to evaluate the risk of making decisions in different situations, how to use critical testing to build a body of shared E-B knowledge, and how to use both tacit and explicit knowing.

The next chapter is more concrete. It describes how to design your research project so that you can efficiently use available resources to solve your problem.

Chapter 5

RESEARCH STRATEGY: APPROACHES, DESIGNS, SETTINGS

"A great discovery solves a great problem, but there is a grain of discovery in the solution of any problem."

George Polya
How to Solve It

An environment-behavior research project begins with the definition of a problem. You assess what you know about it and what you want to know, and you envision what you might do with results. Then you commit yourself to a way of working: focusing on a particular problem and deciding on the research design and setting that will solve your problem best. By answering these questions for yourself, you can design your research project to achieve what you want: What do I want to find out? What design will give me useful information to solve my problem? What setting will use my resources effectively?

Decisions to Be Made about Research Design
Research Approaches
Diagnostic
Descriptive
Theoretical
Action
Research Designs
Case study
Survey
Experiment
Research Settings
Natural
Contrived

RESEARCH APPROACHES

Beginning with little knowledge about your study object, you might choose to carry out a reconnaissance mission (Gans, 1962) to find out about it generally: its purposes, its parts, and the relations among its parts. Or you may want to describe it or some of its parts more thoroughly. In either case your main objective is improving your understanding of the study topic. However, your main objective may be to use the findings of your study to refine theoretical knowledge or to influence real-world decisions and their consequences. If your aim is to understand a topic, you might engage in a *diagnostic* or *descriptive* study; if it is to refine a particular theory or improve action, you might undertake *theoretical* or *action* research.

Research projects generally combine several approaches sequentially. Researchers begin with a diagnostic phase and then decide to describe further certain of the traits they have uncovered. They use theories when they make such decisions and when they formulate hypotheses they want their data to test. Applied research, ideally, influences action. Examining each approach separately can help you select the mix most relevant to your problem.

Diagnostic Studies

Diagnostic studies help you deepen your understanding of a setting; they provide suggestive evidence on a broad realm rather than "rigorous safeguards on the trustworthiness and specifiability of findings" (Hyman, 1955: 67). They make the tradeoff between precision and breadth in favor of breadth. They offer insight into the structure and dynamics of a whole situation, possibly even setting the stage for further research. Gans' *Urban Villagers* (1962) is just such a study.

Gans lived in Boston's West End neighborhood for eight months in 1957 and 1958 just before the low-rise buildings were torn down and replaced by high-rise, high-income housing. In *The Urban Villagers* Gans diagnoses the West End, identifying its purposes, its parts, and the relations among them. He identifies what to him are the constituent parts of an urban village—an area where immigrants "try to adapt their nonurban institutions and cultures to the urban" (1962: 4). He describes what it was like to live there: family life, politics, social services, the mass media, and consumer goods. He compares West Enders with other Americans and concludes that their ethnic differences are less striking than their socioeconomic similarities. He comments on urban redevelopment, criticizing the definition many redevelopment officials then held of a "slum."

In his methodological appendix to the book, Gans points out that he had no rigorous hypotheses to test in his study and that in fact his findings were themselves hypotheses. His evidence, more "illustrative than documentary" (1962: 347), leads to after-the-fact sociological interpretation rather than to tested knowledge. He describes his study as an attempt by a trained social scientist to describe and explain the behavior of a large number of people—using his methodological and theoretical training to sift the observations—and to report only those generalizations which are justified by the data. . . . Properly speaking, the study is a reconnaissance—an initial exploration of a community to provide an overview—guided by the canons of sociological theory and method but not attempting to offer documentation for all the findings. . . .

Many of the hypotheses reported here can eventually be tested against the results of more systematic social science research [1962: 349–350].

For trustworthiness of findings, diagnostic studies rely on the consistency, clarity, and coherence of the insights they develop in the situation being studied. Researchers who want more precise measurement of particular attributes of a group or situation may carry out a descriptive study based on conceptual frameworks developed in diagnostic ones.

Descriptive Studies

Descriptive studies describe and measure as precisely as possible one or more characteristics and their relations in a defined group. Developing clear concepts and translating these into something that can be counted as a manifestation of the concept are particularly crucial problems in descriptive research. Rainwater's study of fear among residents of the Pruitt-Igoe housing project in St. Louis (1966) is a descriptive study. On the basis of a large survey Rainwater describes the feelings of a particular group of people about their homes. He shows that their feelings about the street are dominated by fear of social, psychological, and physical attacks from the outside world and that they consequently see their homes as havens from such abuse.

In an equally interesting but less well known descriptive study, Altman, Nelson, and Lett (1972) interviewed 147 sailors about their and their families' activities at home. Their complex questionnaire requested the sailors, among other things, to draw floor plans of their homes, to label rooms, and to describe in detail how each room was used, by whom, and whether doors were left open, closed, or locked. The investigators recognized sets of relations in their data:

. . . two characteristic family styles of use of home environments. One family pattern . . . seemed to be characterized by a cluster of environmental behaviors which were [open, accessible, informal, sharing, overlapping, and socially interactive. The other type of] families had firmer environmental boundaries between members, a more formal approach to use of space, and a lesser degree of family interaction and role sharing [1972: 2].

Their description of family styles began to uncover possible explanations for their findings:

There was a bare suggestion that family size/density may be important. Other directions potentially worthy of exploration may concern family integration-disintegration, e.g., marital discord and harmony, presence of emotionally disturbed, delinquent, etc., children. Thus, the matter is totally open as to dynamics associated with these differences [1972: 3].

But the authors point out:

Because this study was inductive and normative in goal, no real explanation of these stylistic differences could emerge from the data. Future research can fruitfully address this question in terms of underlying factors associated with these behavior patterns [1972: 3].

Altman et al. recognized that different types of research projects can and must build on one another if a body of environmental design knowledge is to be established.

Theoretical Studies

Theoretical studies test specific hypotheses suggested by experiences elsewhere or primarily derived from more comprehensive theory. Such studies tend to increase general insights and to focus more on the conceptual framework of a problem than on the precise nature of the group they are observing.

A clear example of a theoretical environmental design study is *Social Pressures in Informal Groups* (Festinger, Schachter, & Back, 1950), carried out among married Massachusetts Institute of Technology students living in one dormitory complex. Festinger's research team wanted to test, among other hypotheses, the theoretically derived notion that, the closer similar people live and the more chances an environment offers them to meet, the more likely they are to become friends. The research team chose these dormitories because they provided a naturally occurring experimental setting in which to test their theoretically derived ideas. All students living there were married, many were supported by the G.I. Bill, and all were assigned haphazardly to an apartment unit. Thus, the population was both homogeneous and apparently randomly placed throughout the site. Important for Festinger's natural experiment was the fact that the dorms were designed with two different building types on two sides of the dormitory site.

Festinger et al. found in both types of housing that proximity alone did not lead to greater friendship. Rather, placement of front doors and pathways was crucial: the more chances neighbors had to meet each other on the way in or out, the greater the likelihood that they would become friendly. As mentioned in Chapter 2, the researchers called this dimension of environment "functional distance."

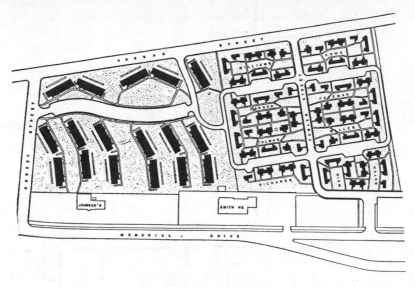

M.I.T. dormitory site. Reprinted from *Social Pressures in Informal Groups*, by Leon Festinger, Stanley Schachter, and Kurt Back, with the permission of the publishers, Stanford University Press. Copyright 1950, renewed 1978 by the Board of Trustees of the Leland Stanford Junior University.

Action Research Studies

In *action research studies* changes are made and analyzed that have direct and lasting consequences on people beyond those in the research project. An example is the construction and evaluation of the Twin Rivers new town where residents were expected to walk more and drive less (Keller, 1978). Changes there included special pathways and stores located near housing; consequences resulted for inhabitants. Action research projects aim to improve future actions by understanding earlier, similar changes in such things as physical environments, management rules, policies, and the way decisions are made.

To assess the side effects of an action, investigators can compare the consequences of different actions taken in roughly similar situations. Howell and Epp studied social spaces in high-rise housing for older persons (Howell & Epp, 1976; Howell, 1980). They located two nearby buildings whose designs differed primarily in whether or not residents were required to pass by social spaces as they walked from entrance to elevator.

On the basis of observed differences in behavior at these and similar sites, Howell and Epp made visible for designers both positive and negative consequences of such decisions in the future. For example, they found that if a building forces its residents to interact in social spaces when they do not want to and provides social spaces that make residents feel they are in a "goldfish bowl," residents are more likely to fight and less likely to use social spaces. This

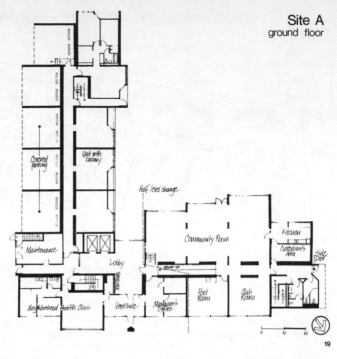

Site A
ground floor

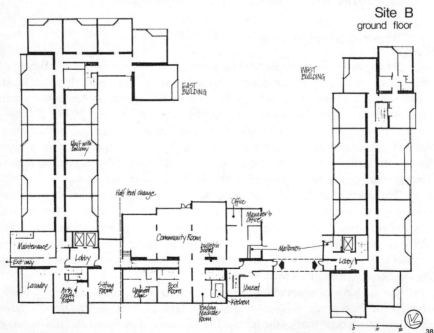

Site B
ground floor

Relation between social spaces and path from entrance to elevator in two
high-rise buildings for older people. From Howell, Sandra C., *Designing for
Aging: Patterns of Use*. Cambridge, Massachusetts: MIT Press (1980, in
press). Reprinted by permission.

happened in building B, where the arrangement of entry, social spaces, and elevator forced residents to see others whenever they came or went. In building A residents were encouraged but not forced to interact and could engage comfortably in private meetings in the activity rooms. They consequently used these spaces more.

Comparative action research settings may occur naturally or may be created analytically by careful sampling. For example, a survey of the consequences for low-income families of moving into new public housing (Wilner et al., 1954) established matched samples of people who did and did not move, thereby assessing consequences over a ten-year period of a major E-B policy while it was being implemented.

Action research studies are particularly prevalent among the works of environmental researchers and designers who see planning and evaluation research as essential to effective decision making.

RESEARCH DESIGNS

What research design an investigator chooses to study a problem with depends on the way the problem is defined, what the investigator wants to know, the nature of the object being studied, previous knowledge the study is based on, and type of results desired. Researchers use a *case study* design when they want to develop intensive knowledge about one complex object, because case studies are designed to understand an object as a whole. Investigators who want to learn about classes or types of elements embedded in a diverse group use a *survey* design. *Experiments* are useful to test the effects of actions by observing differences between a situation in which an action is taken and another in which it is not taken.

Case Study

Investigators use case studies to describe and diagnose single, internally complex objects: individuals, buildings, episodes, institutions, processes, societies. In case studies investigators delineate boundaries of an object and then observe such things as the elements it comprises, relations among elements, the development of the object, and contextual influences.

A case study is appropriate when investigators are interested mainly in information specific to the particular study object and context, rather than information easily generalizable to a large population.

Some benefits of this approach can be seen where a research/design team was asked to design a residence for older veterans in a small, rural New York town called Oxford (Nahemow & Downes, 1979; Snyder & Ostrander, 1974). At Oxford, psychologists Ostrander and Snyder wanted to provide information about one institution—its residents, its staff, its setting—in order to design another institution for essentially the same constituents. They had carried out similar projects on the needs of older people which provided them general direction for asking questions, but at Oxford they were particularly interested in what this specific situation was like and what was important to the lives of users of this institution. This situation was prototypically appropriate to a case study.

In case studies, multiple research techniques, especially participant observation, are often needed for investigators to get sufficient data about different aspects of an object. At Oxford the researchers lived in the facility for several days in a row, observed and recorded physical traces, observed and mapped resident and staff behavior, analyzed health records, carried out an interview survey with all residents, and tested mock-ups of proposed room arrangements. By comparing the various types of data, they gradually began to see what was important in the daily lives of the people there.

Two examples of insights by the investigators at Oxford are that some older persons lived a 24-hour life-style and that there was a link between physical mobility and friendship. While living at Oxford, Snyder and Ostrander observed that a number of residents heated food in cans on radiators and kept food chilled on their windowsills, although a communal eating hall served meals on a regular schedule. (Institutional rules prohibited hot plates or refrigerators in rooms.) When interviewed, residents explained food in their rooms by complaining that the cold meals served on Sundays were not sufficient. But it was clear to observers that food was prepared in rooms on other days and at other times as well. Investigators saw clues to a more plausible reason for this activity when they got up in the middle of the night and found some residents reading in the library (3:00 A.M.) and others taking showers (5:00 A.M.). Insomnia kept residents up! Further probing in focused interviews revealed other activities that reflected a 24-hour resident life-style independent from the institution's main 6:00 A.M. to 7:00 P.M. schedule. As a result, final design proposals included such things as all-night activity rooms, kitchenettes accessible to small groups of residents, and individually regulated temperature controls, all intended to accommodate residents' need for greater self-reliance.

Use of multiple techniques also enabled researchers to see a special problem of residents: the less their mobility, the fewer friends they had. This insight was sparked when investigators analyzed administrative records, finding a higher percentage of residents confined to wheelchairs than observed in the hallways and a strikingly high percentage of residents with degenerative disabilities. They had a hunch that these percentages were important. Observation of behavior and physical traces, as well as interviews, pointed out why wheelchair residents were so isolated: between the one ward on which many of them were located and most communal areas there were physical obstacles such as stairs, and aides assigned to help them were too weak to overcome these obstacles. The link between disability and social isolation gave particular force to design proposals for barrier-free access to all communal areas.

The design and research team at Oxford was particularly explicit about why it made certain design decisions. One set of design decisions was made to increase residents' control over their environment and in turn to increase residents' self-reliance and self-respect. These decisions included one-story buildings, rooms clustered around community spaces, a glass-enclosed "street" connecting clusters, and individual rooms easily convertible from singles to doubles.

Each design decision at Oxford is as much a research hypothesis as any verbal or mathematical formulation might be. It is a proposed response to a problem. Although acceptable for the moment, it is open to further testing and refinement. Future evaluation researchers will be able to build on and improve this set of hypotheses linking environment, behavior, and psychological states.

When case studies are carried out on topics which have been studied before and about which some theory exists, results may be generalizable beyond the particular situation examined. Another way to make a case study more generalizable is to choose a setting that is in many ways typical of other settings—for instance, a hospital whose size, facilities, services, and setting are like those of many other hospitals.

Survey

A survey design is useful when investigators want to find out in detail about a phenomenon, such as housing satisfaction, or about a class of elements, such as single-family homes located in a neighborhood with many kinds of

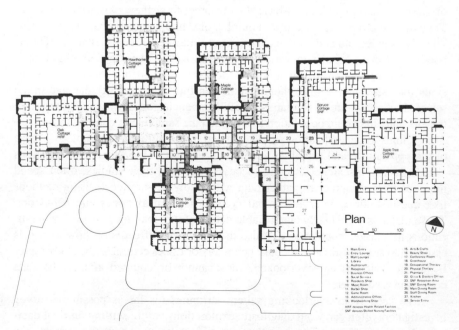

Plan of Oxford veterans' home. New York State Veterans Home, Oxford, New York. Completed 1979. Architects: The Architects Collaborative, Inc., Cambridge, Mass. Used by permission.

dwelling units. Using a survey, investigators—such as census takers—can study groups of elements dispersed over a broad geographic area. The U.S. housing-survey census gathers physical-trace data on buildings and their condition much as the population census finds out about people. Survey researchers who study large populations often choose to gather data that are easy to quantify and therefore less time-consuming to analyze than qualitative data. For this reason frequent research methods used in surveys are mail questionnaires and interviews. Yet, as the housing census makes clear, quantifiable survey data in E-B research can as well be gathered by systematically observing physical traces or even behavior.

To study school property damage in Boston, a team of sociologists, planners, psychologists, and architects used a multiple-method survey design. The goal of the study was to provide guidelines for Boston architects to use in designing schools which would decrease property damage and maintenance costs (Zeisel, 1976a). Zeisel and his colleagues used a survey design to explore the general phenomenon of property damage: of all sorts, in any public school, wherever located throughout the city. They wanted to discover how frequently different kinds of damage occurred and how various types of damage correlated with elements of physical settings. The resulting guidelines were intended to be applicable to any Boston school, not to one particular building.

Team members could not assume the problems at one school to be typical of those at others, nor did they have the resources to visit every school in Boston. They therefore randomly sampled a number of schools to visit, making sure these schools included old and new ones, ones in primarily White and Black neighborhoods, and ones located in various school districts. The logic of sampling is central to surveying. Investigators try to make sure by such devices that conclusions from the sample of a phenomenon—in this case property damage in the selected schools—are as similar as possible to conclusions they would draw were they to study the entire population from which the sample was chosen.

Limits to generalization are determined by such things as sample size, size of the population, and sampling techniques, as well as the salience of questions asked. Survey researchers, trying to be extensive in their studies, often spend much of their resources to gather data with a low per-unit cost, using methods like questionnaires, interviews, and counts of physical traces and behaviors. These methods yield easily quantifiable data useful in making statistical generalizations to a larger population. To use these methods effectively, however, it is essential to ask questions and count behaviors or traces central to the study topic. If salient attributes are overlooked, they cannot be counted after costly data collection is complete.

To keep from overlooking salient attributes (as far as possible), survey investigators often carry out diagnostic explorations before settling on final data-collection instruments. The less the investigator knows about the subject, the greater emphasis is put on preliminary diagnostic studies. Just before the major data-collection effort, drafts of techniques are pretested—tried out to see whether they are understandable and whether any essential topics have been omitted. A range of data-collection techniques are often employed so that each technique can be used to check on the others' completeness.

In Zeisel's survey of Boston schools, for example, investigators used a combination of observation of physical traces, observation of behavior, interviews, questionnaires, and records analysis. During an initial walk-through with custodians at each school, they recorded physical damage in field notes and photographs. This information served as the first indication that custodians dealt with four kinds of property damage: (1) malicious damage resulting from attacks on the school; (2) misnamed vandalism, whose consequences look the same as malicious damage but are caused by acts not intended to do harm, such as hitting hockey pucks for fun against a glass door; (3) nonmalicious damage, such as graffiti, resulting from conscious action not meant to hurt the school or anyone in it; and (4) maintenance damage, such as paths worn across lawns, the consequence of unconscious behavior and design unresponsive to user needs. The first type assumes malicious behavior, the last three not.

Investigators then carried out focused interviews with groups of students in various neighborhoods to redefine the four categories so they would reflect students' points of view. A survey of maintenance records was made to determine the most frequently reported type of damage (window breakage) and how often custodians differentiated between malicious and nonmalicious damage (seldom).

After investigators analyzed all these data, they designed a structured questionnaire and sent it to maintenance superintendents in every school district in Massachusetts to find out how they spent most of their repair budget (on windows), whether they felt damage was increasing or decreasing (increasing), what they had already done to reduce the risk of future damage (fire and theft alarm systems), and how often they differentiated malicious from nonmalicious damage (seldom).

The multiple-method survey convinced the investigators and the city of Boston that the design guidelines they developed would make visible to architects a variety of design opportunities for reducing property damage in future schools.

Experiment

An experimental design is appropriate when investigators want to measure the effects that an action has in a particular situation. An experiment answers the question "What difference does it make?" What difference does it make if residents of a building participate in making management decisions, for example, or if students live in single rather than double rooms?

In an experiment you want to be able to focus observations on a small number of attributes at one time. To do so, you need control, so that you can be as sure as possible that the effects you observe result from experimental changes rather than from the way the changes are administered or the effects are observed.

Control is used to achieve experimental knowledge built on the principle that "knowledge is knowledge of differences" (Runkel & McGrath, 1972). More precisely:

> Basic to scientific evidence (and to all diagnostic processes including the retina of the eye) is the process of comparison, of recording differences, or of contrast. Any appearance of absolute knowledge, or intrinsic knowledge about singular isolated objects, is found to be illusory upon analysis. Securing scientific evidence involves making at least one comparison. For such a comparison to be useful, both sides of the comparison should be made with similar care and precision [Campbell & Stanley, 1966: 6].

In experiments researchers organize their operations so as to control various factors. For example, to measure changes caused by the action they introduce, they may observe the situation both *before and after* the action. And to make sure that changes observed are not the result of other characteristics of the situation, they may also observe an equivalent one in which the experimental action is not taken. This comparison may be created by randomly assigning participants to both situations. The participants assigned to the situation in which the action is not taken are called a *control group*.

Experimental design in applied behavioral science research often seeks to approximate the control of a laboratory experiment but does not, because of real-world restrictions. Campbell (1974) distinguishes research projects in which randomized assignment is absent by calling them "quasi-experiments." One such study is Carp's evaluation of Victoria Plaza, a housing project for older people in Austin, Texas (1966). Carp controlled and identified as best she could differences between residents and a nonresident control group. She first interviewed and tested all 352 older persons who had applied for housing to the Austin Housing Authority—before any of them knew whether they would be accepted to Victoria Plaza. Of these persons, 204 were accepted and became residents; 148 either were rejected or withdrew their application. A year after move-in, Carp reinterviewed 190 residents and 105 nonresidents, treating the latter as a control group. This means she first compared the two groups to determine whether they were significantly different in their initial interview and then compared how each had changed or not changed during the year.

The two groups turned out to be significantly similar before moving in, on such items as age, income, education, self-evaluation, health, and condition of present housing. The housing authority's procedures, however, tended to select more people for residence who said housing was a major problem for them and who seemed to be slightly more mentally alert and cheerful. For some research purposes, it might be preferable to select residents and nonresidents randomly; this is not always possible in real-world settings. In addition, since Carp was interested in how a real-world setting works, it would have gone against her intentions to control the assignments artificially. She overcame this problem by

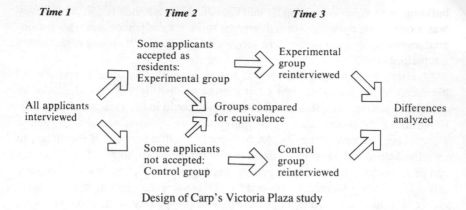

Design of Carp's Victoria Plaza study

comparing the two groups after selection, taking small differences into account in her analysis and assuring herself that there were no significant differences on traits that might reasonably be expected to confound results. And what were those results?

Among the more interesting results was that while residents showed a decrease in desire for medical services (from 7% to 1%), nonresidents doubled their stated need for these services (from 13% to 27%). Carp concludes that either the new housing actually affected residents' physical well-being or it improved their morale so that they no longer felt the need so much.

Not surprisingly, almost no residents felt that housing was a major problem after living in Victoria Plaza a year, while among nonresidents the percentage feeling this way increased from 27 to 29. A significant side effect of residence is also interesting: Before tenants were selected, in 1960, only about a quarter of both residents and nonresidents felt they had "no major problems." In 1961 this figure jumped to nearly three quarters for residents, while the proportion among nonresidents remained near a quarter (see Table 5-1).

Table 5-1. Percentages of Victoria Plaza residents and nonresidents reporting "no major problems"

	Residents	Nonresidents
In 1960, before moving	25	27
In 1961, postoccupancy	74	29

From *A Future for the Aged: Victoria Plaza and Its Residents,* by F. Carp. Copyright 1966 by University of Texas Press. Reprinted by permission.

And of course not all effects of the housing move were good. Carp found that residents who started getting together with neighbors socially after moving in also felt more than nonresidents that they had to "keep up with the Joneses"—to buy new furniture and clothes. Residents became "house proud" in their new

netimes even dipping into capital. Although they felt living this way
, many were worried: among residents the percentage who consid-
money to be a major problem increased from 65 to 89; among nonresidents
it remained at 60.

Carp's experimental design was not as controlled as some laboratory experiments in physics—but then Carp wanted to shed light on the effects of an
actual E-B setting. And this she did as best she could in her real-world situation.
Experiments of course also have limitations, and Carp discusses how these
affected her research. For example, because she had to stay out of the picture to
avoid influencing the results of the experiment, the extent to which her findings
can be generalized to other older people may be limited. Her groups were initially
self-selected (they wanted to move in) and were screened by eligibility requirements (excluded were younger persons, more prosperous ones, and those with
serious handicaps). Once again this reinforces a major methodological point:
each investigator has to select his or her research design on the basis of his or her
particular needs and purposes.

RESEARCH SETTINGS

Whether a research project is to be a case study, a survey, or an experiment, investigators can decide where they are going to study their problem. Will
you slosh in the rain watching events in natural settings? Or will you sit indoors
observing subjects in contrived settings?

Natural Settings

Natural settings offer researchers the unique opportunity to observe people
in settings they choose to come to, engaged in activities a contrived setting could
not re-create: patients decorating walls of hospital rooms with get-well cards,
customers expressing ethnic attitudes in neighborhood bars, teenagers roughhous-
ing around schools.

Natural settings are particularly appropriate for diagnostic studies in which
investigators want to find out what is actually going on—what elements, relationships, and dynamics are salient. You cannot fully observe a situation and its
context if certain portions are excluded from study, as they might be if the
situation were transferred to a contrived setting.

Gans' *Urban Villagers* (1962) and *Levittowners* (1967), Cooper's *Easter
Hill Village* (1975), and Keller's study of Twin Rivers (1976) are all environment-behavior community case studies carried out in natural settings. Each investigator found a residential complex, neighborhood, or new town in which a set
of interesting E-B questions were answerable: does proximity affect friendship,
does residential history affect residents' satisfaction with a new home (Cooper,
1975), how far will residents walk to stores in today's automobile society (Keller, 1978)?

In locating sites to carry out such studies, investigators look for situations, settings, and events that reflect theoretically relevant questions. A prepared investigator will be on the alert for research opportunities that present themselves suddenly: a spontaneous demonstration, an accident, a new town being planned nearby, or an amenable building committee.

In natural settings you can also carry out an experiment, by manipulating a part of a physical environment, a particular social behavior, or a policy. For example, in a hospital an investigator might change a wall or a window in a randomly selected set of similar patient bedrooms, estimating effects by comparing before-and-after observations in rooms with and without changes. In one ingenious natural experiment, experimenters had well-dressed and badly dressed men cross against a red light at a traffic intersection to see how the implied class difference of clothes influenced other people to break the law (Lefkowitz, Blake, & Mouton, 1955). In natural experiments like this one or like Carp's study of Victoria Plaza, investigators are seldom able to control the situation by experimental methods like assigning participants randomly to different groups. In this project they assumed that at about the same time of day and at the same street corner, most people would vary randomly on attributes that might affect their responses to well-dressed or sloppily dressed men. (Pedestrians followed the well-dressed jaywalker more often.)

In natural policy experiments, investigators work with "experimental administrators" to collect baseline data, to help decide the location and timing of policy implementation, and to measure aftereffects both where policy is and where it is not implemented (Campbell, 1969). For example, the U.S. government wanted to determine the effects of a housing-allowance program, under which people who cannot afford market-rate dwellings are given a direct monetary allowance. The government ran a large-scale natural E-B experiment in several selected areas around the country to determine actual consequences of this policy. Among their findings were that increased spending ability did not necessarily lead low-income people to move into higher-income neighborhoods. Rather, social cohesion among residents and exclusionary practices among landlords led to higher prices being paid for housing in what remained predominantly low-income areas. Such an experiment is costly, but less costly than if the program were implemented nationwide in a way that turned out not to have the desired results.

Surveys too can be conducted in natural surroundings, but the location for data gathering may be unimportant for the study itself. For example, Fried (1963) studied how people reacted to being forced out of Boston's ethnic West End neighborhood by urban renewal; he interviewed these people wherever they happened to have moved in the Boston area. The focus of the study was not respondents' location; rather, it was their attachment to the place where they used to live—which then was a demolished pile of rubble. Fried found that most residents experienced intense suffering because they felt that they had lost both their friends and the place with which they identified. For a smaller group the forced move had a positive effect. Dislocation presented an opportunity to move up the social and economic ladder, which living in the West End did not encourage. The setting that tied together Fried's respondents could be reconstituted only through data analysis.

Contrived Settings

Contrived settings are planned and controlled research environments in which to observe people and gather data from them. One such setting is the experimental laboratory, in which investigators control the setting, choose participants randomly, effect controlled changes, and measure some attribute of the subjects after those changes. People in such situations usually know they are subjects in a research project, but not always. For example, to determine effects of room attractiveness on behavior, investigators had their assistants administer some tests to randomly assigned subjects in rooms decorated differently—one "beautiful" and one "ugly" (Mintz, 1956). In addition to measuring subjects' test scores, however, for three weeks they observed how long it took the two assistants to administer the same test in different rooms. In 32 pairs of testing sessions, the examiner sitting in the "ugly" room finished before the one in the "beautiful" room 27 times. The two examiners finished first the same proportion of times when they were in the "ugly" room, and the proportions remained the same during each of the three weeks of the experiment. This last observation led the investigators to conclude that the environmental effects were not merely initial adjustment reactions on the part of examiners. Although the assistants knew they were participants in the project, they did not realize they were actually its subjects.

Contrived settings can also be used to carry out surveys. For example, to determine teenagers' responses to particular acts of property damage, Zeisel (1976a) showed slides to invited groups and interviewed them as groups about their reaction, finding that the teens defined most of the damage as nonmalicious. Altman et al. (1972) individually administered their survey questionnaires to sailors who were also together in a contrived setting.

Such contrived surveys, or "judgment tests" (Runkel & McGrath, 1972), may be carried out to determine people's reactions to film or videotape material as well. For example, using response meters in addition to questionnaires enables each subject to express a judgment, like excitement or dislike, during the film by pressing a button. Responses recorded by a central computer are automatically correlated to the moment in the film when the judgment is made. Such methods, well known to test reactions to advertisements, can easily be transferred to assessing visual presentations of environments—potential or real.

In many people's minds natural settings are associated with diagnostic case studies and contrived settings with descriptive or theoretical experiments, much as they think white wine must be served with fish and poultry, red with other meat. Both beliefs are oversimplifications that inhibit researchers (and diners) from choosing the combination of elements that will best solve their problem and meet their needs.

OVERVIEW

Research strategy comprises commitments to a particular problem and a way of working on it. The first steps that you take when planning a strategy for a research project have important consequences not only for the way you allocate time, money, and energy but also for what you observe later on. This chapter describes some ways to approach research problems and makes visible the consequences of certain choices, so that people involved in research projects can choose strategies suited to achieving what they want. This chapter proposes that investigators can avoid costly revisions in their research projects if they self-consciously answer the following questions: What do I want to find out? What design will give me useful information to solve my problem? What setting will use my resources effectively?

The next chapter examines criteria researchers can use to evaluate and thus improve the quality of their research.

Chapter 6

RESEARCH QUALITY

"Personal knowledge in science . . . commits us, passionately and far beyond our comprehension, to a vision of reality. Of this reality we cannot divest ourselves by setting up objective criteria of verifiability—or falsifiability, or testability, or what you will."

Michael Polanyi
Personal Knowledge

People devised research to improve the way they observe the world around them and to increase their control over the consequences of their actions.

To achieve these ends it is useful to differentiate what you know from what you do not know—that is, to identify problems present-day knowledge cannot solve. If what you know and do increasingly solves recognized problems and identifies new ones, your knowledge has been improving.

When your research methods and results can be understood by other people, those others can help you identify your progress. When you can compare your research conclusions with other interpretations of the same data, you can identify your own progress. When you know how to transfer what you learn to new situations without unconsciously creating more unseen problems than you solve, you can improve your own action.

Investigators can maintain these conditions by continually asking themselves such questions as these: Have I carried out my research in such a way that it can be shared with others? Have I presented my research results in such a way that they can be tested in comparison with other researchers' results? Have I clearly identified what problems my research results can and cannot solve?

Fundamental to continued learning is an open mind. Paradoxically, this is not easy for researchers to maintain if at the same time they want to use developed theoretical perspectives and build on a body of scientific knowledge. The difficulty is that working within a theoretical perspective sometimes limits researchers in identifying problems.

Investigators who share a theoretical perspective—also called a paradigm (Kuhn, 1970) or a research program (Lakatos, 1970)—make assumptions about some problems in order to focus attention on others that they feel are important. They may use this approach to direct research to answer questions and explain

---

Criteria of Research Quality

Shared Methods

  Intersubjectivity
  Reliability
  Validity

Comparable Presentations

  Tenability
  Testability

Controlled Results

  Specifiability
  Generalizability

---

empirical results in ways that provide further insight into the theory rather than ways that identify additional problems. "Don't study that topic, you won't learn anything interesting from it" can actually mean "It won't help develop the theory."

When investigators regularly question their assumptions, they keep their minds open and provide themselves with new problems to solve. One simple way to do this is to think about seemingly obvious observations as hypotheses rather than facts. For example, saying "It may be a street corner" instead of "It is a street corner" generates questions whose answers will be new knowledge. What, precisely, is a street corner? Is this really one? How do different people define street corners? How do street corners differ?

Creative investigators know how to keep avenues open for exploration. Using shared methods, presenting findings comparably, and knowing how to use results to solve problems all help make research explorations learning experiences.

SHARED METHODS

When a group of people jointly understand a set of research methods and use them to solve problems, they can identify ways to improve the quality of their research. For this to occur, investigators make *explicit* their methods, the way they use them, and the conclusions they draw from using them. As a result of the sharing this explicitness makes possible, members of the group can (1) use one another as measuring sticks to establish the acceptability of a method to the group, its *intersubjectivity;* (2) test a method against shared expectations about how it ought to perform in use, its *reliability;* and (3) assess how well a method can be used to inform action in the real world, its *validity*. A high degree of intersubjectivity, reliability, and validity among techniques excludes from the sphere of scientific observations those that are idiosyncratic, murky, or inconsistent and reflect only one person's unique perspective.

Intersubjectivity

When researchers assess another's investigatory methods, they judge such things as how appropriate the methods seem for solving that particular problem, how reliability and validity of methods have been controlled, and how consistent the methods are with accepted theory. A group of scientists judge, for example, the extent to which the application of a method fits their scientific attitudes about how a phenomenon ought to be studied. Does a researcher employ only nonvisual interview techniques to find out about people's perception of a city, or does he use an array of techniques better suited to more recent theoretical developments about cognitive maps and images (Downs & Stea, 1973)?

Investigators might question the efficiency of using participant observation techniques to measure national attitudes toward environmental legislation or using survey research to determine the salient characteristics of toddlers' play behavior in order to design one day-care center. This type of assessment is meant to guard against a not uncommon occurrence: investigators accustomed to using a particular technique sometimes find themselves using that technique like the person with a hammer to whom everything looks like a nail.

Intersubjective judgments, which are based on attitudes shared by a group, can be a limiting criterion in scientific inquiry. However, when the scientific community at large shares in research through publications and discussion, there is hope that diversity of opinion will reward the innovative as well as reasonable and appropriate use of research methods.

Reliability

A perfectly reliable research method would consistently yield the same results if it could be used repeatedly in a situation that did not change at all. In solving actual research problems, the reliability of a method is greater when, after repeated use, little variability of results can be attributed to the method. For example, the more a set of categories for recording behavior used repeatedly or by different persons leads to similar records in the same situation, the more reliable it is considered to be.

We can think of assessing the reliability of a method in the same way we think of assessing the reliability of a child's memory about an event. We cannot re-create the event, but we can test his memory of it in order to share in his experience.

For example, a child returns with his sister from the drugstore and reports

that he saw a friend of ours there. We could wait a short while
to describe again whom he saw, to see whether the two reports ar
might ask his sister what happened and compare reports. Or we
child to describe the beginning and end of the event to see whe
reports agree.

Reliability tests used in research parallel this type of question..ug. One method (test-retest) compares results from the same technique used with the same group after enough time has elapsed for the subjects to forget their answers to the first test. Another method (alternate forms) compares the results of two techniques designed to be as different as possible yet to be the same type of tool; one technique considered reliable is tested against the other. A third method (split-half) compares the results of two parts of one technique applied to the same group at the same time. For example, results of 25 questions in a 50-item test of housing satisfaction are compared with results from the other 25; each set of questions is considered a repetition of the other.

When research techniques are used to observe changes, reliability tests are geared to minimize the chance that changes recorded are actually due to repetitious use of the measuring technique or to the way it is applied. Reliability tests aim to uncover such things as shifts in results as the technique gets older or worn by use, shifts in results over time because initial application affected respondents' responses to the next application, and results reflecting systematic errors in the technique.

Unfortunately, it is usually quite difficult to distinguish between measurement error (unreliability) and actual change in an object. The problem arises because most topics deal with things that are continually changing. Therefore, constant results ought not to be expected even with perfect reliability. When a research technique is test-retested for reliability—say, a standardized semantic differential scale measuring perceptions of a new building—it is highly likely that some attribute of context or respondent will have changed, however slightly. If investigators in such a situation measure no change at all (false constancy), they do not congratulate themselves for using reliable techniques; it is likely that their unreliability is covering up actual changes. Instead they begin to refine their measures to respond to the real change that is likely to have taken place.

Using multiple research techniques to study a problem can increase reliability and decrease the chance of falsely constant results. Collecting different kinds of data about the same phenomenon with several techniques is likely to counterbalance bias inherent in any one technique with the biases of the others. "Triangulation" of methods to increase reliability assumes, of course, that techniques are not biased in the same way (Webb et al., 1966).

We want to make methods more reliable so that when we talk about comparable research data we can assume we are talking about the same thing. Testing for reliability helps to establish and stabilize a shared memory among researchers—a shared set of categories for structuring and recording experience.

Validity

Investigators use research findings to achieve real ends. The more a method increases their and others' control of action, the more valid the method is considered to be. Most variability in research results can then be attributed to actual changes, not to the research methods used.

Validity can also be seen as a criterion applied to the report of a child returning from a trip to the drugstore. We want to be able to act on what the child tells us. If he has reliably reported that a special friend of ours is working at the drugstore, we want to be able to trust that our walking to the store will have the consequences we want—namely, that we will find our friend. If we do, the child's report can be called valid as well as reliable.

If the child reports that a friend whose funeral we just attended was the store clerk, we would immediately discount the story as invalid. But if the report is possibly valid, we could test its validity by, for example, asking his older sister (who is more familiar with our friend) whether the store clerk really was the friend. Or we might phone the store and ask for our friend, assuming that her presence now means the child actually saw her before. We could also try to remember more about our friend—does she have a relative who owns a drugstore; is she a trained pharmacist? In this way we would construct other evidence to back up the child's report. Or we might analyze the report to see whether the attributes the child uses to describe our friend all match the person we expect to find when we arrive at the store.

These everyday practical tests parallel formal ones for assessing the validity of research methods. "Concurrent validity" tests compare results from one technique with results of another technique that has been accepted as valid. For example, proposed new measures for ascertaining housing satisfaction are considered valid if results agree substantially with measures of satisfactory housing that some other planners have already used successfully.

"Predictive validity" tests compare results of a technique with those of another one measuring a phenomenon the first is expected to predict. Answers to housing-satisfaction questionnaires, for example, might be expected to correlate with (that is, predict) the amount of time residents spend fixing up their homes. If this theory is applied, and results from questions about satisfaction correspond to results from questions about time spent, the satisfaction questions could be considered valid. This test assumes correct theoretical assessment of the relation between satisfaction and time spent. It assumes that there are no other significant conditions influencing time spent on the house that might confuse the comparison.

"Construct validity" relies on correlation between the results of a technique and a network of theoretically related concepts. In other words, the property the technique measures is considered part of a more comprehensive construct whose other parts are in turn assumed to have been validly measured: tests of design creativity are considered valid, for example, only if they correlate with measures of performance, achievement, and mental quickness.

"Content validity" tests determine whether different parts of the same technique show the same results—for example, whether different sets of items on a design-creativity test show the same creativity quotient. This test is related to, but not the same as, the reliability test for internal consistency; it presents a similar problem when results are not consistent. It is difficult for investigators to know whether the two halves of the technique measured different concepts or measured several dimensions of one concept.

In general, the more methods are used simultaneously to observe different traits of a complex phenomenon, the more chance to validate techniques a researcher has, as long as all the methods are related to what the researcher wants to do. Investigators can compare techniques systematically by comparing the extent to which several techniques differentiate different traits from one another while showing similar results when measuring the same trait—thus establishing the "convergent and discriminant validity" of the techniques (Campbell & Fiske, 1959).

In sum, validity tests are used to find out whether methods explain what we and others need in order to act on the world with desired results, while reliability tests make certain that investigators using and reusing a set of methods collect comparable data. Intersubjectivity keeps scientists focused on a set of shared approaches and theories and ensures that they "speak the same language." Fundamental to being able to share and thus improve research methods is making as explicit as one can what methods one uses, how one uses them, and how one interprets results—in other words, making the methods comparable.

COMPARABLE PRESENTATIONS

To see whether research results are an improvement on what we know, it is essential that alternative explanations of data be capable of being compared. When we say that research hypotheses are *testable,* we mean that they are presented in such a way that they can be confirmed or disconfirmed by empirical data. When a hypothesis is confirmed, its *tenability* increases.

Testing a hypothesis is an attempt to show that a plausible rival hypothesis does or does not do a better job at explaining results. "A better job" means that one hypothesis explains not only what the other hypothesis explains but still more (Popper, 1972). The tenability of a hypothesis is increased both when it is tested and not disconfirmed and when plausible rival hypotheses are disconfirmed. The more rival hypotheses disconfirmed, the greater the tenability of the hypothesis (Campbell & Stanley, 1966). Mere replication of test findings does not necessarily increase the tenability of a hypothesis.

In testing a hypothesis the more you can present it so that, if it is inferior to a rival hypothesis, the test will prove it, then the more important are results of the test. In other words, the greater the risk investigators take of being wrong, the more they can value the times they are right. Of course, being right merely means not having been shown to be wrong, this time.

Three problems limit the testability of a hypothesis (Galtung, 1967): (1) its wording, (2) the problem of defining data that can confront the hypothesis, and (3) the problem of getting necessary data.

The Wording Problem

Statements considered true or false merely on the basis of their construction are customarily called *analytic*. Examples are "All boys are young males" (true) and "Girls are boys" (false).

Several types of statements are untestable in the sense that testing them gives us no new answers; nothing can be learned from testing them. A hypothesis that building a park will either increase, decrease, or not change the feeling of neighborliness among adjacent residents is a *tautology*—a statement that is analytically true. A hypothesis that if there are more tall modern buildings in a city, the degree of city pride among residents will be simultaneously higher, lower, and the same is a *contradiction*—a statement that is analytically false. It is not useful to test such statements.

Problem of Defining Data

Some hypotheses do not analytically restrict researchers from imagining empirical data to confront them with, but they use terms or references that make them not empirically testable. Examples are easy to think of: city planning is a necessary profession; territoriality is an innate drive among men and women; the Seagram's building in New York City is beautiful. One can imagine no data to test these hypotheses as worded, although they are not analytically true or false. In research terms, they are examples of *indecision*.

The following diagram presents tenability as a variable, taking into account tautologies, contradictions, and undecidable statements.

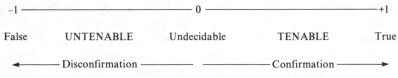

Tenability: Degree of hypothesis confirmation. Adapted from *Theory and Methods of Social Research*, by J. Galtung. Copyright 1967. (New York: Columbia University Press, 1967.) Reprinted by permission of Universitetsforlaget, Oslo, Norway.

For tests of hypotheses to lead to greater or lesser tenability, the hypotheses must be worded so they lie on the line within $(-1, +1)$, not including $1, -1$, or 0. The terms *true* and *false* are left to describe analytic statements because "we cannot imagine a synthetic hypothesis that we cannot also imagine being confirmed to an even higher degree, or even more disconfirmed" (Galtung, 1967: 33).

Problem of Collecting Data

Some hypotheses conceivably can be tested, but only by data which are in practice impossible to collect or which would be destroyed by the process of collecting them. For example, data would be in practice impossible to collect in order to confront hypotheses about unrecorded historical events or the transient internal state of an unavailable respondent. In applied design situations, practical limitations on data collection include amount of time and money available, interest among research funders, and regulations that limit access. A hypothesis is necessarily untestable in a context in which no research is allowed.

In sum, testability is the possibility of improving a hypothesis by confronting it with empirical results and with rival hypotheses. Testing increases or decreases the tenability of a hypothesis. A hypothesis being tested must have a chance of being shown to be better or worse than another: the greater the chance of being worse, if it is worse, the more weight an investigator can give to the test.

CONTROLLED RESULTS

Whether the goal of a research project is improved theory or improved action, investigators want to apply findings—to describe concrete research situations in which they developed the data and to use the findings in new situations. For example, did one "shared spaces" design in apartment buildings for older people actually make a difference to residents' use of them (Howell & Epp, 1976), and if other architects use this type of design, will it have the same effects? Did landscape design in Easter Hill Village actually lead to greater feelings of satisfaction among the residents Cooper interviewed (Cooper, 1975), and in what other situation will it have similar effects? *Specifiability* describes the degree to which research results can be used to control consequences of action in the testing situation studied; *generalizability* describes the degree to which results can be used to control action in new situations.

Specifiability

One improves the specifiability of results by controlling factors that might influence the observed changes in ways we do not see, making us credit an action or physical setting with effects it did not have. As the following hypothetical examples show, several factors can compound the interpretation of research results if investigators are not careful (Campbell & Stanley, 1966; Cook & Campbell, 1979).

1. *History:* Events outside an investigator's control occurring during the study can unwittingly cause observed results. An example would be if a "Plant a Tree" campaign, started by neighborhood ecologists, had led to high resident satisfaction with landscaping in St. Francis Square (Cooper, 1971), and Cooper had attributed this to the attractive initial planting.

2. *Maturation:* Natural growth taking place during a study can cause observed changes even though the growth is not causally related to the environment evaluated. An example would be if Zeisel were to attribute reduced graffiti and property damage to school designs based on his research (1976a), when actually the young people responsible had just abandoned this activity because they grew up.

3. *Testing:* Research techniques early in a study can influence respondents so that later measures record changes resulting from the technique, not the environment. An example would be if Carp's (1966) move-in questions had sensitized residents so that a year later they showed more interest in the housing than they otherwise might have shown, and Carp attributed this to living in Victoria Plaza.

4. *Instrument Decay:* Measurement techniques themselves change during the research project and only appear to reflect change in respondents. An example would be if observers of the buildings for older people studied by Howell and Epp (1976) had grown used to their job and had begun to record briefer encounters as "social interaction," resulting in increases over time of reported interactions, although the number of actual interactions remained the same.

5. *Selection:* Selection procedures for respondents can bias some groups in a study. An example would be if Keller had selected to interview only residents of Twin Rivers whose names had appeared in the town newspaper and had attributed a high level of environmental dissatisfaction to them, when they actually were acting dissatisfied to get their names in the paper again.

6. *Experimental Mortality:* Respondents drop out of studies in a way that systematically influences results. An example would be if anti-social residents in Westgate West had moved out of apartment locations that forced them to meet other residents, and Festinger et al. (1950) attributed the mutual friendliness of present residents there to "functional distance" instead of to tenant self-selection.

Factors of this sort also interact with each other to further confound the specifiability of a research project.

The hypothetical examples used to help define factors that can confound specifiability show that a careful researcher has many things to look out for merely to be able to interpret what she sees. Cooper's, Keller's, Howell's, and other environment-behavior studies referred to in the examples were well enough conceived and carried out that such confounding factors are either implausible or tested for. To increase the specifiability of a study, a researcher must consider and control outside influences on her data by using measures that include certain kinds of experimental designs, control groups, and multiple methods.

Generalizability

We also use research knowledge to control the effects of our actions in new situations. For example, knowledge that in 1966 at the University of California, Berkeley, students in dormitory rooms spent most of their time studying alone might be useful in designing a policy of primarily single-room dormitories for another campus (Van der Ryn & Silverstein, 1967). The more conclusions originally applicable in one setting or to one group can be applied to others without unjustifiable side effects, the greater is their generalizability. Whenever we stretch the knowledge we have, we necessarily make errors; we use research to limit these.

There are several kinds of generalizability. One is generalizability to other, similar elements—whether those elements are settings, people, or events. For example, we can use what we know about property damage in a few Boston schools to plan social programs and building redesign in others (Zeisel, 1976a). Another is generalizability to similar elements related in terms of time—in other words, to new situations. For example, studies of older suburbs (Gans, 1967) were applied five years later to plans for new towns throughout the United States. Another is generalizability from one state of a developing organism to a new state. For example, small research projects to evaluate the housing-allowance experiment—providing poorer families with money to rent their own homes— were used in writing the final policy to be implemented nationally.

Procedures developed to increase the generalizability of information in these different senses, so that we can improve our use of research, include (1) reducing the degree to which research conditions influence the study topic— increasing validity; (2) increasing the similarity between elements being studied and other elements in the group; and (3) showing that results are replicable with representative groups of elements from different populations. Each of these measures, and others used to increase generalizability of findings, attempts to increase the likelihood that the particular research situation studied can be treated without uncertainty and risk "as if" it represented other elements, new situations, and so on.

1. The less chance that the application of research methods unknowingly effected change in the sample of a population studied, the greater the chance that the sample behaved "as if" it were the rest of the group. For example, interviews with a group of residents before they move into a new building may unwittingly make them more aware of their environment than other tenants, leading them to make physical changes in their dwelling units they otherwise would not make. If investigators infer that other tenants in the building behave as this group does, they will be mistaken.

2. When it is impractical or impossible to observe everything or every person one wants to know about, investigators often sample part to observe. For example, in E-B studies investigators have observed samples drawn from diverse populations of such things as hospital buildings, children playing, times of day, visitors to a world's fair, and social encounters. Various procedures may be used to choose the sample so that most of the variability of the total group is represented in the variability of the sample of elements observed, so that, in turn, findings about the sample can be applied to describe the whole.

3. Investigators can define common problems and study them using essen-

tially similar research designs in different populations. Such replications help us to more knowledgeably apply statements about one group to less restrictively defined groups. In E-B research, for example, one group of replications began with the neighborhood research of Whyte (1955), Fried and Gleicher (1961), Gans (1962), and Fried (1963) in Boston's Italian community, the North and West End. Among the questions each of these investigators wanted to resolve was "Why are community members so strongly attached to their physically run-down, yet socially cohesive, setting?" These research projects all treated issues of territoriality, turf, environmental meaning, presentation of self, neighborhood symbolism, culture-bound user needs, and income-determined user needs. Replication studies in England (Young & Willmott, 1957), in India (Brolin, 1972), with Blacks (Cooper, 1975) and Puerto Ricans (Zeisel, 1973a), in another low-income neighborhood near Boston (Zeisel & Griffin, 1975), and in still other settings dealt again and again with these topics and the basic question of attachment to a physical environment. As more opportunities for replications presented themselves, we increased our ability to apply relations between data originally applicable only to a small Italian community in Boston to other ethnic, income, and cultural groups.

OVERVIEW

Useful research solves already-recognized problems and identifies new ones. Research methods that increase researchers' ability to do this improve the quality of research. If you use methods that allow other people to criticize your research, you can learn from them. If you can differentiate better research from worse research, you can improve your own. If you know when your research findings are applicable and when not, you can act on the world with greater control.

This chapter describes how seven quality criteria for research can be used to achieve these ends:

Intersubjectivity	Tenability	Specifiability
Reliability	Testability	Generalizability
Validity		

The chapter proposes that continually asking oneself several questions helps to keep in view the meaning of these criteria. Have I carried out my research in such a way that it can be shared with others? Have I presented my research results in such a way that they can be tested in comparison with other researchers' results? Have I clearly identified what problems my research results can and cannot solve?

PART TWO

RESEARCH METHODS

Part One described what might be called theoretical issues of cooperation between researchers and designers in the field of environment-behavior: What is research and what is design? How does awareness of their differences and similarities help people in E-B professions cooperate? What are some of the direct consequences and side effects of design and research cooperation? How do you go about designing a research project so you can use it to achieve what you want? How do you evaluate and improve the quality of your own and others' research? Part One provided a perspective to answer these questions.

Part Two is more "hands on." It describes how to observe people, their settings, and relations between the two using available E-B methods to improve your understanding of your topic. Underlying this section is a commitment to a multiple-method research approach for solving complex problems: although each method is presented separately, it yields its maximum potential when used conjointly with other methods. This section includes discussions of observing physical traces, observing behavior, focused interviews, standardized questionnaires, and archives.

Chapter 7

OBSERVING PHYSICAL TRACES

Observing physical traces means systematically looking at physical surroundings to find reflections of previous activity not produced in order to be measured by researchers. Traces may have been unconsciously left behind (for example, paths across a field), or they may be conscious changes people have made in their surroundings (for example, a curtain hung over an open doorway or a new wall built). From such traces environment-behavior researchers begin to infer how an environment got to be the way it is, what decisions its designers and builders made about the place, how people actually use it, how they feel toward their surroundings, and generally how that particular environment meets the needs of its users. Researchers also begin to form an idea of what people are like who use that place—their culture, their affiliations, the way they present themselves.

Most people see only a small number of clues in their physical surroundings; they use only a few traces to read what the environment has to tell them. Observing physical traces systematically is a refreshing method because, through fine tuning, it turns a natural skill into a useful research tool.

A simple yet striking example of the use of this method is Sommer's observation of furniture placement in a mental-hospital ward and corridor (1969). In the morning after custodians had neatened up and before visitors arrived, Sommer found chairs arranged side-by-side in rows against the walls. Each day, several hours later, he found that patients' relatives and friends had left the same chairs grouped face-to-face in smaller clusters. Among the inferences this set of physical-trace observations prompted Sommer to make was that custodians' attitudes toward neatness and their beliefs that furniture ought to be arranged for efficient cleaning and food service were incongruent with patients' behavior and needs.

To test these ideas, he rearranged the furniture in the ward, expecting patients to take advantage of the increased opportunities for sociability. For the first few weeks, he was surprised to find, patients and nurses returned chairs to their against-the-wall positions; according to them, the new way "wasn't the way things belonged." Eventually Sommer put the chairs around tables in the middle of the room, and on the tables he put flowers and magazines. When this threshold of environmental change was reached, changes in behavior took place as well: patients began to greet each other more, to converse more, and to read more, and staff members began a crafts program on the tables in the ward. And it all began when Sommer noticed a difference between how custodians left chairs in the morning and how patients and visitors left them at the end of the day.

The following discussion presents (1) significant qualities that observing physical traces has for use in E-B research, (2) types of devices for recording observed traces, and (3) a classification of trace types to make visible those relations between people and environment that are useful for designing.

Observing Physical Traces

Qualities of the Method

    Imageable
    Unobtrusive
    Durable
    Easy

Recording Devices

    Annotated diagrams
    Drawings
    Photographs
    Counting

What to Look for

    By-products of use
    Adaptations for use
    Displays of self
    Public messages
    Context

QUALITIES OF THE METHOD

Observing traces is an exceptionally useful research tool that can produce valuable insights at the beginning of a project, test hypotheses in the middle, and be a source of ideas and new concepts throughout. If you take into account what the method can and cannot do, you can achieve the results you want; like any tool, if used inappropriately it can be destructive. The method can be a source of provocative images, is unobtrusive, is easy to use, and deals with long-lasting phenomena. It provides opportunities for investigators but also sets up some traps.

Imageable

Observing physical traces provides rich impressions and is highly illustrative. Walking through a home for older veterans in Oxford, New York, investigators saw, for example, wheelchairs in odd places, old furniture, new medical equipment, direction signs, people in uniforms, open cans of food on windowsills, and patients' get-well cards taped to walls in rooms (Snyder & Ostrander, 1974). The walk gave researchers an initial picture of what life in that home was like: its design successes, some problems, exceptional situations, patterned wear and tear. At the beginning of a research project, such observations can be used to spark investigators to think about what the observed objects might mean. Skillful observers will notice even commonplace physical traces and figure out which of them will lead to fruitful inferences to pursue further. At Oxford, investigators focused their attention on cans of food on windowsills—developing from this information a central research hypothesis that residents lived a 24-hour life-style out of phase with the institution's 6:00 a.m. to 7:00 p.m. schedule.

From a trace investigators ask questions about what *caused* it, what the person who created the trace *intended,* and what *sequence* of events led up to the trace. The imageable quality of physical traces makes it easy to generate hypotheses about causes, intent, and sequence, but from the trace alone researchers cannot tell how tenable their hypotheses are; to do this, they need other methods. For example, in a brief evaluation of a somewhat run-down housing project in Roxbury, Massachusetts, Zeisel (1973b) found large, well-kept flowering shrubs in residents' backyards. At first he falsely assumed that residents beautified their small yards because they cared about the appearance of the project and wanted their own vistas more scenic. In later interviews with residents he found that shrubs had been planted years before in response to a management-sponsored competition for the best garden. A closer second look revealed that even good-looking plants in the backyards had been very much neglected.

The same potential pitfall can arise when investigators falsely infer intent. One morning a group of architects visiting a housing project for older people in a predominantly Italian section of Boston noticed a bocce-ball court surrounded by apartment windows. It looked as if it had never been used. They tentatively concluded that something was wrong with the facility, that residents did not like playing bocce ball, or that they did not like the location of the court. In fact, the court looked brand new because workmen had just completed it several days before. In addition, it was early morning, and anyone who might have used the court was still at home.

It is also difficult to infer process. In a suburban Boston prison, cell walls are papered from ceiling to floor with *Playboy, Penthouse,* and *Swank* centerfolds. At first glance it seems impressive that prisoners fix up their dwelling units so extensively—that they mark out and personalize territory so dramatically. But the impression the traces give is misleading. Most centerfolds have been glued to the cell wall by a series of previous inmates. Walls are not stripped when a new inmate moves in, every 6 to 12 months. The wallpapered surroundings that inmates move into offer them many diversions but little chance to personalize.

Visual trace records can be used as illustrations of research concepts. This can prove useful to investigators who want to follow up on trace observations with interviews to test their hypotheses. In studies of property damage in parks (Welch, Zeisel, & Ladd, 1978) and in schools (Zeisel, 1976a), for example, investigators showed slides of damaged property to groups of teenagers, park personnel, and persons living next to the property in order to focus discussion on what these people thought about property damage.

In lectures and reports, pictures of vivid traces can help viewers and readers understand physical settings in which projects were carried out. Lenihan (1966), in his report evaluating the VISTA program in the 1960s, wanted readers to understand the wide variety of volunteers' assignments: Appalachian mountain villages, Southwestern desert towns, urban slums. He used photos of physical traces to augment the poetry of his writing.

The force of concrete visual impressions can be a pitfall for careless researchers. The visual impact of even low-frequency observations can be so great—flowering bushes, nearly new facilities, vandalized windows—that they dominate a researcher's mind. To a person walking through a well-kept housing development, the beauty of a few flowering bushes can give the impression that there are flowers in bloom everywhere, even though few residents have bushes and only some are flowering. When such traces are photographed and presented out of context, they can mislead—a problem of false emphasis the visual communications media face every day. It is important that observers also train themselves to see traces that do not stand out, such as the scarcity of certain expected objects or the absence of wear and tear. If you ask yourself "What traces are missing?" in addition to "What traces do I see?" you are more likely not to be seduced by visually impressive traces. You will begin to see what is not there.

Unobtrusive

Observing traces is an unobtrusive method (Webb et al., 1966). It does not influence the behavior that caused the trace.

Unobtrusiveness is particularly valuable when gathering data about which respondents are sensitive or when respondents have a stake in a certain answer. For example, an investigator who wants to know how strictly hospital attendants follow fire-safety rules will learn more from counting the fire exits blocked by stretchers than from interviewing attendants, who may want to paint a rosier picture than actually exists. School principals who want to avoid showing they are not doing a good job may report less damage to school property than a researcher might observe directly. And principals who want the school committee to increase the budget for maintenance may magnify the damage. If a respondent at home knows a researcher is coming, she may neaten up the house beforehand, putting away such physical traces as toys in the living room, which might indicate how different rooms are used.

Observing or measuring traces does not require being present when the traces are created. The method is therefore particularly useful to find out about rare events, hard-to-see events, private behaviors, and behavior of groups who cannot be interviewed. Zeisel's school study (1976a) provides an example of using physical traces to document private behavior that is hard to observe directly. During the day teenagers can be seen hanging out around schools, playing stickball against walls, and sometimes climbing onto rooftops. At night they sometimes find out-of-the-way places around back to sit together, drink, and smoke. Boston teenagers treat these half-hidden settings as clubhouses where outsiders are not allowed. The first hint of such nighttime clubhouse activity came from physical traces: empty beer cans, discarded playing cards, cigarette butts, graffiti, and broken lights.

Durable

Many traces have the advantage for researchers that they do not quickly disappear. Investigators can return to a research site for more observations or counting and can document traces with photographs or drawings. Of course, the more permanent a trace is, the greater its chance of being observed at all. For example, rock gardens and paving stones in someone's garden will be visible for years, long after grass and flowers have virtually disappeared.

There is, however, the problem of selective deposit. Some activities are more likely to leave traces than others. The extent of beer drinking in back of a school can be detected the next day by the number of cans. Playing poker or smoking nonfilter cigarettes may leave no traces at all.

Another consequence of the durability of traces is their cumulative quality; earlier traces can encourage later ones. A large number of people may feel free to cross a lawn because people who did so before left a path, whereas few people would do so were there no path. This cumulative quality can cause problems for investigators who overlook it, who think each act is independent of earlier ones. But if traces are not taken out of context, their cumulative character can provide insights for data gathering and analysis. The finding, for example, that litter tends to beget litter (Finnie, 1973) is particularly useful if you want to arrange maintenance schedules in parks and around schools.

Easy

Physical-trace observation is generally inexpensive and quick to yield interesting information. The inexpensiveness of a brief physical-trace survey makes it possible in most research projects not only to discover but also to explore in greater depth a host of initial hypotheses. Using more costly methods would mean discarding possibly fruitful but implausible hypotheses without looking at them closely. This same quality means, however, that researchers can waste their energy because time and money do not force them to think through each initial proposition rigorously before going into the field.

The speed and ease with which physical traces can be recorded—in still photographs, sketches, notations—make the method useful for collecting a great many data for speedy review. An initial site visit can yield enough recorded observations for weeks of review and analysis. This is helpful in generating a range of testable propositions and hypotheses. Yet the harvest can be so rich that it seduces a research team not to look further: "We already have so much information. Why do we need more?"

In sum, observing physical traces is imageable and unobtrusive, deals with durable data, and is easy to do. The following sections of this chapter discuss ways to record trace observations and a classification of traces particularly relevant to questions of design.

RECORDING DEVICES

Investigators save energy and time by deciding before going into the field how and when they will record trace observations: annotated diagrams, drawings, photographs, precoded counting lists, or a combination of these. If photographs are chosen, researchers decide such issues as whether prints or slides will be more useful for the purposes of the study or whether both are needed. Each decision affects how trace observations can be analyzed, how they can be used in conjunction with other research methods, and how findings will be presented.

Observations ought also to be timed to avoid possible systematic effects of maintenance schedules or predictable activity cycles on the data—for instance, early morning cleanups that obliterate signs of teenagers' night life around schools.

Annotated Diagrams

Recording traces verbally and diagrammatically, as a rule, requires little preparation and no special skills. Except for a notepad, the recording method is unobtrusive; to make it still less obtrusive, trained observers may memorize major traces in a setting and record them later. This is especially possible when the setting is simple and the objective standardized, as when making diagrams of furniture layouts in people's living rooms for a study of what furniture people own and how they arrange it.

During a two-person interview one interviewer can inconspicuously draw a plan of the setting and note where objects are located and where physical traces are. In settings where cameras are out of place or lighting is difficult and the researcher does not want to use flash attachments, written trace notation is appropriate. Annotated diagrams are also well suited when traces can be recorded on two-dimensional plans and then studied. The arrangement of chairs Sommer (1969) observed in the patient dayroom could perhaps be represented in plan more effectively than in photographs.

When annotated diagrams are chosen as one of the recording devices, several rules of thumb can be helpful. Agreement among researchers on a set of standard symbols will increase comparability of the data within a project. For a residential floor plan, for example, a team might use traditional architectural symbols for furniture. When researchers on several projects use such standard and easily understood symbols, their data can be more easily compared and shared.

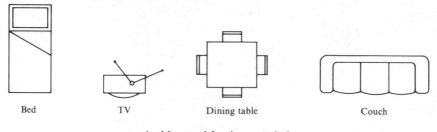

Bed   TV   Dining table   Couch

Architectural furniture symbols

Outdoors and in special settings, investigators may have to be more inventive about the symbols they use. In their study of peddlers and pedestrians on Rome's Spanish Steps, Günter, Reinink, and Günter (1978) developed a set of symbols for recording how peddlers arranged their wares (see next page).

If you want your observation notes not to be confused with your reactions to what you saw, you must not analyze them in the field. Provisions need to be made to facilitate subsequent analysis.

A simple device can facilitate preliminary analysis of field notes with a minimum of fuss: Original notes and diagrams are made on the left half of the notepaper, leaving the right half open for recording hunches and preliminary hypotheses (see the illustration "Furniture Layout in El Barrio Apartment," p. 97). A wide margin can be made on any notepaper simply by creasing it.

If investigators know the floor plans of the places to be observed, and if more than one similar place is to be observed or the same place is to be looked at several times, their notepaper can have a floor plan printed on it. This facilitates making notes and ensures comparability of diagrams. This method can be used equally well for interiors, such as offices, waiting rooms, or dwelling units (Zeisel, 1973a) and for exteriors, such as playgrounds, street corners, or plazas (Günter et al., 1978).

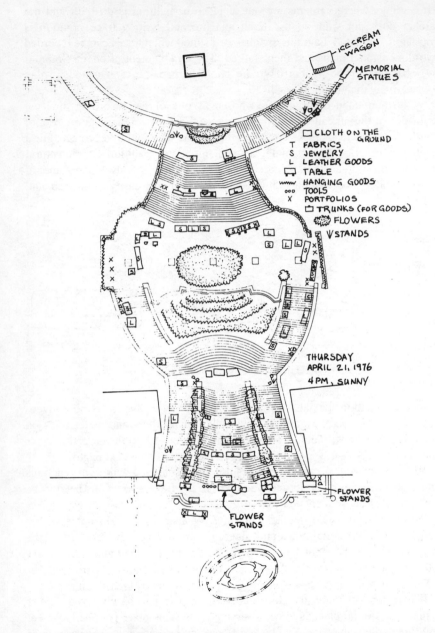

Annotated diagram of the Spanish Steps. (From *Rome-Spanische Treppe,* by R. Günter, W. Reinink, and J. Günter. Copyright 1978 by VSA-Verlag, Hamburg. Reprinted by permission.)

OBSERVATIONS	COMMENTS
Table to eat at Free-standing cupboard Curtains drawn Pictures on wall Four foot high statue of saint covered with clear plastic Curtain over door	*Does the stair location discourage residents from using the furthest door, the one into the living room?* *Does the bathroom location next to the kitchen/eating area bother residents?* *The kitchen seems to be the main place to eat. Is it big enough?* *Is the darkness in bedrooms — caused by drawing curtains — for privacy? If so, is it privacy from neighbors looking in or from the rest of the family?* *The living room door permanently covered seems to indicate that the kitchen door is the main and only entrance to the apartment.* *Does this mean that most people sit in the kitchen most of the time?* *Pictures, saint, and expensive TV in the living room seem to say "this room is a revered, special, almost sacred room." Is it?* *Does blocked living room door covered by a curtain mean it is improper to invade the "sacred" room?*

Furniture layout in El Barrio apartment: Sample field notes from Zeisel, 1973a

Drawings

If observers have the skill to make sketches of the traces they see, the time it takes may well be worthwhile. Drawings can be extremely useful in final reports because they are highly imageable and inexpensive to reproduce.

Photographs

Photographs of physical traces taken at the beginning of a research project can give all parties working on it an initial overview of the types of things they are likely to see in the field. Discussion of photographs among team members can quickly generate hypotheses about possible fruitful issues for further study. A group can leisurely discuss what behavior a trace might reflect and what intent might be behind it. For these reasons, it is generally valuable to document both easily photographed outdoor traces and indoor traces, although indoor ones may be harder to photograph. Photographs are particularly valuable if the research site is not easily accessible because it is too far away, requires special permission to visit, or is altogether temporary (for example, a circus).

When investigators expect to count traces, they can first analyze photographs of observations to decide on categories for counting. Photographs can be used as stimuli in focused interviews, to determine the categories respondents use when they see such things. At the end of a project, photographs are excellent to illustrate verbal presentations of findings. Many of these qualities hold for photographs in research, whether they are of physical traces or of behavior.

In the field several rules of thumb and a few tricks can possibly save time, money, and embarrassment. Expensive cameras are seldom more useful as research tools than inexpensive ones. Researchers need to take some photographs themselves because they know what to record for analysis—what to include in the picture and what to leave out. For illustrative photographs, one can always hire a professional photographer (or choose the most skilled researcher). Even then one will have to tell the professional precisely what to photograph. When extra equipment is needed—for instance, flash attachments or tripods for interior photographs—it must be selected with consideration of both research requirements and respondents' sensitivity.

A researcher's choice of film has perhaps the greatest consequences for the rest of the study. Black-and-white photographs, useful as illustrations, can also be made useful as objects for group discussion. Color photographs are expensive and difficult to print. From contact sheets or directly from negatives, researchers can choose a number of photographs which seem to cover the range of concerns they are aware of, which seem to be most interesting, or which require more discussion and analysis to understand. These photographs can be inexpensively printed as large blowups on a microfilm printing machine, available at most libraries. Although such prints cannot be used as permanent records because they fade after several months, they can be put on a wall for analysis and discussion.

Arrayed in this way, photographs enable all members of a research group to participate in initial visits to the site.

Color slides have other benefits. In addition to being convenient and captivating during oral presentations, slides can be easily grouped and regrouped for analysis on light tables or in projectors. Some slide films can be developed commercially in just a few hours. When it is essential to know that you have all your data before leaving a site, or when you want to make a presentation shortly after making observations, slide film that can be quickly developed or even instant-print film may be a lifesaver.

Counting

Certain traces yield their full value only when their quantity is taken into account. In such situations it will suffice to record in detail one or two examples and count the rest. For example, in a housing project where some families have fenced in their backyards and some not, photographs of a few along with a careful count will do the job.

If you know what you want to count beforehand, precoded counting pads or checklists can be arranged—possibly linked to the site plan for accurate location data.

As important as choosing appropriate categories is intersubjectivity of the categories among observers. Each member of a team of observers faced with the same physical trace ought to record it as a trace in the same category if data are to be comparable. To achieve a degree of intersubjectivity, observers in the U.S. housing census are shown photographs representing distinct levels—and therefore categories—of housing deterioration. On the basis of these "exemplars" this very large group is expected to develop a shared way of looking, at least to some extent.

Another practical way to develop intersubjectivity among investigators is to take them on a site visit to settings similar to those at the research site. Through group discussion they can learn from one another and arrive at a consensus of how items they see would be recorded.

Each way of recording traces catches another dimension of the trace and provides researchers with new data.

WHAT TO LOOK FOR

What an investigator chooses to observe depends on what he wants to do with the data he gathers. If I want to identify my mother in a crowd, I will try to notice only women whose hair is brown with a gray streak. If you want a police officer in New York City, you will look for and "see" only people in dark blue uniforms.

The following categories for looking at and gathering data about physical traces are organized to increase designers' control over the behavioral effects and side effects of their decisions and to increase people's own control over their relation to the environment. Both these purposes are means to another end: to increase everyone's ability to intervene through design to make settings better suited to what people actually do. These purposes translate into such questions as the following: How do environments create opportunities for people? Where do people and their surroundings impinge on each other? Where do they limit each other? How do people use the environment as means to an end? And to what ends? What design skills do people have? How do they manipulate their surroundings? How do people change environments to meet their needs? What takes place in particular settings? To answer such questions, the following organization for observing physical traces is useful.

Physical Traces to Look for

By-products of Use

Erosions
Leftovers
Missing traces

Adaptations for Use

Props
Separations
Connections

Displays of Self

Personalization
Identification
Group membership

Public Messages

Official
Unofficial
Illegitimate

By-products of use, the first category, reflect what people do *in* settings —such traces as litter or worn spots left behind by someone who used, misused, or failed to use a place. The other three categories represent things people do *to* settings. *Adaptations for use* reflect changes by users to make an environment better suited to something they want to do: a fence built, a wall broken down, a lawn changed into a patio. *Displays of self* are changes people make to establish some place as their own, to make it express who they are personally: a flag or a religious symbol on front lawns; mementos of trips on windowsills. *Public messages* are changes such as wall posters and graffiti, by which people use environments to communicate with a large public audience, sometimes anonymously.

What you look for depends on what you want to do with the data. Ruesch and Kees, in their perceptive book *Nonverbal Communication* (1970), describe using data on facial expressions, body movement, and physical traces to understand how people communicate without words. Their emphasis on communication leads them to underplay traces in the categories of adaptations for use and by-products of use but provide a more detailed analytic scheme for displays of self. Another important description of how to observe physical traces is included in Webb et al., *Unobtrusive Measures* (1966). Webb et al. describe the usefulness of a range of measures—for example, counting bottles in garbage cans to see how much people drink, observing litter in the park, and analyzing suicide notes. The categories they develop are not all equally suited to solving E-B questions. For example, they use the term *accretion* to describe any type of physical trace left behind, without specifying the manner in which it was left —the actor's environmental intent. All but one of the categories discussed in the following pages and several discussed in Chapter 12, on archival methods, are examples of accretion. For clarity I have, therefore, scrupulously avoided the use of this important but broad term.

By-products of Use

Sherlock Holmes, Miss Marple, Hercule Poirot, and Lord Peter Wimsey are masters at detecting and correctly interpreting side effects of behavior— worn-away stair treads, a smudge on a door, or a glass wiped suspiciously clean of fingerprints. These examples represent three types of by-products: erosions, leftovers, and missing traces.

Erosions. Use can wear away parts of the environment: grass is trampled where people walk from a parking lot to a nearby building entrance; grooves are cut into the top of a butcher's block table.

Erosions

Some erosion traces, such as the scars in the butcher's table, indicate to the interested researcher that planned and predicted activities have taken place; others that the environment is being used in a new way, such as the path across the lawn. Because most environments sustain some wear and tear, observers must be careful to distinguish between erosion traces that signify bad design, those that reflect uses designers planned for, and traces left when new and appropriate activities took place. Erosion traces, and in fact all by-products of use, can be the first step in finding out what those who use the setting feel about it.

Leftovers. Physical objects as the result of some activities get left behind: cigarettes in ashtrays after a party, dishtowels hung on kitchen-cabinet knobs next to a sink, open cans of food stored on windowsills in a veterans' residence.

Leftovers

Like erosions, leftovers may indicate activities that have been planned for, such as parties, and unplanned for, such as residents eating soup in their rooms. Such leftovers as the dishtowel, however, tell you about planned-for activities that have unplanned-for side effects—in this case the need for towel storage.

Leftovers help to locate (1) places that accommodate planned-for activities, (2) places that only partly accommodate expected activities, and (3) places that are used in unanticipated ways.

Missing traces. Erosions and leftovers in settings tell us about what people do. When we see neither of these, or even very few such traces, it tells us about what people do *not* do. Apartment balconies with no chair to sit on, without even a stored winter tire or a clothes-drying rack, and an office with nothing on the wall or table to betray the occupant's individuality demonstrate missing traces.

Inquiring about why traces are missing can uncover seemingly irrelevant physical design decisions that limit behavior. For example, some balconies have bars spaced so wide apart that families with small children are afraid to use them. Sometimes missing traces are explained when researchers probe rules about how a place may be used: "No family photos allowed on office walls." Asking "why"

Missing traces

may lead to not very useful answers: "The apartment is vacant because tenants just moved out." But it may also lead quickly to fruitful insights, because not to use an available space is quite a strange thing to do.

Adaptations for Use

When some people find that their physical environment does not accommodate something they want to do, they change it; they become designers. Some professional designers try to predetermine as little as they can in buildings and other facilities so that residents have the greatest opportunity to join in design by adapting the setting the way they want (Habraken, 1972; Turner, 1972; Wampler, 1968). At the other extreme are designers who try to plan for everything they think will occur—from built-in furniture to the color of curtains. The former is called "loose-fit design," the latter "tight-fit." But no matter what the original designer wants or expects, people who use environments redesign them. Researchers and professional designers can learn a great deal from this adaptive redesigning.

Adaptive traces are significant for designers because they are direct manifestations of design by users. They take place in the fuzzy area between what professional designers and lay designers do. Such traces are difficult to interpret, but one does not have to estimate whether they will lead to action, as one does with attitudes.

People change settings to better support activities: to facilitate and sustain them. They may remove inappropriate props, such as built-in lights that are unadjustable, or add new ones, such as a backyard barbecue pit to make eating out easier. For the same ends, they can alter the relations among settings—creating both new connections and separations, such as windows and walls.

Props. When users add things to or remove things from a setting, they create new opportunities for activity. Inasmuch as the things support activities, we can think of them as staging props purposefully arranged by users: a wood-burning stove installed in someone's apartment living room; play equipment added to an empty lot to change it into a playground.

Props

New props may have been added because users or uses have changed or because certain activities were overlooked or considered unaffordable in original designs. Props added for either reason may reflect a particular user's idiosyncratic wants, such as the living-room stove, or they may reflect more normative behavior common to a larger group.

Separations. Changes may separate spaces formerly together, increasing such qualities as privacy, control, and darkness or more sharply dividing territories: ground-floor apartments with covered-over windows, stones along someone's property line, "Keep Out" signs on back doors of buildings.

Separations can be particularly informative about side effects of design decisions. The parking areas in the interior of Castle Square, a housing project in Boston's South End, were deeded officially to the city so that it would maintain them, plow them, and pick up garbage on them. But as an unanticipated side effect, people who work in the surrounding neighborhood park there during the day and sometimes all weekend. Residents feel that this infringes on their informal right to park their cars just in front of their houses, and so they place wooden sawhorses across the parking places in front of their doors to stop other people from parking there.

Separations

Separations do not necessarily block physical movement or all the senses at once. They may, for example, be only visual (an opaque cardboard wall around a work area), auditory (a blaring radio in an office so nobody can overhear a conversation), olfactory (a fan to keep kitchen smells out of the living room), or symbolic (a three-inch-high brick border around a front yard).

Connections. Physical adaptations for use may connect two places, enabling people to interact in new ways: holes that teenagers strategically cut in a playground fence to enable players to get in without walking around to a distant gate; pass-throughs cut in walls between living rooms and windowless kitchens to provide a view out when residents eat in the kitchen. Buildings converted to restaurants often have windows cut into swinging kitchen doors so that people serving can avoid bumping into each other when coming from opposite directions.

Connections that users of a facility make can indicate that the original designer overlooked a common behavior that requires being able to move, see, hear, or talk between one space and another or that such activity developed since the place was designed (as with the window in a swinging restaurant door). Of course, sometimes users may want a connection that setting managers do not. An example would be hacksawed bars on a prison-cell window after a jailbreak.

Connections

Displays of Self

Residents change environments to put their stamp on them—to say "This is mine and it says something about me." Displays of self may be directed toward other people, but just as often the changes mean something mainly to the person who makes them: mementos of trips, family portraits, doll collections. Displays may help others identify a person's environment—name plaques on the front door—or may tell people about the person by announcing what groups she is a member of.

Personalization. People use environments to express their uniqueness and individuality: a style of furniture in the living room, trinkets on the windowsill, silly signs on businesspeople's desks. Each such use shows how someone is different from his neighbor—in taste, in personality, in habits.

Personalization

To show off personalization traces and other displays of self, people find and make such display cases as windows, walls, doorways, car bumpers, shelves, and window ledges in almost any kind of setting, from offices to homes, from hospitals to schools. By observing how parts of the environment are useful as display cases, you can improve your ability to design environments that provide opportunities for displays of self.

Identification. People use their environments to enable others to identify them more easily: names of students on school lockers, initials on commercially bought sun awnings for homes. Such markings are people's individual street signs, even if they are just numbers: house numbers, office numbers, cell numbers.

Who leaves a trace can be significant. If a student writes his name with felt-tip pen on a school locker, the locker might mean something to him. How important is a home territory like this to him? Felt-tip ink is difficult to remove.

Identification

OVERVIEW

A good way to begin almost any E-B research project is to walk around the research site looking for physical traces of behavior. It is easy to do, can be done unobtrusively, and provides investigators with rich imagery to build on in solving their problem. Trace observation can be carried out both qualitatively and quantitatively.

This chapter has discussed categories of traces particularly appropriate for E-B observations: by-products of use, adaptations for use, displays of self, public messages. The first category represents remnants of what people do *in* an environment, the others of what people do *to* it. This way of looking is aimed at increasing our ability to intervene through design to make settings better suited to what people actually do.

The next chapter discusses how to observe the other half of the E-B equation: behavior.

Did he do this on purpose to leave his mark for the next student? Would he use a name tag provided by the administration? If so, what would he feel about it? More important, what would this indicate about the relationship between students and administrators?

How permanent a trace is may also be significant. Does the name of a family etched into the wood of their front door mean they hold different attitudes toward the neighborhood than their neighbors whose name is spelled out with store-bought plastic letters in the lawn? The family with plastic letters may feel no less permanent, but rather have greater respect for wooden doors.

Group membership. In addition to displaying their individuality, people also display their membership in formal groups and organizations: religious, academic, fraternal, political, ethnic, cultural, professional. Religious statues on front lawns, professional diplomas on living-room walls, ethnic dolls in windows, pictures of President Kennedy, awards from one's company for reaching a sales quota all tell you about the groups an individual identifies with.

Group-membership signs are often carried around on more mobile display cases: car bumpers, high school jackets with emblems, T-shirts.

Group membership

Observers can easily overlook group-membership traces of unfamiliar groups. For example, hot-rod owners identify themselves by extra-wide wheels on their cars, with the manufacturer's name in large, raised, white letters. This practice is derived from actual race-car drivers, who are paid to advertise brand names on their cars and hence have wheels like this. Such signs of group identification can be meant mainly for other group members. To attune yourself to see traces like these with in-group meanings, you can assume that displayed objects you see have such meanings and then ask about them.

Public Messages

Physical environments can be used to communicate to the public at large. Most, but not all, public messages appear in public places.

Official. Probably the most frequently seen public messages are official ones erected by institutions, which may even pay for the right to do so: advertising signs, names of commercial establishments, place names. They reflect official uses of settings—the behavior of paying clients.

Official public messages

Official public messages usually appear in environments designed for that purpose. The private right to display official public messages is increasingly being challenged by the public, asserting its right not to see them.

Unofficial. Individuals and groups also communicate publicly by means of settings not designed specifically for that purpose. Unofficial messages usually announce short-term events and are often accepted and even expected on surfaces in public places: theater placards on wooden walls surrounding construction sites, political posters stapled to telephone poles, and "Lost Cat" announcements taped to laundromat windows.

Unofficial public messages

Informal public messages tell investigators about such things as types of cultural events taking place in an area, proportion of students living there, and political activity. Some bookstores and supermarkets establish tack boards for

such messages. But the usual traces left from unofficial public commu are shreds of paper stuck to lampposts, brick walls, and newspaper stand

Illegitimate. Messages to the general public which are not planned which environmental adaptive changes are not made, and which, although times expected, are seldom if ever approved of, are considered by many illegitimate uses of public environments. The most frequent example of ill mate public messages is graffiti. Political graffiti with antiauthority sloga antiethnic slogans often appear in prominent public places. Members of tee gangs in large American cities stake out their turf by writing their name and st number on walls.

Illegitimate public messages

Illegitimate as I am using it here does not imply a value judgment. It merely refers to official disapproval of the activity. Those who engage in the activity may find it completely legitimate. For example, almost everywhere students paint lines on walls of schools to enable themselves to play games: a hockey goal to play street hockey or a square strike zone to play stickball. They consider such lines as legitimate as the neatly painted official lines on the basketball court (Zeisel, 1976a). Others may consider the lines attacks on society.

Such "illegitimate" expression may have useful social side effects. Gang graffiti, establishing territorial boundaries, possibly reduce gang conflict. Political slogans give minority political groups visibility.

Context

Traces clarify their context and are clarified by them. A square painted on a wall may mean nothing. Near a school it is a stickball strike zone and signifies that the area is used for street games. When looking at physical traces, researchers must keep in mind that they are trying to look beyond the trace itself to understand a larger picture. That larger picture can emerge only if you see the context of what you observe.

Personalization. People use environments to express their uniqueness and individuality: a style of furniture in the living room, trinkets on the windowsill, silly signs on businesspeople's desks. Each such use shows how someone is different from his neighbor—in taste, in personality, in habits.

Personalization

To show off personalization traces and other displays of self, people find and make such display cases as windows, walls, doorways, car bumpers, shelves, and window ledges in almost any kind of setting, from offices to homes, from hospitals to schools. By observing how parts of the environment are useful as display cases, you can improve your ability to design environments that provide opportunities for displays of self.

Identification. People use their environments to enable others to identify them more easily: names of students on school lockers, initials on commercially bought sun awnings for homes. Such markings are people's individual street signs, even if they are just numbers: house numbers, office numbers, cell numbers.

Who leaves a trace can be significant. If a student writes his name with felt-tip pen on a school locker, the locker might mean something to him. How important is a home territory like this to him? Felt-tip ink is difficult to remove.

Identification

Separations do not necessarily block physical movement or all the senses at once. They may, for example, be only visual (an opaque cardboard wall around a work area), auditory (a blaring radio in an office so nobody can overhear a conversation), olfactory (a fan to keep kitchen smells out of the living room), or symbolic (a three-inch-high brick border around a front yard).

Connections. Physical adaptations for use may connect two places, enabling people to interact in new ways: holes that teenagers strategically cut in a playground fence to enable players to get in without walking around to a distant gate; pass-throughs cut in walls between living rooms and windowless kitchens to provide a view out when residents eat in the kitchen. Buildings converted to restaurants often have windows cut into swinging kitchen doors so that people serving can avoid bumping into each other when coming from opposite directions.

Connections that users of a facility make can indicate that the original designer overlooked a common behavior that requires being able to move, see, hear, or talk between one space and another or that such activity developed since the place was designed (as with the window in a swinging restaurant door). Of course, sometimes users may want a connection that setting managers do not. An example would be hacksawed bars on a prison-cell window after a jailbreak.

Connections

Displays of Self

Residents change environments to put their stamp on them—to say "This is mine and it says something about me." Displays of self may be directed toward other people, but just as often the changes mean something mainly to the person who makes them: mementos of trips, family portraits, doll collections. Displays may help others identify a person's environment—name plaques on the front door—or may tell people about the person by announcing what groups she is a member of.

Did he do this on purpose to leave his mark for the next student? Would he use a name tag provided by the administration? If so, what would he feel about it? More important, what would this indicate about the relationship between students and administrators?

How permanent a trace is may also be significant. Does the name of a family etched into the wood of their front door mean they hold different attitudes toward the neighborhood than their neighbors whose name is spelled out with store-bought plastic letters in the lawn? The family with plastic letters may feel no less permanent, but rather have greater respect for wooden doors.

Group membership. In addition to displaying their individuality, people also display their membership in formal groups and organizations: religious, academic, fraternal, political, ethnic, cultural, professional. Religious statues on front lawns, professional diplomas on living-room walls, ethnic dolls in windows, pictures of President Kennedy, awards from one's company for reaching a sales quota all tell you about the groups an individual identifies with.

Group-membership signs are often carried around on more mobile display cases: car bumpers, high school jackets with emblems, T-shirts.

Group membership

Observers can easily overlook group-membership traces of unfamiliar groups. For example, hot-rod owners identify themselves by extra-wide wheels on their cars, with the manufacturer's name in large, raised, white letters. This practice is derived from actual race-car drivers, who are paid to advertise brand names on their cars and hence have wheels like this. Such signs of group identification can be meant mainly for other group members. To attune yourself to see traces like these with in-group meanings, you can assume that displayed objects you see have such meanings and then ask about them.

Public Messages

Physical environments can be used to communicate to the public at large. Most, but not all, public messages appear in public places.

Official. Probably the most frequently seen public messages are official ones erected by institutions, which may even pay for the right to do so: advertising signs, names of commercial establishments, place names. They reflect official uses of settings—the behavior of paying clients.

Official public messages

Official public messages usually appear in environments designed for that purpose. The private right to display official public messages is increasingly being challenged by the public, asserting its right not to see them.

Unofficial. Individuals and groups also communicate publicly by means of settings not designed specifically for that purpose. Unofficial messages usually announce short-term events and are often accepted and even expected on surfaces in public places: theater placards on wooden walls surrounding construction sites, political posters stapled to telephone poles, and "Lost Cat" announcements taped to laundromat windows.

Unofficial public messages

Informal public messages tell investigators about such things as types of cultural events taking place in an area, proportion of students living there, and political activity. Some bookstores and supermarkets establish tack boards for such messages. But the usual traces left from unofficial public communications are shreds of paper stuck to lampposts, brick walls, and newspaper stands.

Illegitimate. Messages to the general public which are not planned for, for which environmental adaptive changes are not made, and which, although sometimes expected, are seldom if ever approved of, are considered by many to be illegitimate uses of public environments. The most frequent example of illegitimate public messages is graffiti. Political graffiti with antiauthority slogans or antiethnic slogans often appear in prominent public places. Members of teenage gangs in large American cities stake out their turf by writing their name and street number on walls.

Illegitimate public messages

Illegitimate as I am using it here does not imply a value judgment. It merely refers to official disapproval of the activity. Those who engage in the activity may find it completely legitimate. For example, almost everywhere students paint lines on walls of schools to enable themselves to play games: a hockey goal to play street hockey or a square strike zone to play stickball. They consider such lines as legitimate as the neatly painted official lines on the basketball court (Zeisel, 1976a). Others may consider the lines attacks on society.

Such "illegitimate" expression may have useful social side effects. Gang graffiti, establishing territorial boundaries, possibly reduce gang conflict. Political slogans give minority political groups visibility.

Context

Traces clarify their context and are clarified by them. A square painted on a wall may mean nothing. Near a school it is a stickball strike zone and signifies that the area is used for street games. When looking at physical traces, researchers must keep in mind that they are trying to look beyond the trace itself to understand a larger picture. That larger picture can emerge only if you see the context of what you observe.

OVERVIEW

A good way to begin almost any E-B research project is to walk around the research site looking for physical traces of behavior. It is easy to do, can be done unobtrusively, and provides investigators with rich imagery to build on in solving their problem. Trace observation can be carried out both qualitatively and quantitatively.

This chapter has discussed categories of traces particularly appropriate for E-B observations: by-products of use, adaptations for use, displays of self, public messages. The first category represents remnants of what people do *in* an environment, the others of what people do *to* it. This way of looking is aimed at increasing our ability to intervene through design to make settings better suited to what people actually do.

The next chapter discusses how to observe the other half of the E-B equation: behavior.

Chapter 8

OBSERVING ENVIRONMENTAL BEHAVIOR

Observing behavior means systematically watching people use their environments: individuals, pairs of people, small groups, and large groups. What do they do? How do activities relate to one another spatially? And how do spatial relations affect participants? At the same time, observers of environmental behavior look at how a physical environment supports or interferes with behaviors taking place within it, especially the side effects the setting has on relationships between individuals or groups. In a park, for example, an observer sees a child playing, watched over by her father, who anxiously jumps up every time the child moves out of his sight. The child's being hidden from view triggers a reaction by her father. The event tells an observer something about the child's activity and the importance for the relationship of maintaining a visual link between father and child.

Observing behavior in physical settings generates data about people's activities and the relationships needed to sustain them; about regularities of behavior; about expected uses, new uses, and misuses of a place; and about behavioral opportunities and constraints that environments provide.

You do not have to be an expert to observe behavior. Before entering a party or a restaurant, you may survey the scene to see what behavior is appropriate there. An alert new student in a school watches who plays where in the gymnasium, who sits where in class, and who sits with whom in the cafeteria. Environment-behavior researchers systematically make the same types of observations with different ends in mind.

Hall's classic description of how people behave in and use space, *The Hidden Dimension* (1966), draws heavily on behavior observation in natural settings. Sensitive behavior observation led Hall to discover the important spatial dimension to human communication. He observed, for example, that how far or how close people stand reflects their social relationship—distance generally meaning coldness and closeness generally meaning friendliness. Further behavior observation turned this rather simple conclusion into an exciting insight: the way people from different cultures interpret spatial distances can lead to misunderstanding, even insult. For instance, an American might feel he is being friendly by standing several feet from an Arab friend during a casual conversation. The

Arab, attributing meaning to space, feels the American to be cold and distant and moves closer. The American takes this move to be aggressive. He steps back. To the Arab, this is clearly an attempt to be unfriendly—an insult.

This chapter presents qualities of the research method for E-B studies, some practical steps observers can take to prepare for observing environmental behavior, and how to organize observations to learn the most about the relation between settings and what people do in them.

Observing Environmental Behavior

Qualities of the Method

    Empathetic
    Direct
    Dynamic
    Variably intrusive

Observers' Vantage Points

    Secret outsider
    Recognized outsider
    Marginal participant
    Full participant

Recording Devices

    Notation
    Precoded checklists
    Maps
    Photographs
    Videotapes and movies

What to Observe

    Who: actor
    Doing what: act
    With whom: significant others
    Relationships
    Context
    Setting

QUALITIES OF THE METHOD

Observing behavior is empathetic and direct, deals with dynamic phenomena, and allows researchers to vary their intrusiveness in a research setting.

starts have really been well tested and enables them to review their own work later with a clearer mind.

Variably Intrusive

Researchers have to decide how far they will intrude and from what social and physical vantage point they want to participate in observed events. At one extreme they can choose to record and observe behavior unobtrusively from a distance—for example, with a telephoto lens. In addition to possibly creating ethical problems, observing in this way removes the observer from the scene of action, depriving the method of a large part of its research potential. However, close participation increases the chance of unwittingly affecting the observed situation. Choice of vantage point depends on such things as research problem, available time, and investigator skills.

To offset research bias resulting from their presence, participant observers adopt social positions with which people are familiar. In a hospital, this could mean sitting in the waiting room like a patient; in a restaurant, working as a waitress or being a customer. To be able to take account in data analysis of changes they themselves induce, observers record any incident in which people may be reacting differently because the observers are present in their adopted position. For example, patients in a waiting room may be whispering because another patient (the observer) is waiting too. The more crowded a setting—for example, a rush-hour subway platform—the less observers' actions affect the situation.

Of course, intrusion may be part of the research project's design. For example, the observer has the ability to change situations and watch results, as Lefkowitz et al. (1955) did in their natural experiment, mentioned earlier, on pedestrians' reactions to differently dressed jaywalkers. Felipe and Sommer (1966) used themselves as both observer and stimulus to test a personal-space hypothesis that people get uncomfortable enough to leave if their personal-space norms are broken. Observers sat very close to students in a library and compared the time before the students left with the time before another student across the room moved, whose space was not invaded. The same natural-experiment approach to observing behavior can be taken by moving furniture, erecting signs, or changing an environment in some other way. Natural experiments are an example of artificial intervention made possible because observing behavior is such a variably intrusive research method. (The students next to whom Felipe and Sommer sat regularly moved away first.)

In sum, observing behavior is both empathetic and direct, deals with a dynamic subject, and allows observers to be variably intrusive. These qualities make the method useful at the beginning of research to generate hunches, in the middle to document regularities, and late in a research project to locate key explanatory information.

Empathetic

Researchers observing people soon get a feeling for the character of a situation. Observation, especially participant observation, allows researchers to "get into" a setting: to understand nuances that users of that setting feel. When personal quirks of observers influence the recording of observations, their reliability can be questioned. Yet personal feelings may provide essential initial research insights that a study can revise and elaborate.

Jacobs' *Death and Life of Great American Cities* (1961) is based largely on behavior observations that Jacobs made while a resident in New York's Greenwich Village. Her perspective enabled her to describe empathetically what it is like to live on a street where people look out their windows at passers-by, children play on the sidewalk in view of neighbors and parents, and shopkeepers serve as news outlets and street guardians.

That observing behavior seems so easy and obvious can present problems. It is common for observers to report observations in seductively authentic descriptions that, unfortunately, omit details and transfer untested feelings. Missing are standardized procedures for observing and a theoretical framework for interpreting observations. Having explicit procedures and theory increases the likelihood that different observers' descriptions are comparable, enabling readers of observation reports to interpret and evaluate them more easily.

Empathy can be taken too far: observers may assume that the way they personally feel in a situation is the way everyone else feels. For example, an observer who dislikes being with many people might assume that the high level of contact on Jacobs' close-knit urban street makes most people anxious and uncomfortable.

Observers also run the risk of overlooking differences between people, unless they formulate their feelings into testable hypotheses. On Greenwich Village streets, how many people choose to look out their windows to participate in a neighborhood life important to them, and how many do so because they have nothing else to do? How many parents talk to other parents while watching children play because it is what is expected of them, and how many do so because they are lonely and want the contact?

Direct

Respondents often hesitate to report that they break formal rules: smoking in school hallways near "No Smoking" signs; two families living in an apartment designated for one family. Yet they do not care if they are seen doing such things, because they and their friends or neighbors find such behavior acceptable.

The same can be true for behavior that, although acceptable to a particular group, breaks the informal rules of a larger one. A cross-cultural example of the resulting need for direct observation is evident in Chandigarh, Le Corbusier's modern capital of India's Punjab province. Many residents of this administrative center are aspiring middle-class civil servants who live in buildings that reflect modern norms to which some of the more traditional Indians do not keep. For example, some residents reported that they used the kitchen counters to prepare meals, but when Brolin (1972) looked more closely, he found that they followed the traditional Indian practice of cooking on portable stoves on the floor. One resident assured Brolin that, caste distinctions being obsolete, everyone including servants used the front door. Brolin was surprised to observe household servants using the back door. Had Brolin used only interviewing techniques, he might never have observed such rule-breaking activity.

People also tend not to report to interviewers activity they think is trivial and therefore not worth reporting. Nonetheless, a seemingly trivial datum may be central to an environmental research question. For example, if someone asked you now to describe what you had been doing for the last two minutes, you would probably say that you had been reading. You might describe as well the position you are in—sitting, lying. You probably would not say that you were leaning forward or backward and that you had just turned the page, although to design a comfortable library these details may be important.

Because observing behavior can be intensely personal, trained and sensitive researchers able to perceive relevant nuances can use the method more fruitfully. Being on the spot allows researchers to adjust their observations to a particular setting and to a refined understanding of the situation. Whyte's personal research capabilities are evident in his participant-observation study *Street Corner Society* (1955). His day-to-day involvement with a street gang enabled him to uncover more than ordinary evidence.

Whyte noticed, for example, that one gang member, Alec, regularly bowled higher scores than gang leaders during the week. But when the whole gang bowled together on Saturday night, their scores paralleled the gang's hierarchy. The leaders bowled the highest scores, while Alec came in last.

When a "follower" was bowling too well, his companions would heckle him, saying such things as "You're just lucky!" and "You're bowling over your head!" When Doc, the leader, bowled poorly, they would shout encouragement, telling him he could do better. Whyte noticed that gang members exerted subtle—and not so subtle—social pressures on one another to conform to the hierarchy. He was able to make this insightful observation on what sociologists call "social control" because he had many opportunities to observe general and specific gang behavior and could adjust his observations to each situation.

Dynamic

As you look at people doing things, what you see changes: activities affect other activities; episodes take place. You get a glimpse of the role of time in the life of an environment: a mother leaning from her window calling her child to supper, the child coming. More complex chains of events are exemplified by a

hospital emergency room when an ambulance arrives. As Wiseman's perceptive documentary film *Hospital* (1970) shows, an ambulance arrival can have simultaneous effects on nurses, doctors, other patients, nearby staff members, police officers, and many others who participate, actively and passively.

In complex situations observers begin to get a sense of chain reactions: the effects of effects. No other effort gives a researcher so much of an idea of how people bring places to life. Ellis' (1974) explanation of "occasioning" among poorer Black people shows how they manipulate both behavior and time to cope with limited space. For example, although kitchens are predominantly associated with cooking and eating, residents might regularly use that room for other occasions: card parties, sewing bees, meeting the boys. Although "occasioning," according to Ellis, is a strategy used by poorer Blacks in the United States, observing behavior among other groups of people could test the hypothesis that they use the strategy as well.

When you observe behavior, you soon become aware of repetitive activities in identifiable places—what Barker calls "standing patterns of behavior" (1968). Place-specific activities within such a pattern are more closely related to one another than to patterns of activities in other places—for example, the set of activities in a drugstore connected to ordering, making, drinking, and paying for an ice cream soda are more closely related to one another than to those activities which constitute getting a prescription filled—although there may be no precise boundary defined between the two places where they occur. Training helps observers to identify sets of activities that are closely related to one another, to identify significant patterns, and to distinguish significant patterns from unimportant ones.

For example, in doing research on bank design, an observer might watch customers make bank transactions, from filling out slips at the desk to getting or depositing money at the window. It is easy to overlook parts of the sequence that occur before clients enter the bank or after they leave the teller's cage: seeing that documents are in their pockets and that money is safely put away into a purse. Does the security guard standing watch consider himself part of every transaction? To look carefully at events, observers continually question whether they see the whole event, whether they see all the participants, and whether something significant has been missed.

Observers in dynamic research situations can test their hunches on the spot. An observer who believes she has detected a regularity can try to predict what the next few persons will do and can revise or refine the hunch right away, depending on how these persons act. Instant feedback like this enables researchers in the beginning of a study to test many hunches, quickly identifying the more fruitful research ideas.

The more explicitly predictions and tests are made in notes and reports, the more you can use team members to check your interpretation. Writing down predictions and tests also helps observers avoid the trap of thinking that fal

OBSERVERS' VANTAGE POINTS

Observers can choose to be outsiders or participants in any situation. As outsiders, they may be secret observers or recognized ones; as participants, either marginal or full.

Secret Outsider

The distant observer unobserved by participants in a natural setting is a secret outsider. Moore (1973) initially chose this vantage point for a study of children's play at an elementary school in Berkeley, California. School officials replaced half an acre of blacktop with dirt that children could dig in and objects to play with, such as timber, aluminum pipe, and tree stumps. For five months, every week at the same time, before, during, and after the change, Moore climbed to the roof of the school and recorded what the kids did, using time-lapse photography. He chose this vantage point so he would not alter their behavior with his recording equipment until he showed them the film and because he thought this would enable him later to analyze patterns of use. He found, however, that by choosing to record only an overview of the playground, he missed what individuals did over time and any indications of depth of personal involvement in what they did. To catch some of these dynamic attributes of his topic, he took the camera down to the ground, becoming a recognized outside observer.

Recognized Outsider

When Blau (1963, 1964) compared two job-placement offices, he introduced himself as a researcher to those who were to be observed, explained his study, and was given a desk by the department head to work at and observe from.

A pitfall of such a recognized-outsider position is what is known as the Hawthorne effect—that subjects who know they are being observed as part of an experiment often change the way they act. The Hawthorne effect derived its name from the now-classic environmental experiments at the Western Electric Company's Hawthorne Plant in Chicago, where Roethlisberger and Dixon (1939) wanted to determine, among other things, how lighting levels affected workers' productivity. They carried out their studies as recognized observers. When they raised light levels, production increased. When they lowered light levels, production increased also. They concluded that consciously being under a microscope changes workers' behavior.

You can try to minimize the Hawthorne effect by spending enough time at your research site that people there get used to you and take you more for granted. Observers can develop tasks for themselves to do while observing so that people begin to see them as other people with something to do. Whatever observers do, there will always be the danger of some Hawthorne effect, which must be recognized and considered during data analysis.

Another problem for recognized observers is that no matter how honestly and convincingly they present themselves, their study, and their ethical commitment to respect privacy, someone may not believe them. Observers can exacerbate this problem by oversight. Blau obtained permission to study the placement offices from the department head. The staff members therefore assumed that Blau would report everything he saw to their boss. This was a mistaken, but not surprising, interpretation. Observers need to avoid giving off clues that they are partisan watchdogs. They must remain as unaffiliated as possible by being careful about who introduces them, where they sit, whom they have lunch with, whose office they use to make phone calls from, and generally from whom they accept favors.

Sometimes you cannot help being a victim of natural institutional mistrust, particularly when you are interested in informal uses of physical settings. Welfare recipients with relatives staying over in the living room, students smoking in the school bathroom, teachers making private calls from an office phone, patrolmen resting in coffee shops between emergencies are worried about being caught by someone in authority. In such situations, subjects tend to fear that researchers are spies—perhaps tax inspectors or school administrators. Subjects normally play along with the "spy," feeding him harmless information but not admitting the mistrust they feel. The more researchers explain their harmlessness, the guiltier they seem. To reduce the effects of mistrust on the validity of the research, observers must sensitively record situations in which mistrust is likely to have changed behavior. They can also make a special point not to ask questions about rule-breaking activity clearly irrelevant to the study problem.

Secret- and recognized-outsider vantage points both have disadvantages along with their advantages. Secret observers are by definition distant and removed from the action. Their position also raises ethical questions. Recognized observers may affect action in unknown ways.

Marginal Participant

Researchers who adopt the vantage point of a commonly accepted and unimportant participant want to be seen by actual participants as just another patient in a hospital waiting room, another subway rider, or another art student drawing in a park. A marginal-participant vantage point is a comfortable one for E-B researchers to adopt because observant professionals and laypersons adopt it naturally in daily situations.

Marginal positions that observers choose are likely to be somewhat familiar. We have all been bus passengers, members of the audience at a street concert, and restaurant patrons. Familiarity, however, can prevent observers from looking carefully at what is actually going on. It is tempting to assume that a quick glance will tell you everything because, after all, you have seen it all before. Such an attitude dulls the observer's ability to be surprised by what she sees—an ability crucial if research is not merely to record the obvious.

An observer who is familiar with her vantage point can also be misled into assuming that she knows how others in a setting feel about *being watched*. For example, the marginal observer assumes when watching an informal football game in the park that he is taken to be a casual spectator. Meanwhile, the football players think he is a park attendant about to tell them to stop playing on the grass. To increase the validity of their research, observers must test their assumptions about how they are perceived by others. For example, observers can slightly change their natural behavior to see how people in the situation respond.

Ways to control unwanted side effects include deliberate choice of clothing, physical posture, and objects one is carrying. Researchers observing in Harvard Yard will be seen very differently if they carry green bookbags than if they carry leather attaché cases. One useful trick is to use one's behavior-recording device as a prop to indicate a familiar, yet inconsequential, participant position: camera for tourist, notebook for student, sketchbook for amateur artist.

In general, being a marginal participant observer requires the least amount of research preparation time. But precisely for this reason it requires that observers be introspective and self-aware.

Full Participant

To observe behavior, researchers can use positions they already are in and positions they adopt central to the situation they are studying. Full participants in a study of housing design might be residents of a neighborhood. A study to plan an office might be helped by researchers taking jobs as office clerks and typists.

Participant observation by a waitress would have been appropriate in an E-B situation described by Whyte (1949). In 12 restaurants in which tension was high between dining-room and kitchen staff members, he observed that when waitresses gave orders to the cooks in the kitchen, the cooks resented it. They were higher-paid and resented taking orders from less-skilled waitresses. Although they could not avoid communication flow in this direction, they could avoid taking orders directly. Tension was reduced when a clipboard was installed in some restaurants on the counter between dining room and kitchen. Waitresses put order slips on the clipboard. Whenever a cook decided to take the next order, he went to the board and picked up a slip. He put the plate back on the separating counter. He no longer took orders directly; the environmental change gave him control over his own actions.

In some cases researchers may not be able to choose full participation, as when all participants are highly skilled professionals (doctors in a hospital) and when membership in the setting being studied is restricted (men's athletic clubs). Gaining full participant-observer status by taking up residence, taking a job, or joining an organization usually means making a long-term commitment. Return on investment potentially comes in the form of an insightful and empathetic position from which to gather behavioral data.

RECORDING DEVICES

Devices suited to recording behavior observations include verbal descriptions and diagrams, precoded checklists for counting, floor plans or maps, still photographs, and film or videotape. What devices to choose depends mainly on how much detailed information the problem demands and how much the observer already knows about the behaviors to be observed.

Notation

Recording behavior in verbal and diagrammatic notes demands that observers decide what to describe and what to overlook on the spot. For example, in describing how people use a hotel lounge, the observer must decide whether to record how people meet each other and move around, how people sit and watch others, how they hold their newspapers and shift their weight, how they move their eyes and twitch their noses. Each level of analysis is useful to design researchers for solving different problems. Each individual observer decides on and then isolates that level of analysis particularly relevant to his or her own study. If multiple observers work on the same research project, they must be trained and sensitized together, comparing their observations so that each knows what types of behaviors to note. That well-trained observers make decisions about levels of analysis can be an opportunity to see richness in a situation and catch that richness in discrete notes.

Procedures for descriptive behavioral notation are relatively simple. Notes are recorded by researchers working alone or by one team member when the other member is conducting an interview. As with notes of physical traces, it is useful to crease a note page, creating a wide right-hand margin. When observations are written in the left-hand column, the right side is open for individual or group analysis. Table 8-1 shows a sample of field notes.

Table 8-1. Sample field notes from site visit to hospital emergency room. (Observations made from nurse's station at 1:00 p.m.)

Observation	*Comment*
Woman waiting in wheelchair has been waiting in corridor between nurse and row of examining rooms since at least 10:30. She is watching all the activity.	*Does watching emergency activity make waiting easier?*

Table 8-1 (continued)

Police arrive with stretcher. Announce in loud voices that they have a woman who fell down and passed out. She is lying still on stretcher with eyes closed, covered. All other patients sitting in corridor lean forward in chairs to look. The stretcher will not fit through corridor where patients are sitting. Police struggle to maneuver stretcher through the crowd of nurses and doctors in the nursing station to get to uncrowded corridor on other side. Patient is put in examining room. Curtain pulled part-way closed by last policeman to leave. Patients waiting in corridor have full view of patient in exam room.

Why do they announce it? For nurses to clear a path?

Patients looking again! Is it just something to do?

Hallway waiting causes traffic problems for stretcher cases.

This probably bothers patients being examined.

A policeman wheels stretcher out back door into middle of waiting area, while another tells a nurse the details about the woman they brought in, leaning over counter at nurse's station.

This public discussion surely seems like an invasion of privacy.

Nurse leaves nurse's station, walks around counter into corridor, scans all patients waiting there. She walks up to one man who is seated, stands three feet away and tells him the results of lab tests and what they mean. Doctor walks over and asks same patient to go into exam room with him.

Nurse in her "station" cannot see the informal or overflow waiting area in corridor. What are the design implications? Behavior of nurse in telling lab results is another type of invasion of privacy.

Doctor's voice, shouting angrily, comes from an exam room.

What acoustical control is needed in exam rooms?

Doctor leaves nurse's station, approaches woman waiting in wheelchair, pulls up a chair, sits down beside her, and talks in low tones. Other patients sitting nearby watch and occasionally speak to each other.

Consultation in waiting areas may be standard emergency-room procedure? Is there a way to allow this to take place but provide more privacy?

Sound of friendly chatter, laughing from one exam room.

Does this perhaps relax people in waiting area?

Field notes by architect/researcher Polly Welch for "Hospital Emergency Facilities: Translating Behavioral Issues into Design," by P. Welch. (Graham Foundation Fellowship Report.) Cambridge, Mass.: Architecture Research Office, Harvard Graduate School of Design, 1977.

Several small tricks help avoid embarrassing mistakes in descriptive behavior notes: always include yourself in observations to avoid finding out that a crucial observed behavior actually was a response to the observer's presence; when sitting and taking notes in public, make a drawing on the top page of the notepad so that anyone who looks over your shoulder will find an acceptable sketch; never leave notes around. What to a researcher are harmless descriptions of the obvious, to participants can be highly insulting snooping.

Precoded Checklists

Descriptive notes provide a qualitative understanding of what is going on: what types of behavior patterns there are, what characteristics of participants are salient, and what level of descriptive abstraction is appropriate to solve a problem. If researchers want to know in greater detail how often an activity takes place, they can use qualitative observation data to develop a precoded checklist for counting. The qualitative approach serves in such situations as the diagnostic phase of the research project.

In their study of behavior on a psychiatric ward, Ittelson, Rivlin, and Proshansky (1970) recorded over 300 descriptions of behaviors during extended periods of time. For example, patient reclines on bench, hand over face, but not asleep; patient cleans table with sponge; patient plays soccer in corridor; patient sits on cans in hall watching people go by. For counting purposes, they coded the descriptions into categories representing types of activities observed, such as lying awake, housekeeping, games, and watching an activity.

For each activity on a checklist, observers record characteristics of participants (alone or in groups), place, time, and other relevant conditions, such as the weather. Perhaps the most significant task in developing a checklist is specifying the descriptive level of abstraction to record. Ittelson et al. decided, for example, that activity types (housekeeping, personal hygiene) were more relevant to their problem than activities were (cleaning a table with a sponge, setting one's hair). Rather than describe subjects in terms of approximate age, sex, weight, and height, which might be relevant to a study of children's play equipment, observers in the psychiatric ward coded sex of subject, whether acting alone or in a group, and, if in a group, of what size and sex mix.

To set up a checklist demands previous diagnostic observation, a thorough understanding of how the data will be used, and an understanding of how to develop coding categories. Once a precoded checklist is set up, it provides relatively comparable quantifiable data with only a moderate amount of training for observers.

Maps

Recording activities on floor plans, diagrams, or maps is particularly convenient if researchers want to observe and analyze several people in one general area at the same time: groups at a cocktail party, patients in a waiting room, office workers eating in an open-air plaza. Looking at behavior recorded on maps can give investigators a better sense of how a whole place is used at once than looking at statistical tables.

Maps are also useful to record sequences of behavior in settings where people have a choice of several paths: from home to bus stop, from desk to desk in an open-plan office. Analyzing map records in the light of an actual setting can give an idea of the characteristics of popular paths.

If investigators want precise physical-location data, they can construct base maps with grids corresponding to regular elements in the actual setting, such as floor tiles or columns.

Photographs

Still photographs can capture subtleties that other methods may not record: the way someone sits on a chair or leans against a column; the way two persons avoid looking at each other by adjusting their body postures. In addition, as presented in Chapter 7, photographs are useful throughout a research project because of their illustrative quality. The same procedures hold for deciding on photographs to record behavior as were described for using photographs to record physical traces.

Videotapes and Movies

Whenever time is a significant element in an E-B problem, motion photography—videotape or movies—ought to be considered. For example, urban design of streets for handicapped and older people demands understanding their pace: how fast do they move, how long can they move before resting, how fast can they move out of other people's way? To design a safe escalator, it is essential to know how different types of people approach it, prepare to get onto it, and embark (Davis & Ayers, 1975).

WHAT TO OBSERVE

Observing behavior looks like a simple E-B research technique. Everyone watches people every day. Doesn't everyone know how to do it? In a way, yes; but few know what to look for and how to analyze what they see so that it is useful to design.

Designers make places for people to do things in—either alone or together with other people. A structure for looking at environmental behavior useful to designers results in data to help physical designers make decisions that improve places for people. The better information designers have about how the people they design for behave in physical settings and how those people relate to or exclude other people, the better they can control the behavioral side effects of the design decisions they make.

But that is not enough. Designers must also know how the contexts of observed activities affect the activities, because in different sociocultural and physical settings the same behavior can have different design implications. For example, children may do homework at the kitchen table for different reasons in a house with several available rooms to study in than in a one-bedroom apartment where four people are living. In some groups people react to neighbors sitting on the front stoop with disdain, while for others the front rather than the back is where everyone sits.

When you structure the way you look at something, you replace complex reality with a simpler version to guide your reactions and action. To increase our control over the behavioral side effects of design decisions, we can describe behavior in terms of actor, act, significant others, relationships, context, and setting (see box).

Elements in Environmental Behavior Observation

Who is   *Actor*

doing *what*   *Act*

with *whom?*   *Significant Others*

In what *relationship,*   *Relationships*

                                    aural, visual, tactile,
                                    olfactory, symbolic

in what *context,*   *Sociocultural Context*

                                    situation
                                    culture

and *where?*   *Physical Setting*

                                    props
                                    spatial relations

The following illustrations are verbally annotated to show how you can use these observation categories to describe environmental behavior in actual situations.

Each observation comprises a relationship between an actor and a significant other to which the physical setting in some way contributes.

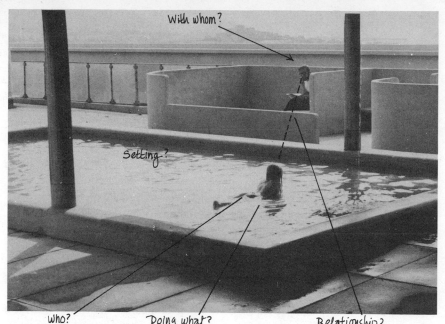

With whom?

Setting?

Who?   Doing what?   Relationship?

Swimming pool and sitting area on
roof of Le Corbusier's Marseille
Block Housing, Marseille, France   Context?

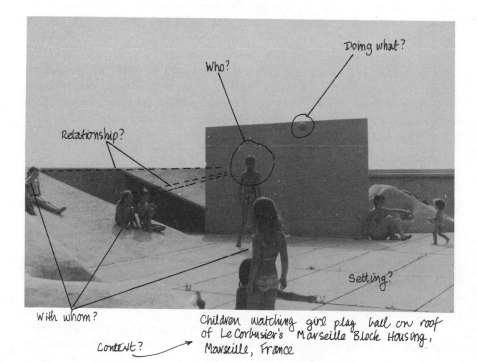

Doing what?

Who?

Relationship?

Setting?

With whom?

Children watching girl play ball on roof
of Le Corbusier's Marseille Block Housing,
Marseille, France

Context?

125

Who: Actor

The subject of a behavioral observation, the "actor," may be described in numerous ways, depending on the purpose of the description. Designers can use research in large design projects to better understand similarities and variations among types of people. For example, instead of designing a school for 273 unique individuals, a designer can use research to differentiate the needs of students, teachers, principals, and maintenance workers. Nursing homes can be planned for patients, nurses, doctors, maintenance crews, and visitors; furniture can be designed for the range of people who work in offices. In a sense, individuals in observations are treated as representatives of a social group.

We can use individuals as such representatives by describing a person's social position or status: age status, marital status, educational status, professional status, and so on. It helps to be complete in observations if we describe both a person's ascribed statuses (the characteristics that a person has automatically, such as sex and age) and his or her achieved statuses (those that the person had to do something to get, such as finding a job, graduating from college, getting married, or inviting people to a party). Many positions are defined as part of a relationship to others: party hostess (guests), wife (husband), teacher (student), nurse (patient), salesperson (customer).

An observer unable in field notes to describe statuses accurately can describe clues from which he and other researchers reading the notes may be able to infer status. For example, Snyder and Ostrander, in their Oxford nursing-home study (1974), observed people who were patients, family members, visitors, and staff members. After a few days they knew most individuals personally or could infer their status from such things as dress (uniform means nurse; bathrobe means patient) and tools (stethoscope means doctor; sitting in wheelchair means patient). But when they were not sure, they described in their field notes whatever clues they had and whether they were guessing about the person's status. It is better to record "It could be a nurse's aide resting in the wheelchair" than to write "It is a patient asleep in the corner," so that other researchers can help evaluate the data.

Sometimes relevant descriptions of actors in behavioral observations are names of groups—teens, teachers, girls—not individuals. In Zeisel's property-damage study (1976a) researchers observed groups of boys playing street hockey and stickball in open spaces around schools. It was not important for their research and design problem to identify each street-hockey participant as an actor in a separate act. Researchers treated the group as the actor, describing the group's size and composition. Groups can be described in the same status terms as individuals. For example, the psychiatric ward study by Ittelson et al. (1970) identified groups by the number of male and female patients, doctors, and visitors they contained.

One pitfall for observers to avoid is subsuming significant individuals under general group descriptions. If four teenagers are shooting hockey pucks at the front doors of a school while five others look on from a bench nearby and one gets ready under a tree to play, it would be misleading to write in one's field notes: "A group of ten boys are playing street hockey at the school entrance." To design a place to play street hockey, the relationship among players, spectators, and reserve players is relevant.

A group of two also raises problems for observers: are they a group acting together with common significant others, or do they themselves represent actor and significant other for each other? If they are very similar and are doing the same thing, it may be appropriate to describe them together: two boys playing street hockey with each other, two elderly men playing chess, two women walking down the street together. However, when the couple is made up of two different types of individuals interacting, it may be useful to describe them separately, seeing one of the two as the actor in the observation: parent and child in the park, nurse and patient in a hospital. But even here, as with all descriptive observation techniques, the researcher's judgment is the most significant determinant of what is important to describe.

Doing What: Act

The people you observe will be doing something. An observer needs to decide the level of abstraction he will use to describe behavior and how he will distinguish individual acts from a connected sequence of acts.

The level of description observers choose depends mainly on the design and research problem facing them. Let us take as an example an observational study to write a behavioral program for a shopping-center design. Observers could describe very generally that some people there are "shopping" and others are just hanging around. More precisely, they can describe that some shoppers browse, while others buy something. Or observers might record where and count how often a supermarket patron stops in the aisles. Observers might record how high patrons reach and how low they stoop when getting items off the shelves. Or observers might go to the trouble to observe and record in what direction patrons turn their heads and focus their eyes while walking down the aisle. Each observation is either interesting or useless, depending on the problem researchers are trying to solve. The series of design questions in Table 8-2 shows how each level of described activity might be useful.

Along with deciding on appropriate levels of analysis, researchers must explain how the acts they describe relate to one another. In the sequence of acts called "shopping," a person prepares a shopping list, leaves home, goes to the store, looks at items in the store, reaches for them, examines them, walks down the aisle, pays at the cash register, returns home, and unpacks. Each of these can be seen as a discrete act linked to the others as part of a larger "shopping" sequence. If researchers observing behavior maintain clarity of descriptive level

Table 8-2. Behavior descriptions and corresponding questions for a shopping-center design, by level of detail

	Behavior Observation	Design Question
General Description	"Shopping" as opposed to "hanging around"	In a shopping-center plan, how many places are needed for people to hang around, and how can they be designed to augment rather than interfere with shopping?
	Shoppers browsing as opposed to buying something	. How should items be displayed so that browsers and buyers can see them but buyers have greater access to them?
	Where and how often shoppers stop in supermarket aisles	How can flooring materials, lighting, and aisle length be designed for maximum convenience to customers, maximum exposure of sales items, and minimum maintenance?
	How high patrons will reach and how low they will stoop	What shelf design and what product placement (what size container on what shelf) will ensure that customers have the easiest time reaching items?
Detailed Description	Where customers' eyes focus while moving down an aisle	Where should standard signs be placed to convey the most information, and where ought sale signs be located to catch customers' glances?

and completeness in describing related acts, they will be able to analyze their data more easily.

I have stressed the skill that observers need to decide how and what to describe. It is equally important that they have the ability to describe what they see with minimum interpretation. Well-recorded observations leave ample time and space for analysis after data have been collected. If observers try to interpret what they see before writing it down, they run the risk of recording interpretations rather than description, losing the data for good. The data cannot be retrieved to be analyzed by others or reviewed later. If data on behavior are to be sharable, it is vital that observers record "a smiling person," not "a happy person," because a smile can mean many things.

With Whom: Significant Others

Acts people engage in are partly defined by how other people are or are not included. Other people whose presence or absence is significant in this way can be seen as participants in the act itself. Girls for whom boys playing street hockey show off make the activity what it is. If they were not there, it would be another situation. The same is true in reverse for studying alone in the library. Those who are not there—friends, roommates, strangers—contribute to the situation by their absence. To understand and present what is going on, descriptions of girls watching the boys and of absent roommates must be included in research observations of behavior.

"Significant others" are especially important in environmental design research because so many design decisions about adjacencies, connections, and separations have side effects for relationships. To continue one of our earlier examples, boys playing street hockey need a hard, flat surface to play on. If this surface is provided for them in the middle of a deserted field far from other activity, it is unlikely to be used, because the "significant others," the girls and passers-by, have not been taken into account. A tot lot with no places for parents to sit and watch may go unused in favor of a more convenient one or will be used in a different way than the designer had hoped.

The positions or statuses by which actors are described often have standard role relationships associated with them. In a family, for example, one finds role relationships between parent and child, sister and brother, husband and wife, grandparent and grandchild. In hospitals there are role relationships between doctor and patient, doctor and nurse, patient and nurse, patient and visitor, nurse and visitor, patient and patient. A sensitive researcher observing a doctor making notes in a hospital will use the concept of significant other to direct attention to the relationship the doctor making notes has set up between herself and patients, nurses, and other doctors. Does she sit among patients in the waiting room, or does she retire to a private lounge? Does she discuss notes with nurses or just hand them in? To design appropriately for notetaking in hospitals, the answers to these relational questions can be important.

Relationships

Between actors and significant others in a situation there will be specific relationships for observers to describe. In extreme cases relationships can be described simply: "together" (two lovers on a park bench at night) or "apart" (a prisoner in solitary confinement).

Most E-B relationships, however, are not so simple. Are two persons talking to each other through a fence together or apart? What about two persons sitting back-to-back in adjacent restaurant booths? The problem researchers face is to systematically describe relationships like these so that differences and similarities between two situations are clear. Then researchers and designers can use the information to develop broader strategies for design rather than continually approaching each situation as totally new. To gather such information, researchers need to agree on a set of categories to describe connections and separations between people, and they must understand how the effects of relationships on activities differ in different behavior settings.

Hall (1966) shows us that behavioral connections and separations between people in environments can be conveniently and efficiently described in terms of four physiological senses and a symbolic perceptual dimension: seeing (visual), hearing (aural), touching (tactile), smelling (olfactory), and perceiving (symbolic).

Describing two people as completely together, or "copresent" (Goffman, 1963:17), means that, like two children in the bathtub, they can see, hear, touch, and smell each other, and they feel that they are "in the same place."

When we move away from extreme relationships, the sensory terms we have for describing relationships enable us to discriminate among and compare various types and also to begin to identify the role that the physical environment plays in relationships between people. A mother on the third floor calling to her child playing on the street is connected visually and aurally but is separated in terms of touch, smell, and perception. Two students studying at opposite ends of a long library table are separated symbolically and in terms of smell and touch but are connected visually and aurally. Persons in an L-shaped living room, around the corner from someone cooking in the kitchen, are separated by sight, touch, and perception but are connected in terms of food smells and sound.

Simultaneous connections and separations

When observers see and can describe relationships like these, they try to find out what the relationships mean to participants. Although they must use other research methods as well to determine meaning, behavior observation provides clues to meaning. The clues are the ways people react when other people talk to them, touch them, and so on.

Context

People react to other people differently in one situation than in another and differently in one culture than in another. It is as if they filtered what they saw through a series of screens—situational and cultural. The screens are usually used unconsciously, as Sommer (1969) and Hall (1966) have pointed out. People assume that other people see things the same way they themselves do. It is the observer's job to identify how people's situational and cultural screens are constructed—how they interpret their own and others' behavior.

This is particularly important in environmental design research because the meanings people attribute to relationships determine how they react to environmental features, such as walls, doors, and lights, that affect those relationships.

Situations. A person's sitting alone and apart from others, facing a wall in a library, probably means she wants to be left alone to read or study. In a bar, this same physical behavior can be interpreted as an invitation for conversation (Sommer, 1969). The person might still reject the advances, but she is unlikely to be distressed and insulted, as the person disturbed in the library may be.

An extreme example of how a situation can influence the meaning people attribute to behavioral relationships can be seen if you watch people's shocked reactions when you talk in a normal voice to a friend over the hush in a crowded elevator. In a department store, a market, or a crowd viewing a parade, your voice would not even be noticed. In an elevator, however, the definition of personal space is different, and so are the definitions of unacceptable behaviors. An observer must try to understand the situational rules being applied by participants to interpret the meaning they attribute to even a simple observation such as "Two persons stood next to each other talking."

Culture. Cultural context also influences how people interpret and react to behavioral relationships. For example, Hall (1966) reports that in England sitting alone reading in a room at home with the door open means "Do not disturb; do not even knock." In the United States you would close your door to indicate you wanted to be alone; an open door means you are available. It would not be inappropriate for people to knock on an open door and ask whether they might come in. An interior designer laying out open offices in these two cultures needs to be aware of these differences if he wants to control the behavioral side effects of his physical design decisions.

It is particularly important to record cultural contexts for behavior when you carry out observational studies in another country, in ethnic neighborhoods, or in parts of your own country with strong regional differences. Otherwise, designers using your data will be making decisions irrelevant to users. As in Le Corbusier's Chandigarh, people may end up cooking on stoves on the floor in efficiency kitchens and establishing illegal street markets in the plazas in front of modern government buildings (Brolin, 1972). To see behavior from a cultural perspective other than one's own requires general observation and study of another culture, awareness of one's own cultural biases, and at times requesting members of or experts on another culture to help interpret behavioral data once they are collected. As the basis for this interpretation, it is necessary to describe as fully as possible people's reactions to relationships they find themselves in.

Setting

The meaning of behavior in a particular setting depends on the potential of the setting for use—the options it provides (Gans, 1968). If people in an airport waiting lounge are sitting on the floor surrounded by empty seats, their behavior may have a different meaning than if no seats are available. Understanding participants' choices and possibilities to act helps you interpret what they finally choose to do.

Behavior potentials of settings. *Objects* imply obvious options for use: seats in telephone booths are for sitting down when calling, bathroom sinks for washing hands. At the same time they have a host of less obvious latent implications limited only by users' physical capabilities, daring, and imagination. The telephone seat provides tired noncallers a place to rest. Sinks in school bathrooms often fall off the wall because they are sat on by teenagers taking a cigarette break between classes. On a hot summer day urban fountains turn into swimming pools. These objects can be seen as *props* for behavior.

Elements that divide and connect places organize potentials for behavioral relationships. The glass walls, closable doors, acoustic paneling, and corner placement of a phone booth provide users with the option for acoustical and physical privacy but not visual privacy. The visual privacy school bathrooms provide enhances their suitability for taking cigarette breaks.

Relational design decisions. *Barriers* clearly determine potentials for relationships between people in settings. Barriers include walls of various materials and consistencies, screens in different sizes and materials, objects used to mark the edges of places, and symbols from color changes to verbal signs. Design decisions defining *fields* in space influence behavior relationships less obviously. Field definitions include such characteristics of places as shape, orientation, size, and environmental conditions—sound, light, air.

To define the ways these physical characteristics affect relationships between people, we can use the simple relational scheme developed earlier: seeing, hearing, touching, smelling, and perceiving.

Barriers. Barriers are physical elements that can keep people apart or join them together on one or more of the five dimensions—seeing, hearing, and so on. As one progresses from walls to symbols, barriers become more permeable.

Walls separate people in places. The absence of walls allows people to be connected. The thickness, consistency, and materials of walls influence the quality of separation. For example, walls with no soundproofing between bedrooms provide neighbors with aural opportunities (and inhibitions) that denser walls do not.

Screens—glass panels, a garden hedge, a shower curtain, doors, counters, windows—separate and connect people more selectively than complete walls. Glass can enable visual connection but tactile separation; a shower curtain, the opposite. Materials can be combined to provide different degrees of connection and separation along any mix of dimensions. Screens can also be designed to give selective control over the screen to users. For example, the lock and bell on a glass-paneled house door provide a range of permeability options for family members, friends, and thieves (Hoogdalem, 1977).

Screens

Objects form another class of barriers. Things placed in space may be perceived as space dividers or connectors: a piece of sculpture on a public plaza as a separator or as a place to meet; a couch in a living room; a tree in a garden.

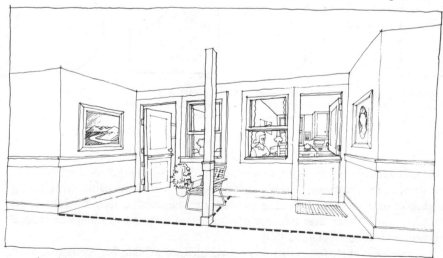

An object, here a column in a shared interior porch, can help people divide space perceptually. (Congregate House for Older People. Design-research team: Barry Korobkin, John Zeisel, and Eric Jahan. Donham & Sweeney, associated architects.)

Finally, *symbols* can be barriers. Color changes in the rug around a public telephone and change in ceiling height in a room signal that someone considers this space to be two separate places, perceptually.

Depending on how people interpret spatial symbols, they may change their behavior: not walking too close to the phone caller because of the floor color, calling one part of a room by another name because of the shift in ceiling height.

Symbols can also be overt signs: "Do Not Walk on the Grass" potentially keeping people off; "Open for Business" potentially bringing people in. Sitting on the grass near a "Keep Off" sign conveys another impression to observers than if there is no such separator.

Fields. Field characteristics of an entire place can alter people's ability to be together or apart. Field characteristics do this not by standing between people, like barriers, but by altering the physical context within which visual, aural, tactile, olfactory, and perceptual relationships take place. Field characteristics of places include their shape, orientation, size, and environmental condition.

The *shape* of a setting affects primarily visual and perceptual relationships. If people want to, they can use the cues that shapes provide to consider areas within one space as separate places. Corners in a square area, for example, can be more easily seen as separate from one another than parts of a round place can. In a study of children playing in different rooms, groups of children quickly claimed as distinct territories the places in the leaves of clover-shaped rooms (Hutt, 1969).

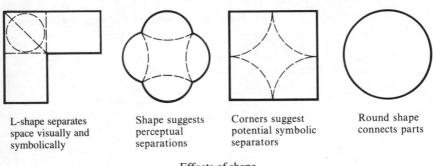

| L-shape separates space visually and symbolically | Shape suggests perceptual separations | Corners suggest potential symbolic separators | Round shape connects parts |

Effects of shape

Orientation of one place to another influences the behavioral relationship between people in them. Two places oriented so that people using them have a higher chance of casually seeing or meeting one another may be considered "functionally" closer than two equidistant places oriented to minimize chance encounters (Festinger et al., 1950).

Festinger et al. found that this concept helped explain why certain pairs of neighbors regularly liked each other better than other pairs, although both sets of apartments were the same distance apart. Apartments 1 and 6 and apartments 2 and 7 (see diagram below) are exactly 53 feet apart. The location of the left-hand

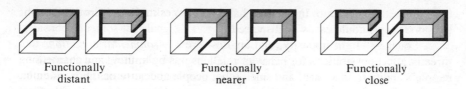

| Functionally distant | Functionally nearer | Functionally close |

Degrees of functional distance

stairway forces residents of apartment 6 to pass apartment 1 whenever they come or go. But people living in apartments 2 and 7 can leave home and return without ever running into one another. As the hypothesis of Festinger et al. leads them to expect, residents in the functionally closer pair, 1 and 6, selected one another more often as friends than did residents in apartments 2 and 7.

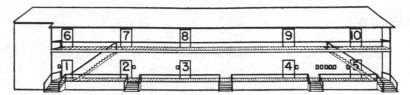

Schematic diagram of a building in Festinger's dormitory study. (Reprinted from *Social Pressures in Informal Groups,* by Leon Festinger, Stanley Schachter, and Kurt Back, with the permission of the publishers, Stanford University Press. Copyright 1950, renewed 1978 by the Board of Trustees of the Leland Stanford Junior University.)

Possible distance between people is a major determinant of potential behavior relationships. The *size* of a setting offers opportunities for people to put distance between themselves or limits their options. A 4-meter-square conference room does not offer any of seven participants at a meeting the option to separate

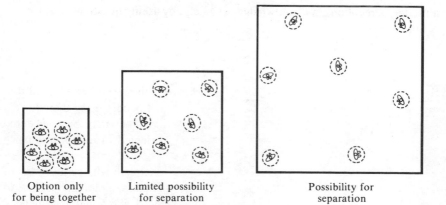

| Option only for being together | Limited possibility for separation | Possibility for separation |

Degrees of setting size

from the rest of the group. In the main hall of New York's Grand Central Station, the same people could easily be dispersed.

Loudness, light intensity, and air flow are *environmental conditions* that directly affect possibilities for behavior relationships by limiting and augmenting people's ability to hear, see, and smell other people and activities. For example, light turned low in a restaurant effectively separates people at different tables as if there were a physical screen between them. A single worker in an open-plan office listening to a radio at high volume acoustically invades the space of other workers and separates himself from them aurally. Machines that emit high-pitched sound and mask background noise without participants' awareness protect acoustical privacy as a closed door might. An exhaust hood and fan over a kitchen stove keep kitchen smells out of adjacent rooms—olfactorily separating people cooking in the kitchen from others.

OVERVIEW

To design environments suited to what people do in them, we must understand environmental behavior: *Who* does *what* with *whom?* In what *relationship,* sociocultural *context,* and physical *setting?* This chapter proposes that by looking at how environments affect people's ability to see, hear, touch, smell, and perceive each other, we can begin to understand how environments impinge on social behavior.

Environmental elements that affect relationships include barriers, such as walls, screens, objects, and symbols; and fields, such as shape, orientation, size, and environmental conditions. Design decisions about these elements have identifiable side effects for social behavior.

Environmental-behavior descriptions that can enable designers to improve control over behavioral side effects of their decisions include six elements: actor, act, significant others, relationships, context, and setting.

The next three chapters discuss how to find out about people's feelings, attitudes, perceptions, and knowledge—namely, by asking questions.

Chapter 9

FOCUSED INTERVIEWS

Asking questions in research means posing questions systematically to find out what people think, feel, do, know, believe, and expect. Normally when we think of an interview or a questionnaire, we think of the yes/no or multiple-choice questions of most public opinion polls. But such questions are fringe forms of a research tool of potentially much more penetrating power. You can use a focused interview with individuals or groups to find out in depth how people define a concrete situation, what they consider important about it, what effects they intended their actions to have in the situation, and how they feel about it. Originally formulated to tap reactions to films of military instruction and propaganda, radio broadcasts, and other mass communication devices, focused interviews are particularly suited to the needs of environment-behavior researchers interested in reactions to particular environments. Many of the concepts this chapter explains and the way it explains them are based on Merton, Fiske, and Kendall's insightful and inventive book *The Focused Interview* (1956).

PREINTERVIEW ANALYSIS AND INTERVIEW GUIDE

To understand thoroughly how someone reacts to a situation, one must first analyze the structure of that situation, using theory and observational research methods. This analysis can then be used as the basis for discussing the situation in detail with the respondent. Such a situational analysis guides the discussion; the interviewee's responses are used to test, refine, and modify the analysis. A skilled focused interviewer negotiates with a respondent to find correspondence between his own analytic structure and the respondent's mental picture of the situation. By structuring the information themselves, focused-interview respondents become participants in the research.

The *interview guide* is a loose conceptual map, such as a family might draw up before taking a cross-country camping trip. It lays out major sights to see, places to stay, and so on. After the trip begins, the family members find some of the sights closed, others uninteresting, others so arresting that they stay longer than expected. They also find that they do not drive as many miles as planned each day and that the children like to stop to eat more often. Every day they adjust their plans, and they end up having a fine trip that mixes the plans

they made on the basis of advance analysis with reactions to events as encoun-
tered. Skilled focused interviewers similarly modify their original plans to correspond to the conceptual map reflected in the respondent's answers. That conceptual map is the respondent's definition of the situation for which the interviewer
is searching.

In the focused-interview guide, the map is a set of topics, elements, patterns, and relationships that the interviewer tentatively intends to cover. Adjustments to the guide during the interview are carried out by skillful use of the major
focused-interview tool, the *probe:* the interviewer's prompting for further elaboration of an answer. An interviewer probes to find out how a respondent's definition of the situation differs from the hypothesized one; this information allows the
interviewer to adjust and refine the guide. The researcher's goal is to determine
which of the many hypothesized elements are important to the respondent and
then to understand as thoroughly as possible what these elements mean in the
respondent's definition of the situation.

To avoid misunderstandings, one should know that for surveys in which
questions are posed with prescribed rigidity, a "good interviewer" is one who
adheres to the text and never develops initiative of his own. In a focused interview, the opposite is true.

OBJECTIVES OF FOCUSED INTERVIEWS

Definition of the Situation

An individual's definition of a situation is the way she sees and interprets
it—the personal light in which a particular event is cast. This definition influences the way she responds to that event.

For example, during focused interviews custodians, school administrators,
and neighboring residents reported that kids messed up public lawns by playing
ball on them and broke public street furniture by jumping on it (Zeisel, 1976a).
Teenagers involved in these activities described them differently. They played
ball in open fields to avoid the danger of traffic and the bother of people walking
by. They hung around benches and play equipment in tot lots because the equipment was convenient for sitting, climbing, and jumping. In the beginning of this
school-property-damage study, the research team heard repeated reports from
administrators of costly "vandalism" at the schools. The investigators assumed,
along with the respondents, that the property damage was indeed "vandalism"—
maliciously carried out—until, of course, they got the teenagers' definition of
the situation.

Knowing how participants define a situation—the meaning they give it—
helps to interpret data gathered through other methods, no matter how unreasonable the respondent's definition sounds. To keep an open mind and see
situations as others see them, one must be prepared to find as many definitions as
there are participants.

Strength of Respondents' Feelings

Throughout any design project, decisions about priorities are made. Is it more important to plan direct access to cars from apartments or to keep cars parked far from the front door? Is it more important for patients in a cancer-treatment center to wait with relatives, or is modesty more important for them, maintained by waiting alone? Designers forced to make such tradeoffs can better control the side effects of their decisions if they know the strength of respondents' feelings about convenient access, a view free of automobiles, relatives' support, and modesty.

Intentions

Observing behavior and physical traces tells investigators about unintended consequences of activities. In Boston's West End "urban village," men spent much time on the street washing and polishing their cars. They said they did this to keep the cars clean, which the cars are. Observations showed that the men polished their cars next to one another and talked to passers-by as well, creating a close-knit network of neighborhood friends. This social contact is another consequence of car washing in this neighborhood. Both consequences could be observed in the situation. Only by asking the actors what their intentions are can researchers distinguish conscious intent from unintentional side effects.

BASIC CHARACTERISTICS OF FOCUSED INTERVIEWING

Focused interviewing has the following characteristics:

1. Persons interviewed are known to have been involved in a *particular concrete situation:* they have worked in the same office building, lived in the same neighborhood, or taken part in an uncontrolled but observed social situation, such as a tenants' meeting, a street demonstration, or a design review session.

2. An E-B researcher has carried out a *situational analysis* to provisionally identify hypothetically significant elements, patterns, and processes of the situation. The researcher has arrived at a set of hypotheses about what aspects of the situation are important for those involved in it, what meaning these aspects have, and what effects they have on participants.

3. On the basis of this analysis, the investigator develops an *interview guide,* setting forth major areas of inquiry and hypotheses.

4. The interview about subjective experiences of persons exposed to the already-analyzed situation is an effort to ascertain their *definitions of the situation.*

PROBES

Probes are primarily questions that interviewers interpose to get a respondent to clarify a point, to explain further what she meant, to continue talking, or to shift the topic. The probe is the systematic development of an everyday device used in conversation when one person is interested in precisely what another has to say.

- *Addition probes* encourage respondents to keep talking—to keep the *flow* of the interview moving.
- *Reflecting probes* determine in a *nondirected* way which of the analyzed topics in the interview guide are significant to the respondent and which new ones to add because they were overlooked.
- *Transitional probes* make sure that the respondent discusses a broad *range* of salient topics.
- *Situational probes* stimulate the respondent to *specify* what parts of a situation prompted the responses.
- *Emotion probes* encourage discussion in *depth* of how the respondent feels about each specified part of the situation.
- *Personal probes* get respondents to describe how the *context* of their lives influenced their reactions.

This chapter goes on to discuss each type of probe, showing with examples how it can be used to enrich an interview.

Addition Probes to Promote Flow

Addition probes urge respondents to continue talking by conveying the researcher's interest in what is being said. Skillful interviewers use addition probes to get respondents to express themselves more fully and to keep the overall flow of the interview moving. They are so simple and natural that interviewers sometimes use them inadvertently.

Addition probes may be *encouragements:* such as "Uh-huh," "I see," "Yes," "Good," "That's interesting," "I understand," interjected during and after answers. Encouragements can be combined with *body movement* probes, such as nodding your head, leaning forward, looking directly at the respondent, and putting your hand to your chin thoughtfully. Skillful interviewers invent an unending number of such probes. If it seems inappropriate to make utterances, interviewers can combine attentive body movements with one of the most difficult types of probes—*attentive silences*. This probe, during which an interviewer waits for the respondent to begin speaking, requires much tact and skill because the lack of conversation between two persons alone in a room is uncomfortable. It is socially unacceptable in many Western cultures. As a result, inexperienced interviewers often fill up a silence by asking another question or by changing the topic. They are afraid of not being able to keep a flow of conversation going.

Focused-Interview Probes and Their Purposes	
Probe	*Purpose*
Addition	*Flow*
Encouragement	
Body movement	
Attentive silence	
Reflecting	*Nondirection*
Echo	
Question-to-question	
Attentive listening	
Transition	*Range*
Cued	
Reversion	
Mutation	
Situation	*Specificity*
Re-presentation	
Environmental walk-through	
Reconstruction	
Emotion	*Depth*
Feeling	
Projection	
Attentive listening	
Personal	*Context*
Self-description	
Parallel	

They may be unwittingly stopping the respondent from finishing a difficult answer that he would just as soon avoid because it is a particularly weighty topic for him and therefore probably significant for the interviewer.

Reflecting Probes to Achieve Nondirection

Nondirection pervades the focused interview. Respondents, rather than interviewers, decide what issues and elements are salient to them and are to be discussed and which are irrelevant. The ideal interview would be one in which the interviewer analyzes a situation—its parts, patterns, relationships, and over-all structure—and then begins by asking one general, unstructured question. Then in a long monologue the ideal respondent discusses his feelings about each topic, pointing out in detail which are and are not relevant to him and adding new topics the interviewer overlooked.

Ideal interviews do not occur. Respondents mention important issues but seldom raise and then discard unimportant ones. The interviewer must bring up topics in order to find out whether a particular topic was not raised because the respondent thought it was obvious and could be taken for granted or because he thought it irrelevant. Few respondents are specific enough about issues or explain their responses in sufficient depth. The interviewer's job is to test and modify the interview guide by inferring from the discussion how well the respondent's definition of the situation meets the guide's hypothetical one. To do this, the interviewer uses probes to see that the discussion covers all the hypothesized topics, leaving room for the respondent to raise additional ones. Then the inter-viewer makes sure each topic is discussed in enough detail and depth.

The focused interviewer's success is closely linked to her skill in using addition and reflecting probes to urge respondents to be complete in their report-ing without telling them directly what to talk about. Beginning the interview with general, unstructured questions, the interviewer urges the respondent to express which topics are important and which unimportant and what types of answers are relevant for the different questions. As the interview continues and topics are discussed at length, the interviewer divides and focuses general questions into more specific ones, sometimes even suggesting the types of possible answers. These more structured questions are based on the sometimes implicit leads that respondents provide when they answer general, unstructured questions.

Example	*Comment*
Int: What is your general feeling about this hospital?	General unstructured question.
Resp: I really like it.	Respondent expresses a general feeling.
Int: What do you particularly like about it?	Focus on aspect of environment that generated expressed feeling.
Resp: Well, I don't know.	Stalling tactic to think.
Int: (Nods head and listens silently)	Body movement and silence probes.
Resp: I suppose the thing I like best is the waiting areas; a real person has taken the time to put personal things on the walls and tables.	Focused answer explaining with greater specificity what it is about hospital environment respondent likes.
Int: What do you mean when you say you like that best?	Question probing depth of feeling.

Resp: I mean it makes me feel comfortable, like I don't mind being here.	Focused answer beginning to explain feeling more completely.
Int: Is there anything else here that makes you feel that way?	Question structuring response category but keeping stimulus unstructured.

While the interviewer probes and focuses, the respondent sets the stage, directing the conversation into areas she feels are important. This procedure enables interviewers to find out two things at the same time: which topics respondents think are relevant and what they feel about these topics.

To avoid directing the focused interview, a useful position for an interviewer to take is that of a *potential convert* to the respondent's point of view. The crucial word here is *potential,* because interviewers who voice strong agreement or disagreement may thereby inhibit further explanation of a topic. Respondents may not go on if they feel they have convinced the interviewer or feel they have come up against a stone wall. The trick is to use probes to show the respondent that by continuing her report, she may indeed make a convert of the mildly skeptical interviewer.

Direction can also be avoided by reflecting back the respondent's own words. One reflecting probe is the *echo probe* (Richardson, Dohrenwend, & Klein, 1965), in which the interviewer literally repeats in the form of a question the respondent's last phrase:

Example	*Comment*
Resp: The thing I like best about this place is its location.	General response.
Int: Its location?	Echo probe.
Resp: Yes, you know, the fact that it is right near two bus stops and a store.	Focused response specifying stimulus.

An equally simple reflective probe is the *question-to-question probe.* The interviewer uses it by answering a respondent's question with a question, to avoid stating an opinion:

Example	*Comment*
Resp: What did the architect think when she put these windows next to the playing field?	Respondent's question to interviewer, apparently for clarification.
Int: You mean it is not clear what the architect had in mind when she did this?	Question-to-question probe.

Example	*Comment*
Resp: No. She obviously didn't think about the fact that kids on the playing field are always being rough and showing off to other kids by breaking everything in sight that's breakable.	Focused response explaining situation from respondent's point of view.

A third reflective probe, the *attentive-listening probe,* demands more interviewer participation. The interviewer listens for the implied meaning of the respondent's remarks, repeating back to the respondent as a question what the interviewer believes is meant:

Example	*Comment*
Int: Is there anything you do regularly on a daily basis in the building?	General question about routines.
Resp: I always go down to get my mail late in the morning, at least half an hour after the mail arrives. This way I don't meet anyone and no one knows if I get mail or not.	Descriptive response about personal routine.
Int: You mean it bothers you if there are other people there who see that you might not receive any mail for a day or two?	Attentive-listening probe.
Resp: Yes, it's none of their business. I like to meet my friends when I want to, but I don't like to be forced to see them when I am doing chores around the building.	Focused response explaining resident's avoidance behavior in terms of forced meetings.

Transition Probes to Extend Range

The range of an interview is the number of topics it covers relevant to the respondent and to the situation. Extensive range is often a measure of the quality of an interview. Probes extend range by making certain that the topics listed in the guide are discussed, as well as unanticipated topics the respondent brings up and topics that suggest interrelations between the focused interview and data from other research projects. In maintaining sufficient range in an interview, it is difficult to move from one topic to another without giving the respondent the impression that the interviewer is running the show entirely. The major danger is that respondents may become passive and wait for the interviewer to ask a series of structured questions—destroying the purpose of the interview.

In easy interviews respondents demonstrate their involvement with each topic by giving short shrift to irrelevant items and discussing in depth topics that hold meaning for them. When this occurs, a skilled interviewer simply stays out of the picture. Still, he listens closely to the order in which topics are covered as an indication of their importance within the respondent's definition of the situation.

When such ideal conditions do not occur, the interviewer uses *transition probes* to facilitate movement from topic to topic with a minimum of overt direction. In focused interviews several typical situations requiring transition probes arise regularly.

For one, respondents may continue to discuss a topic the interviewer feels has been discussed with sufficient specificity, depth, and context at detailed levels of abstraction. The interviewer can then use a *cued* transition probe, in which "the interviewer so adapts a remark or an allusion by an interviewee as to ease him into consideration of a new topic" (Merton et al., 1956: 58). Cued probes use analogy, association of ideas, or shifts in emphasis to effect smooth transitions.

Example	*Comment*
Resp: (School maintenance worker discussing maintainability in various areas of the school) . . . another thing particularly convenient about cleaning the bathroom is the special water faucets there, although the outlets might be a bit larger to allow water to get out faster.	Final remarks of a sufficiently detailed explanation.
Int: Another place with readily available water must be the school swimming pool. How is that as far as maintenance is concerned?	Cued probe using the topic of water to move from a discussion of lavatories to one of play facilities.
Resp: In the swimming pool, water is not the main maintenance problem. There it is the type of tile; it is difficult to clean . . .	Response related to new interview topic.

When a respondent finds herself discussing a topic with intense personal meaning, her answers become highly charged. She may try to change the subject either because of unpleasant associations or because she does not feel at ease talking about important things with a stranger. Since such topics may be particularly relevant, an interviewer tries to keep respondents on the topic by showing how interested he is—with silence and body probes.

If a respondent nevertheless moves on to a new topic, the interviewer is better off dropping the topic and picking it up later in the interview in a new context or when rapport with the respondent has improved. A mental or written note to use such a *reversion probe* will help. Reversion probes take advantage of at least a superficial connection to bring up a topic insufficiently covered earlier:

Int: That reminds me of something we
spoke about earlier.

or

Int: Isn't this point a continuation of the
point you made before?

A reversion probe is particularly useful when a respondent is distracted from an interesting topic to one that interests her still more. The interviewer knows there will be no difficulty returning to the first topic but hesitates to do so quickly for fear of interrupting the respondent's train of thought.

Another common situation is one in which the respondent, happy to have an audience, warms up to a topic having nothing to do with the subject of the interview. A lonely hospital patient asked to discuss a hospital setting, for example, may show the interviewer pictures of his grandchildren and discuss them in detail—their ages, education, and exploits. The interviewer should be grateful for such excursions because they strengthen rapport with the respondent. Nevertheless, cued transitions help to bring the conversation on track:

Example	*Comment*
Resp: . . . and my fourth grandchild just started nursery school . . .	Irrelevant discussion.
Int: That raises the issue of families visiting patients in the hospital. Where do you entertain your family?	Cued probe.
Resp: Usually my family sits in the bedroom with me, but when the grandchildren come we sit in the dayroom.	Response moved back to interview topic: the hospital setting.

With garrulous respondents, however, an interviewer may need to resort to *mutation probes* that blatantly change the subject. Mutation probes, generally unstructured questions, raise questions out of context, with no reference to previous discussions. Interviewers must use mutation probes sparingly. Otherwise they can cut off discussion of relevant topics because they are too tired to listen carefully or because the topic is mistakenly not on their interview guide. Potentially informative leads are easily lost this way. The temptation to use mutation probes unwisely is particularly great at the end of an interview when some topics have not been covered. The interviewer wants to translate his guide topics into specific questions and ask these in rapid succession. As a rule, if an interviewer does not have the time to follow up on a topic, it is inefficient to raise it using mutation probes. It is better skipped altogether.

Situation Probes to Encourage Specificity

Specificity in the focused interview is a respondent's ability to state with precision which elements in a situation she reacted to and in what way, rather than just saying that the situation as a whole had an effect on her. This is particularly vital if you want to understand respondents' reactions to such complex environments as housing projects. Merton et al. (1956: 7) point out that this was the case in Chapin's early research on public housing:

> Chapin (1940) studied the gains in social participation which can be attributed "to the effects of living in the [public] housing project." As he recognized, "improved housing" is an unanalyzed "experimental" situation: managerial policies, increased leisure, architectural provision for group meetings, and a host of other items are varying elements of the program of "improved housing."

Chapin used focused interviews to find out specifically what it was about the housing project that influenced people's social participation. Researchers interested in influencing design decisions need to know which decision in a complex set of decisions has had what effects.

Interviewers who want respondents to specify further a particular stimulus situation can ask them directly to do so:

Int: What was there particularly about the building that you liked?

or

Int: What part of the schoolyard do you play in most?

The more an interviewer repeats references to the stimulus situation, especially in a series of progressively specifying questions, the more likely the respondent is to make reference to specific parts of the environment.

Researchers can either first request respondents to specify aspects of the environment and then discuss their reactions to each aspect or ask respondents to first describe a reaction, followed up by further specification of what is being reacted to. Merton et al. (1956: 71–72) surprisingly found the latter sequence of questions more effective in achieving specificity—namely, first eliciting a description of reactions, then asking respondents to specify just what was being reacted to.

Example	*Comment*
Int: How do you feel about the office you work in?	General question requesting reaction to environment.

Example	*Comment*
Resp: I feel that if I don't always stay aware of where I am, I'll get lost.	General response describing reaction to environment.
Int: What is it about your office that makes you feel that way?	Probe requesting specification of environmental stimulus.
Resp: The windows. I can't see any windows from where I work, so I never know what time it is or which direction I'm facing.	Focused specification of environmental stimulus.

When interviewers repeatedly request specification of an environmental stimulus, respondents may revert to mere description of the environment. Interpreting a request for specification as a request for information, they may proceed to try to remember as many details about the environment as they can—even irrelevant ones. To avoid this pitfall and to elicit sufficiently specifying responses, interviewers can use probes aimed at helping respondents remember clearly the settings they are asked to specify.

Using *re-presentation probes,* interviewers present respondents with a photograph or drawing of some part of the setting being discussed—a doorway, an area, a piece of hardware. This active probe is least directive when the picture is presented only after the respondent has verbally identified an element or place as relevant to him.

Example	*Comment*
Int: What in the school causes the most maintenance problems?	Request for general information about problems.
Resp: Well, we have the most trouble keeping the thermostats in order.	Mention of an object.
Int: (Presenting photograph of thermostat to respondent) Here is a photograph we took recently of the thermostat you use throughout the building. What is there about it that gives you the most trouble?	Re-presentation probe, combining photograph of object with request for specification.
Resp: If you look closely, you can see how flimsy the adjustment switch is. When kids fool with the switch or even when faculty members try to adjust the temperature, the switch often breaks off. This means we have to replace the whole unit at $ . . .	Focused response specifying aspect of object that causes reaction.

Graphic re-presentations can be used together with cued transition probes or even with mutation probes if interviewers want to find out respondents' reactions to a broad range of environments. Re-presentations then take on the added directive nature of these other probes.

A special case of re-presentation, the *environmental walk-through probe*, can be used if the focused interview takes place in the environment that is the topic of the interview. During a walk-through the interviewer asks the respondent to point out and describe places and objects that are important to him. For particularly salient items the interviewer and respondent stop to specify more precisely what it is about the item that is relevant.

A walk-through is not just a guided tour. To get the most out of an environmental walk-through, interviewers first question the respondent in one place, asking him to describe the environment they will walk through, together with his general reactions to it. As places and objects are mentioned, the interviewer discusses them up to the point of requesting detailed specification, noting these items for later reference during the walk-through. In this way, the interviewer uses first the respondent's personal definition of the situation to define important elements and then the walk-through to elicit further specification.

Reconstruction probes may be used when respondents have trouble remembering the setting they are asked about or when they remember it only in general terms. Reconstruction probes ask respondents to think back to particular events in a place to recall their reactions to it *at the time* the event took place.

Int: When you first entered the hospital
three weeks ago, which entrance did you
come in?

or

Int: What do you remember about the last
time you sat at your old desk, before
moving to this office?

When the respondent refers to a complex set of phenomena that she remembers only as a whole or when she replies "don't know" or "can't remember" after being asked to specify her answers, reconstruction probes often help switch attention to specifics.

Example	*Comment*
Int: How do you feel about the park?	General request for information on feelings.
Resp: I think it is a particularly good place to come with my children.	General report of feelings.
Int: What makes it a good place for children?	Specifying probe.

Example	*Comment*
Resp: I don't know, it's just the way it's planned.	"I don't know" meaning "I can't verbalize it."
Int: Well, do you remember the last time you went to the park with your kids?	Reconstruction probe.
Resp: Yes, we played hide-and-seek on the curved pathways, and . . .	Response beginning to reconstruct specific situations.

Reconstruction probes help respondents to look retrospectively at the situation they are commenting on—to put themselves backward in time and reexperience the setting. Specifying probes in general do more than isolate for analysis specific parts of a whole situation. By linking specific parts to specific respondent reactions, they set up the interview so that each reaction can be explored in depth.

Emotion Probes to Increase Depth

Depth in a focused interview is the degree to which the respondent's feelings about a situation are explored. Reports that a respondent "likes" or "dislikes" a place, that it is "very satisfying," or that it is a "frightening" place can signify a variety of things. Someone, for example, can dislike her workplace but choose to work there because it is better than any other place she has found. Or a street can be frightening to someone, but the fear can be such a peripheral concern that it does not hinder his walking there.

Interviewers use emotion probes to determine how strongly a person feels about a response he has given. The probes encourage respondents to explore and explain in depth the meaning and richness of general expressions of feelings. Emotion probes keep respondents from merely describing a setting by directing them to explain their feelings about it as well.

Feeling probes continually use the term *feel* or *feeling* in questions or repeatedly ask respondents to explain what they mean by a given generally-expressed feeling.

Example	*Comment*
Resp: I am frightened by the teenagers who walk through the project.	General reaction.
Int: What do you mean, "I am frightened?"	Feeling probe.
Resp: The teenagers are rough and could hurt us. We are old.	Descriptive response.
Int: Are you actually afraid they will harm you?	Feeling probe.

Resp: No. In fact, they are actually well-behaved if you talk to them. They just walk across the lawn where there is no path and sometimes throw rocks at the lights.	Specifying response.
Int: What do you feel about this?	Feeling probe.
Resp: I am very angry that they do not obey the rules, but I am glad that the kids respect our being old and that they stay out of our front yards.	Depth response.

A series of feeling probes can bring to the surface strongly felt sentiments that appear at first to be peripheral, and it can show seemingly deeply felt sentiments to be no more than offhand remarks. As a rule, no briefly expressed sentiment ought to be taken at face value until it has been probed in depth.

Another probe for depth of emotion is the *projection probe,* in which interviewers ask respondents to project feelings about a situation onto another, hypothetical person. This is useful when discussing sensitive emotions that the respondent himself might not admit having but would be at ease admitting that "others" or "someone else" might have.

Example	*Comment*
Int: How do you feel about playing at the central basketball court with the older kids?	General request for feeling.
Resp: I don't mind. I'll play anywhere. I play there sometimes, and sometimes I play on the smaller court down the block.	Neutral feeling response.
Int: Why do you use the smaller court?	Feeling probe.
Resp: Because I just don't feel like hassling with the older kids.	Response indicating avoidance reaction.
Int: Does anybody avoid the central courts because he's afraid?	Projection probe.
Resp: Sure, some kids are really afraid of getting picked on by the older kids. Some even avoid walking down the block if they know that someone playing on the central court is after them.	Projective response describing feelings of "some kids" in depth.

When respondents seem to avoid answering a feeling question, this is a clue to interviewers to try a projection probe—particularly when respondents *deny that they personally* have a certain feeling. At the same time, interviewers must be careful not to think that every response referring to "a friend" or "someone else" actually describes respondents' unexpressed feelings. The ability to make such distinctions increases with interviewing experience.

A final emotion probe is the *attentive-listening probe*, in which interviewers listen for the meaning implied in the respondent's answer and then make this meaning explicit in a follow-up probe:

Example	*Comment*
Int: How do you feel about the rules that the school principal makes about what you can and cannot do on school grounds?	General request for feelings about a specific subject.
Resp: He has a right to make any rules he wants. But they should apply equally to all grades, not just to us seventh- and eighth-graders.	Response obliquely describing reactions and feelings.
Int: You mean you feel you are being treated unfairly?	Attentive-listening probe.
Resp: Yes, it really makes me angry that they can . . .	In-depth feeling response.

Sometimes stating implied feelings in terms of limits to action—in terms of extremes—allows respondents first to reject the extreme statement and then to clarify what they were trying to say.

Example	*Comment*
Resp: I can't think of any place I'd rather live.	Seemingly extreme statement of feeling.
Int: Does that mean you like it here so much you wouldn't move for anything?	Extreme attentive-listening probe.
Resp: Not exactly. If my best friend bought a house where it is warmer, I'd consider moving.	Rejection of extreme restatement and clarification of attachment to residence.

Interviewers should be careful not to put words in a respondent's mouth by restating implied feelings approximately and then using a feeling probe too forcefully: "You did mean this, didn't you?"

Attentive-listening probes, like many others, have side effects as significant as their direct effect. Respondents who see interviewers interested and listening tend to relax, be more talkative, and feel greater rapport.

Personal Probes to Tie In Context

Reactions to environments have, as a rule, a dual chain of causes, the environment and characteristics of the reacting person. One such characteristic is his or her position in the environment: nurse, doctor, patient, visitor; teacher, student, principal, parent; tenant, janitor, landlord, delivery person. More general characteristics, such as age, sex, and family status, can also heavily influence a respondent's reactions. The most important factors, however, may derive from the respondent's biography, his or her history, different personal backgrounds, experiences, or idiosyncrasies that influence his or her feelings about things. For example, one high-rise urban tenant may have lived his whole life on a farm, while another was brought up in high-rise city buildings. One doctor may be particularly sensitive to problems of cancer patients because she had a parent who suffered from the disease. If a researcher wants to understand a respondent's answers throughout a focused interview and to generalize data to any larger group of people, the researcher must know the personal context within which a respondent is answering questions: position in the system, personal characteristics, background, personal idiosyncrasies. Biography is a dimension that can provide useful insights, but it requires an interviewer's particular tact.

Self-description probes directly request respondents to describe themselves and why they react to situations the way they do. This achieves results when respondents are self-analytic and conscious of underlying reasons for their actions.

Example	*Comment*
Resp: I hate people talking in the library.	General statement on depth of feeling.
Int: Is there anything particular about you that makes you feel so strongly?	Self-description probe.
Resp: Yes, my mother was a librarian, and . . .	Context response explaining personal background.

When self-descriptive answers result from nonpersonal probes, they are also significant.

Example	*Comment*
Resp: I am afraid to live in that area.	Response stating general feeling.
Int: Why are you afraid?	General probe.
Resp: My age means that my legs are not so strong, so I am afraid of falling down when I walk. And in that area the kids play ball and ride bicycles on the sidewalk.	Contextual response explaining reactions in terms of personal characteristics.

Parallel probes help respondents talk about themselves in one setting by requesting them to find parallel situations in their own lives. This often has the effect of getting respondents to explicate the parallel by talking about personal contexts.

Example	*Comment*
Resp: I find this office extremely inefficient and wasteful.	General response.
Int: In what way?	General probe.
Resp: I don't know, just "inefficient."	Difficulty expressing self.
Int: Is there any setting you can think of which is inefficient like this office or which explains what you mean by "inefficient"?	Parallel probe.
Resp: A submarine is efficient. When I was a sailor, we learned that . . .	Response explaining personal context.

FOCUSED INTERVIEWS IN GROUPS

Many of the initial experiences of Merton et al. with focused interviews took place with groups, not individuals (1956: Chapter 7). Carrying out interviews in groups is a good idea if you want to identify the range of definitions of a situation that interviewees hold, to find out whether a particular opinion is held at all, and to save time. In a study to design social-service offices for a staff of 40, researchers can carry out interviews with four groups of ten respondents much more easily than with 40 individuals. Group interviewing often works out best if the size of the group is kept under 15, if the interview is held informally around a table or in a circle in a small enough room that respondents feel they are all part of one event, and if respondents in the group have something in common.

In a group, interviewers face many of the same problems and use many of the same probes as they do with individuals. You have to keep the flow of discussion moving, remind people of specific details you are interested in, and maintain sufficient range. Sometimes the fact that others are in the room makes an interviewer's job easier—when, for example, an emotional statement by one person incites others to express their feelings more openly.

But a group can also present special problems, most stemming from the "leader effect" (Merton et al., 1956: 148)—namely, that in most groups of people one or two persons will inevitably emerge as louder, more dominant, or more opinionated. Such a person can easily take over an interview, divert it from its focus, and inhibit others from talking. What can you do to prevent this without damaging your rapport with the group and interrupting the flow of the meeting?

Appeals for Equal Time

When one person takes over an interview, that person and others usually know it. Sometimes people even do so as a subtle challenge to the interviewer. It is your task to appeal to the person's sense of fair play in order to give others a chance to talk:

> *Int:* Good point. Perhaps we should hear some other opinions now.

> *Int:* To get a broad enough picture, it might be good to see what other people think about this as well.

Attention to Body Language

Reticent respondents in a group often remain quiet, leaving the floor to the self-chosen leader. This does not, however, mean that quieter interviewees have nothing to say; they just do not create their own openings in the conversation. So it is your job to create openings for them when you notice they want to say something. Cues that they have an opinion to express include these:

- A respondent sitting forward on his chair, looking at you intensely.
- A respondent raising her hand as in a classroom.
- Two respondents chatting quietly—probably expressing minority opinions to each other.

Asking for a Vote

When discussion has been limited to several respondents, or when more respondents have contributed but it is unclear who holds what opinion, you can ask for a vote on an issue. But first you must show you have been listening attentively by clearly stating the opinion or alternative opinions the respondents are to vote on:

> *Int:* Charley has stated that the most important thing about an office is that it have a window—more than privacy or anything else. Which of you agree with this and which disagree? (This type of question in part challenges respondents to contribute.)

> *Int:* Some of you say that you dislike moving from desk to desk when more people are hired; others seem to be saying they don't mind. Could I see a show of hands: How many of you dislike moving? And how many don't mind it?

Group focused interviewing can be disappointing and exhilarating, insightful and frustrating, because the mixtures of people you find lead to infinitely varied interactions among them and between you and them. As with every research tool, to use it successfully you need to know more than you can read about in books. This is particularly true for the skills necessary to carry out a group focused interview.

OVERVIEW

You cannot find out how people see the world and feel about it unless you ask them. The focused interview is uniquely suited to discovering a respondent's personal definition of complex E-B situations. Skilled interviewers analyze situations to develop a guide of interview topics. The purpose of the guide is limited to reminding the interviewer of topics and issues to cover. The skilled interviewer then enables the respondent to approach and discuss these topics in her own special way.

To achieve full coverage and depth of insights, the interviewer's main tool is the probe: an indication by the interviewer to the respondent to provide more information about depth of feelings, other topics, the respondent's personal context, or details of a situation. Interviewers use probes to keep an interview flowing without directing it.

Focused-interviewing techniques are as useful with groups as with individual respondents if the interviewer knows how to keep one member of the group from dominating and can encourage diversity of opinion rather than forced consensus.

Focused interviews, however, are not suited to gathering large amounts of easily comparable and quantifiable data. For this researchers need to use standardized questionnaires—the topic of the next chapter.

Chapter 10

STANDARDIZED QUESTIONNAIRES

Standardized questionnaires are used to discover regularities among groups of people by comparing answers to the same set of questions asked of a large number of people. Questionnaires can be delivered by mail or administered over the phone or in person by interviewers trained to ask the questions in the same way. Questionnaires administered in person are also called "scheduled interviews," especially when interviewers are instructed to follow up certain questions with probes for depth or specificity.

Questionnaires provide useful data when investigators begin with a very well defined problem, knowing what major concepts and dimensions they want to deal with. Analysis of questionnaire responses can provide precise numbers to measure, for example, the degree of satisfaction among residents in a new apartment complex or the percentages of residents who moved from single-family homes and from apartments.

Skilled researchers use standardized questionnaires to test and refine their ideas by beginning with hypotheses about which attributes relate to each other. What they do not know is which hypotheses are going to stand up best to empirical study and how, precisely, the concepts will relate. For example, a research team may hypothesize that type of previous dwelling influences satisfaction with apartment living. Using questionnaires, they might find out that residents moving from single-family houses are more satisfied than previous apartment dwellers with high-rise living because they expected to have drastically less space than they had before (Merton et al., 1960).

Fried (1963/1972) demonstrates insightful use of questionnaires to show how reactions among residents of a neighborhood to being forced out in the wake of urban renewal were related to their "sense of spatial identity" with the neighborhood, "based on spatial memories, spatial imagery, the spatial framework of current activities, and the implicitly spatial components of ideals and aspirations" (1972: 234). Fried's quantitative analysis of responses from 259 relocated women residents before and after moving showed that the more they liked living in the West End and the more they viewed the West End as "home," the more they reported severe grief reactions after moving (see Tables 10-1 and 10-2).

Table 10-1. Post-relocation "grief" by pre-relocation "liking"

	Percent Severe Grief Reactions
Among those who said they *liked living in the West End:*	
"very much"	73%
"positive but less than very much"	53%
"ambivalent or negative"	34%
n = (259)	

Table 10-2. Post-relocation "grief" by pre-relocation "feeling like home"

	Percent Severe Grief Reactions
Among those who said their *real home* was:	
"the West End"	68%
"in some other area"	34%
"they had no real home"	20%
n = (259)	

This chapter discusses some of the qualities of questionnaires, how to organize a questionnaire, and ways to code and formulate categories.

The following chapter will show how asking questions in interviews and questionnaires is suited to such environment-behavior topics as perception, aspirations, knowledge, attitudes, and intentions. That chapter also discusses how to formulate questions in order to find out what you want to about these topics.

QUALITIES

By organizing questionnaires and their administration, investigators can find out a great deal in a short time. But this takes preparation. The quality of questionnaire data depends on the thoroughness that E-B researchers apply to defining the problems they are studying. This is a significant burden because resulting quantitative data often convince other people of arguments qualitative data do not—even when the conceptual basis of the numbers is weak.

Standardized Questionnaires

Qualities

    Control
    Intrusiveness
    Convincing rigor

Organization

    Rapport
    Conditioning
    Fatigue

Coding Open-Ended Responses

    Mutual exclusiveness
    Exhaustiveness
    Single abstraction level

Precoding Responses

    Nominal
    Ordinal

Visual Responses

    Maps
    Drawings
    Photographs
    Games

Control

Interviewers structure questionnaires and control their administration. There is an implicit contract between researcher and respondent that the researcher defines what happens during the interview: how it begins, the ordering of questions and answers, and how it ends. Control has positive side effects, not the least of which is efficiency—minimal cost to gather large amounts of specific and comparable data. Some control over the situation is given up when questionnaires are delivered by mail; accordingly, to increase control, mail questionnaires are usually shorter and more tightly organized.

Repeating standardized questions the same way to many respondents enables researchers to easily compare answers from different respondents. When individual questionnaire items are repeated in separate and similar studies, answers can be shared and compared to build a cumulative body of data.

Intrusiveness

Control in administering questionnaires raises the issue that respondents can change and distort answers. Respondents can be directed by the questions themselves, for example, to treat some issues in greater depth than others, define things in certain ways, respond in provided categories. This is not a problem if questions and response categories correspond to respondents' definitions of the situation. However, when they do not correspond, respondents sometimes feel that the implicit contract to answer questions means they ought not to correct obvious mistakes: the researcher surely knows what she is after.

Researchers using standardized questionnaires must decide before going into the field what level of refinement they want answers to achieve to solve their problem. There is little room for adjustment once data gathering begins. One of the most frustrating things that can happen to researchers in structured interview research is to find that they have spent a great deal of time and energy finding out everything except one item essential to explaining relations between crucial variables.

To avoid some of the side effects of control in any method and in any type of interview (not only questionnaires), researchers carry out particularly thorough preliminary diagnostic research. Focused interviews may be used to determine how people similar to intended questionnaire respondents define a situation: what is important; the names they use for places or things; the types of answers they give. Observation methods can also be used during diagnostic studies. Using diagnostic data, investigators structure standardized questionnaires. But that is not all there is to it.

After the questionnaire is written, investigators *pretest* it with more people like the expected respondents. Pretesting a questionnaire means administering it to self-conscious respondents while asking them to comment on points such as these: what do they understand each question to mean; is it clear or confusing; what do they think is its intent; do response categories give them ample opportunity to express themselves? Pretests are invaluable aids not only in questionnaire construction but in designing any research instrument to fit the needs of a particular situation, group of respondents or elements to observe, and research problem.

Pretests carried out skillfully also alert investigators to unforeseen problems in other dimensions of the research approach: problem definition, research design, methodological mix, observer training, interviewers' skills, "even of the first steps of analysis." A pretest is a small, self-conscious pilot study, a microcosm of the actual project carried out to identify, if possible, unintended side effects (Galtung, 1967: 138).

Convincing Rigor

Quantitative analysis of questionnaire data not only contributes precision to knowledge; it also can make research data convincing to others. The apparent exactness and rigorousness of statistical analysis is a useful device to win arguments with people who do not understand the value of qualitative knowing in scientific research. This is an important characteristic of the method when research results are to be used in a court of law, in a political setting, in applied design—in any competitive decision-making situation. Such situations are increasing as E-B research issues are brought into the public eye by citizens' groups and environmental legislation.

Naive researchers sometimes are themselves convinced by the numbers they can get using questionnaires. They think they can learn something significant by asking a lot of questions and running answers through a computer. Something can, of course, be learned in this way. But it has a low probability of solving the researcher's, the client's, or the respondents' problems.

Quantitative questionnaire data not augmented by researchers' qualitative insight or by qualitative data from other methods can provide a hollow and unscientific understanding of important problems (Campbell, 1975).

ORGANIZATION

If you are not careful, the way your questionnaire is structured can antagonize, bore, confuse, and tire respondents. If it does, you might as well not ask any questions.

Rapport

Questionnaire respondents participate in a research project as informants about themselves. Research results are as valid as the relationship between interviewer and respondent is open and nondefensive. Rapport can be established by introducing oneself and the purpose of the interview clearly, honestly, realistically, and without threatening the respondent. Environment-behavior research projects may be introduced to respondents as attempts to ask their *advice*—how to make future similar environments better, what could have been improved in that setting, or just what people like and think. Respondents like to see themselves as advice givers rather than guinea pigs.

Questions requesting positive responses ("What do you like best about working in this building?") can start an interview on a friendly note. Later, requests can be made for suggestions on improvements. Initial questions can request general impressions; ask for simple demographic information, such as previous residence; or, especially, be on interesting topics to elicit respondents' attention. For every situation and problem each investigator must work out the most appropriate way to begin.

Conditioning

Early questions can influence the way respondents answer later ones. For example, if early questions give respondents the feeling that interviewers really want to find out what is wrong with a place, they may criticize it more than they praise it. If information is presented in the wording of an early question, knowledge of that information cannot be tested later. A good rule to follow is to go from general to specific questions so that questions asked later in the interview require greater specificity of information, intent, and purpose.

Fatigue

In the half hour or so during which a questionnaire is administered, interviewers often have to choose between gathering a great deal of information and not tiring out the respondent. To try to maximize information gathering and minimize fatigue, you can group questions relating to a topic: all those dealing with a neighborhood, with an event, with a set of activities in one place. For clarity each group can be introduced with a unifying sentence: "And now I would like to ask you some questions about . . ."

Interviewers can also group questions having similar types of response categories, such as those discussed in the next section: a series of preference questions, then semantic differential questions, then attitude questions. Both types of groupings can lead to "response sets" among answers—namely, respondents' natural tendency to answer questions in a way that seems logically consistent. For example, respondents may tend not to admit to criticism of one part of a setting while praising another. It is therefore sometimes necessary to mix up questions about different dimensions of the same topic and to limit the length of any one set of questions with identical response categories.

Another way to use wisely the time respondents give you is not to ask them questions that do not apply to them. *Filtering questions* can help you avoid inapplicable questions by, for example, finding out who drives to work before asking how long it takes by car, how many people are in the car, what parking conditions are like. When *follow-up questions* are used for explanation ("Why?"), specification ("What precisely?"), or clarification of intensity ("How much?"), it saves time to target them only to respondents to whom they apply.

All this can be achieved with clear layout and written interviewer instructions to keep the interview flowing and to avoid confusing respondents with irrelevant questions. Saile et al. (1972) faced many of the problems discussed here. Their questionnaire helped resolve many of them (facing page).

CODING OPEN-ENDED RESPONSES

No matter how researchers pose questions in an interview, they must record the answers and prepare them for counting and analysis. By grouping similar responses together, they make responses comparable to one another. For example, four respondents who are asked a free-response question about why they like a room might give four answers: "I like it because it is big," "I like it

OMIT QUESTION #s 127-135 for SCATTERED SITES:

"Now, we have just a few more questions to go, and we'd like to get your views on the Housing Authority..."

127. In general, would you say that the management here does a good job, a fair job, or a poor job in running the project?

> Good job.................1
> Fair job.................2
> Poor job.................3

128. Do they repair things fairly quickly   YES   NO
      when something goes wrong?...................1⌐   2
                                                   GO TO
                                                   # 130

129. What problems have you had? (Record exact answer)

130. Do you think the rules and regulations   YES   NO
      about living here are fair?..................1⌐   2
                                                   GO TO
                                                   # 132

131. Why not? (Record exact answer)

132. When you first moved here did you go through
      a training program to learn how to look after   YES   NO
      this house?...................................   1   2

133. Would you recommend a training program like   YES   NO
      that for other people moving in here?.........   1   2

134. Would you like to have a booklet explaining   YES   NO
      how to look after this house?.................   1   2

135. Do you think it would be helpful to have a
      handbook to explain the rules and regulations   YES   NO
      about living here?............................   1   2

136. Do you think you'll stay in this house or do
      you expect to move sometime?.......STAY   MOVE SOMETIME
                                          1⌐   2
                                          GO TO
                                          # 138

(From *Families in Public Housing: An Evaluation of Three Residential Environments in Rockford, Illinois*, by D. Saile, J. R. Anderson, R. Borooah, A. Ray, K. Rohling, C. Simpson, A. Sutton, and M. Williams. University of Illinois at Urbana-Champaign Committee on Housing Research and Development, 1972. Reprinted by permission.)

because sound travels well there," "I like it because of its size," and "I like the way many people can fit into it." The researcher must decide whether each response is unique, whether the responses can be partitioned into categories of answers (two mention largeness, one good acoustics, and the fourth accommodating many people), or whether they can be partitioned into two categories (large size and acoustics). His decision will be based on how the different groupings, or partitions, help him solve his research problem.

This process of deciding how to partition responses into groups is called *coding* because researchers use a few responses to develop a category "code," which is then applied to the rest of the responses in a study. Coding categories— partitions—are confusing rather than helpful unless they are mutually exclusive, exhaust all the possible types of responses, and are all at the same conceptual level. The following examples will explain these three coding characteristics.

Mutual Exclusiveness

Mutual exclusiveness means that responses clearly fall into either one or another category. There can be no overlapping, either numerically or conceptually.

The age categories "under 11, 11–20, 21–40, 41 or over" are mutually exclusive; the categories "under 10, 10–20, 20–40, 40 or over" are not. An example of mutually exclusive categories for residential location is "in this neighborhood, in this city but outside this neighborhood, outside this city but in this state, within any other state in the country, in another country."

Exhaustiveness

Exhaustiveness means that any possible response fits into some category. Researchers can include an "other" category to achieve exhaustiveness in complex questions.

Qu: How did you travel to the supermarket the last time you went?

Categories that are not exhaustive: car, bus, on foot, other

Exhaustive categories: Own car, other's car, taxi, bicycle, public bus, special shopping bus, subway, on foot, combination of two or more modes (please specify):

(a) ——————
(b) ——————
(c) ——————

other (please specify):
(a) —————————
(b) —————————
(c) —————————

Single Level of Abstraction

Single level of abstraction means that response categories are conceptually parallel. They do not partition responses into, for example, apples, pears, oranges, and fruit.

Qu: What do you feel is the nicest part of a house?

Multi-level abstraction
code: bedrooms, shared rooms, esthetics,
                                           windows, hardware

Single-level abstraction
code: bedrooms, private work rooms, other
                                           rooms, passageways, outside grounds

PRECODING RESPONSES

In a standardized questionnaire, if there are open-ended questions needing coding, analysis of the survey can be time-consuming and costly. In addition, a great number of free-response questions reflects a lack of researcher preparation and wastes the potential benefits of using a standardized questionnaire. In some cases what the researcher wants to find out cannot be rigidly structured—for example, when the subject of the study is how respondents picture their surroundings in their mind or how they react in complex decision-making situations. In these situations, as discussed at the end of this chapter, special methods of recording and coding information may be developed.

In some situations, however, it is possible to *precode* responses to questionnaire questions: to partition possible response alternatives into a set of categories for respondents to choose from that are exhaustive, are mutually exclusive, and have a single level of abstraction. This means asking questions of the form "Are you very tired, somewhat tired, or not tired at all?" (precoded) rather than "How tired are you?" (open-ended).

Codes may organize things parallel to one another or in rank order. The first are nominal and the latter ordinal categories.

Nominal

Such things as building types or types of research methods may be partitioned for certain purposes into separate and parallel categories. Chapters 7, 8, 9, 10, and 12 of this book represent a nominal code of methods. A simple nominally precoded response asks respondents to reply yes or no to a question, such as "Do you have a driver's license?" Or it offers a binary choice: "Sex? male _____ female _____." Usually, however, nominal codes classify more than two alternatives: "What is your religion? Protestant _____ , Moslem _____ , Catholic _____ , Jewish _____ , Hindu _____ , agnostic _____ , atheist _____ , other _____ , none _____ ." "Do you find it difficult to climb the stairs? Yes; no; don't know, no opinion; does not apply, never climb stairs."

Nominal codes are most useful to collect information, to offer nonranked choices to respondents, and to find out attitudinal data useful in a binary "yes" or "no" form.

Ordinal

To analyze intensity, direction, and quality of such variables as verbally expressed attitudes and perceptions, it may be helpful to arrange responses in a rank order representing different degrees or magnitudes.

When each category is separated from others by what seems to be an equal magnitude, ordinal categories are called "intervals." There are some difficulties with this idea. For example, a uniform difference in temperature—say, 2° F—may be experienced differently if it represents a rise from 6° F to 8° F than a rise from 65° F to 67° F. The same problem holds for age differences. A year has a different quantity and quality at ages 5, 30, and 80. Therefore, interval categories are not presented here as distinct from ordinal ones.

Information. Ordinal precoding can be used for questions gathering *information* that reasonably are seen as "how much" or "how many" questions—age, income, size of household, number of clubs a respondent belongs to.

Age: Under 11 □ , 11–20 □ , 21–30 □ , 31–40 □ , 41–50 □ , 51–60 □ , 61 or over □ .

Club membership: None □ , 1 or 2 □ , 3 to 6 □ , 7 or more □ .

Attitudes. Ordinal coding may also be useful for response categories following questions that ask respondents to judge the intensity of an *attitude* about something, such as a situation, person, object, or setting.

Would you say the rules in this factory are

very fair □ , fair □ , unfair □ , very unfair □ , or do you have no opinion □ about this?

Would you say the work areas you have are

very supportive □ , supportive □ , unsupportive □ , very unsupportive □ , or are you uncertain about this □ ?

When a questionnaire is administered orally, the "no opinion" or "uncertain" category is sometimes not read to respondents, to encourage them to make some kind of choice—no matter how weakly felt. If they still have no opinion, interviewers check the box.

Some coding categories are associated not only with a format for responses but as well with quantitative procedures for analyzing responses. One of these is the *Likert attitude scale,* in which groups of statements are presented to respondents for them to indicate the intensity of their agreement or disagreement. If standard scores are assigned to responses in such a way that high agreement with positive statements is equivalent to high disagreement with negative statements, and if several questions tap dimensions of the same general attitude ("feelings about company management," for example), then cumulative scores on these statements can be used to indicate a respondent's position on that attitude.

Example of Likert Attitude Scale

Please check the appropriate box:

	Strongly Agree	Agree	Uncertain	Disagree	Strongly Disagree
The rules in this factory are unfair	1	2	3	4	5
Management is very helpful in job training	5	4	3	2	1
The work areas we have could easily be much better	1	2	3	4	5

(Number scores in the boxes are not presented on the questionnaire.)

When Likert-scaled questions are used, they can be grouped together in a questionnaire so that once respondents understand how to use this system of recording responses, they can use it for several questions. When this is done, however, the list must be short enough and must mix up positive and negative statements to avoid respondents' going down a long list checking only one column and not thinking.

If researchers feel that using Likert-scale items on a questionnaire can help them solve their problems, they should carefully study the assumptions underlying this type of attitude quantification. If they decide they can make these assumptions, they carry out careful empirical procedures to choose and score groups of statements that actually do relate to one another (as explained, for example, in Shaw & Wright, 1967).

The same caveat holds for the use of every empirically developed measurement scale, including the semantic differential scale, discussed next.

Meaning. When you look at the Eiffel Tower, Mount Fuji, or the chair you are sitting in, you react to it in part on the basis of what it "means" to you. You may, for example, feel uncomfortable and tense in the chair because it is an antique that you see as dainty, weak, and silly, although tasteful. Most people find it difficult to express verbally the range of meaning things have to them. In a taste test of different ice creams, few tasters could spontaneously manage to say anything but "creamy" and "tasty" in attempts to differentiate brands. But when presented with lists of descriptive terms to choose from, they could easily indicate what the different tastes meant to them (Osgood, Suci, & Tannenbaum, 1957).

The principle that people express the meaning things hold for them more completely when presented with a set of appropriate alternatives underlies another analytic coding technique—the *semantic differential scale*. Like the Likert and other scales, this one must entail careful procedures for determining what alternatives are "appropriate" for particular respondents and situations. It also entails important and often questionable assumptions about quantification and ensuing analysis of data (Osgood et al., 1957).

If the scaling technique is critically examined, it can be selectively used to identify the *quality* and *intensity* of meaning that E-B topics such as environments, persons, places, and situations hold for people.

The format for semantic differentiation presents respondents first with the name or picture of an object (place, concept, and so on) or with the object itself, followed by a series of polar opposite terms: good/bad, happy/sad, big/little. For each pair of terms, respondents are requested to indicate how the terms apply to the object on the basis of what the object means to them. They do this in the following format:

Your Chair

Wide ____/ ____/ ____/ ____/ ____/ ____/ ____/ *Narrow*
(1)   (2)   (3)   (4)   (3)   (2)   (1)

Contemporary ____/ ____/ ____/ ____/ ____/ ____/ ____/ Traditional
Functional ____/ ____/ ____/ ____/ ____/ ____/ ____/ Nonfunctional
Tasteful ____/ ____/ ____/ ____/ ____/ ____/ ____/ Tasteless
Gay ____/ ____/ ____/ ____/ ____/ ____/ ____/ Dreary
Orderly ____/ ____/ ____/ ____/ ____/ ____/ ____/ Chaotic
Private ____/ ____/ ____/ ____/ ____/ ____/ ____/ Public
Sparkling ____/ ____/ ____/ ____/ ____/ ____/ ____/ Dingy

Respondents are instructed that marking the line above a response of 1 means the object is extremely wide, contemporary, or whatever; 2, quite wide; 3, slightly wide; 4, neutral, equally wide and narrow, or wideness is unrelated to the object.

Choice and interpretation of scale items are difficult. Osgood et al. carried out several studies and much computer analysis to develop a scale of 50 paired items particularly relevant to general concepts. They found that the descriptive terms fell mainly into categories of evaluation, potency, and activity. A great deal more work is necessary to adapt this scaling technique to E-B studies.

When semantic differential scales are used, it is necessary to choose categories appropriate to the particular research situation and respondents' definition of the situation. For example, in their study of housing for older persons, Howell and Epp (1976) pretested the following semantic differential question:

How would you describe the way the building looks from the outside?

like a private ____/ ____/ ____/ ____/ ____/ ____/ ____/ like a public
home   (1)   (2)   (3)   (4)   (3)   (2)   (1)   building

hard ____/ ____/ ____/ ____/ ____/ ____/ ____/ soft
simple ____/ ____/ ____/ ____/ ____/ ____/ ____/ complex

The older respondents were able to choose between the attributes in the first pair, but they could not understand what the other two pairs had to do with the way their building looked.

Question construction has developed into a complex skill—perhaps too complex. The semantic differential scale exhibits a problem many such techniques face: They may cause you more damage than they are worth. It is unclear, for example, that seven-point polar-opposite judgment tests yield more information than a three- or five-point agree/disagree rating scale. If respondents feel that the adjectives they are asked to rate are nonsensical (*gay* and *dreary* applied to a chair, for example), the loss of rapport with the interviewer may invalidate other parts of the interview. Careful pretesting is one way to avoid such mistakes. Another is to include on the team constructing questions some people who are like potential respondents. This is good advice no matter what type of question you are constructing. In sum, rating scales of any sort must be used only after carefully examining their wording and the operational assumptions they embody.

Rank-ordering of items. It may be useful to precode responses to questions asking respondents to rank a group of items relative to one another on a single attribute: importance, beauty, usefulness, worthwhileness. For example:

Which of the spaces on the following list do you feel it is most important to include in a house? (Please circle "1" for the most important, "2" for the second most important, "3" for the next, and so on until you have ranked all places in terms of their importance to you.)

bathroom	1	2	3	4	5	6	7	8	9	10	11	12
kitchen	1	2	3	4	5	6	7	8	9	10	11	12
laundry room	1	2	3	4	5	6	7	8	9	10	11	12
living room	1	2	3	4	5	6	7	8	9	10	11	12
bedrooms	1	2	3	4	5	6	7	8	9	10	11	12
den or rec. room	1	2	3	4	5	6	7	8	9	10	11	12
study	1	2	3	4	5	6	7	8	9	10	11	12
storage attic	1	2	3	4	5	6	7	8	9	10	11	12
vestibule	1	2	3	4	5	6	7	8	9	10	11	12
dining room	1	2	3	4	5	6	7	8	9	10	11	12
Other: specify _____	1	2	3	4	5	6	7	8	9	10	11	12
Other: specify _____	1	2	3	4	5	6	7	8	9	10	11	12
Other: specify _____	1	2	3	4	5	6	7	8	9	10	11	12

When items in the group are unduly complex—alternative life-styles, for example—it is easier to present them in pairs for sequential comparison than in a simultaneous list.

Each technique for precoding responses creates opportunities for researchers, but each also limits what researchers can do with the data. Only experience with using classification and scaling methods—asking the questions, recording answers, tabulating responses, and analyzing data—will give researchers the knowledge and self-confidence needed to choose a form for precoded responses.

VISUAL RESPONSES

Some cognitive, expressive, and perceptual information about respondents' physical surroundings may be better expressed visually than verbally, through nonprecoded techniques, such as freehand area maps, base-map additions, drawings, photographs taken by respondents, and games.

This is especially true for people's *cognitive maps,* the mental pictures of their surroundings that they use to structure the way they look at, react to, and act in their environment (Downs & Stea, 1973; de Jonge, 1962; Ladd, 1970; Lynch, 1960). One can envision this continually changing picture as a two-dimensional map or drawing, a three-dimensional model, a hologram, or a file of pictures kept in one's mind. "A cognitive map is not necessarily a 'map' " seen as a flat piece of paper (Downs & Stea, 1973: 11). It is more an ongoing "process . . . by which an individual acquires, codes, stores, recalls, and decodes information about the relative locations and attributes of . . . his everyday spatial environment" (Downs & Stea, 1973: 9).

You refer to your cognitive map whenever you deal with an environment. Your so-called map tells you, for example, that if you find yourself in the dining room of a modern middle-class Western home you have never been in, one of the doors around you probably leads to the kitchen. You will be surprised if it is not so—if, for example, you find that the kitchen is on the third floor.

It is interesting enough that we can use the idea of implicit mental maps to help design places more comprehensible to people. Still more interesting is that people's cognitive maps only partly correspond to the measurable attributes of environments that might be represented by a street map drawn to scale or an aerial photograph. People's cognitive maps are influenced and distorted by their background, their experience, their purposes, and so on. For example, in a hospital, workers estimated a path outside the building to be twice as long as a path inside the building, although the two were measurably the same distance (Stea, 1974).

If designers know how people who use their environments see them, they can better control the side effects of design decisions. In the hospital mentioned above, for example, if the designer knows that outside paths are seen as longer than inside ones, he might make different decisions about enclosing them in order to provide alternative ways to get around that are actually seen as alternatives.

There is no one way to study the complex set of perceptions and attitudes that make up a person's cognitive map. Lynch (1960) carried out a 90-minute focused interview with respondents, one part of which requested them to draw freehand maps of the city. Some of Lynch's respondents were shown a series of photographs of downtown areas and asked to choose those they felt were most typical of the way they saw the city. The volunteers in this group were also interviewed with a walk-through probe (see Chapter 9) of the downtown area. During the trip, interviewers asked respondents why they took a particular path, what they saw, and when they felt confident or lost (Lynch, 1960: 140–142).

The visual-response techniques discussed in this section are essential— used together with verbal responses and observational methods—to study people's attitudes, perceptions, and knowledge concerning physical environments. Broadly defined, people's "cognitive maps" comprise all these mental processes—requiring for their study the same array of methods and techniques. In this section, I will discuss freehand maps, the use of base maps, drawings, respondents' photographs, and games.

Freehand Area Maps

Lynch's instructions to respondents were to draw "a quick map of _____ . . . . Make it just as if you were making a rapid description of the city to a stranger, covering all the main features. We don't expect an accurate drawing just a rough sketch" (Lynch, 1960: 141).

Lynch analyzed the resulting maps for such things as omissions, precision, distortions, and differential knowledge of areas. He also established a coding scheme for map responses, which he called "city image elements": paths, edges, districts, nodes, landmarks, and element interrelations.

Lynch's study began a tradition of freehand-area-map drawing in interviews, both to develop the method (de Jonge, 1962) and to look at cross-cultural and group differences in maps.

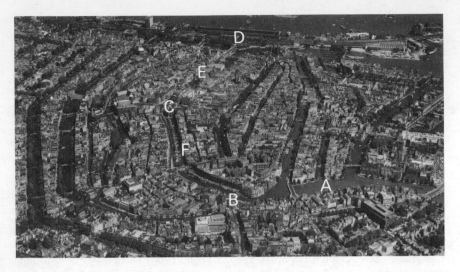

A. Amstel River   B. Mint Square
C. Dam   D. Central Station
E. Damrak   F. Rokin

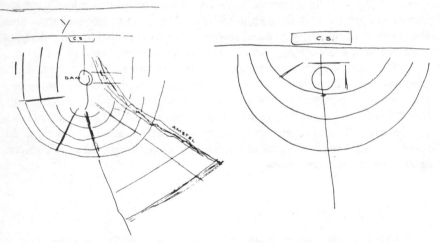

Aerial photo and freehand area maps of central Amsterdam. (Freehand map
from "Images of Urban Areas, Their Structure and Psychological Foundations," by D. de Jonge, *Journal* of the *American Institute of Planners*, 1962,
28, 266–276. Used by permission of the *Journal of the American Planning
Association*. Air photo by K. L. M. Aerocarto N. V.)

Interpreting area maps has shown that people with limited movement—
often poorer people—have detailed knowledge of their immediate neighborhood
but only an ill-formed image of the city they live in as a whole (Orleans, 1973)
and that children see things differently from adults and women from men. For

designers, this means that if they want to control the behavioral side effects of places they design, they must understand the ways different groups see them.

Area maps can be used to find out where respondents feel at home, are afraid, spend time. Limits on topics are imposed only by investigators' imagination. However, there are unresolved difficulties of interpretation. Some people draw particularly well; others refuse to draw. Some people can draw landmarks easily only when starting with a base map with major streets already indicated; others do so just as easily on a blank piece of paper. As with all methods, the more area maps are used and by more people, the more we learn about how to turn the data they provide into useful information.

Additions to Base Maps

Providing respondents with simple base maps to fill in answers can be an efficient way to find out how they use or feel about a place: paths they take, things they do in settings, names they use for places. If one wanted to find out, for example, the terms used for rooms in a house, one could give respondents an unlabeled floor plan.

Zeisel and Griffin, in their housing-evaluation study (1975), wanted to find out how residents moved through the project, particularly how often they passed through a central space planned by the architects to be an active social area. In interviews, the research team presented a completed scale map to respondents

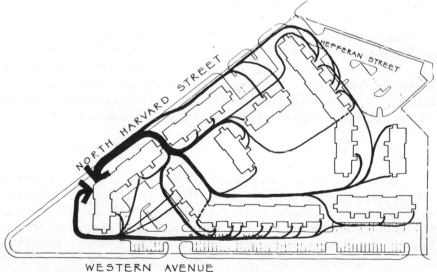

Composite path-map of respondents' trips from home to local store. (From *Charlesview Housing: A Diagnostic Evaluation*, by J. Zeisel and M. Griffin. Cambridge, Mass.: Harvard Graduate School of Design, Architecture Research Office, 1975.)

and asked them to draw or point out on it the paths they took on the way to their cars, to the shops, and to the bus stop. These pathway maps were requested instead of verbal descriptions because they seemed more reliable, more accurate, and more expressive of the process of taking a trip.

Maps like these may be quantitatively coded. They also lend themselves particularly well to comparison and visual analysis on composite data maps.

Drawings

Sometimes people's mental pictures about the future can actually be expressed in a picture. Sanoff and Barbour (1974) worked with an architect commissioned to design a grade school. They were interested in finding out what a "dream school" was like for students. One approach they used was to ask students involved in the programming research to draw typical African, Japanese, and American schools and their dream school. They found particular contrast between the factorylike drawings of typical American schools and the multilevel, almost "treelike" dream schools. Although this type of response is still more abstract and difficult to interpret quantitatively than maps, it can provide investigators with important qualitative insights.

Photographs

Lynch asked respondents to choose typical views of a city from a stack of photographs. This approach can easily be extended—with the advent of inexpensive automatic cameras—to asking respondents to take photographs themselves. An instruction might be to take pictures of "the things you like best in your neighborhood" or of "the things that mean the most to you."

As with the focused verbal interview, respondents using photographs to answer questions can decide for themselves what is important and what is not. However, this method is not one that can simply be used as one question in an otherwise fully precoded questionnaire. It is a separate method in itself.

Games

Another way E-B researchers have recorded respondents' ideas has been to develop games through which respondents express themselves by making a series of linked choices (Robinson et al., 1975). One of the oldest such games is Wilson's neighborhood game (1962). Alternative degrees of attributes such as neighborhood physical quality and sanitation services each have a price tag attached. Respondents are given a set of chips representing the total amount of money they can spend to "buy" the amenities on the game board. With the amount of play money they have, they are forced to choose among attractive alternatives, not all of which they can afford. Their final judgments express not a linear series of individual choices but a balanced set of simultaneous ones.

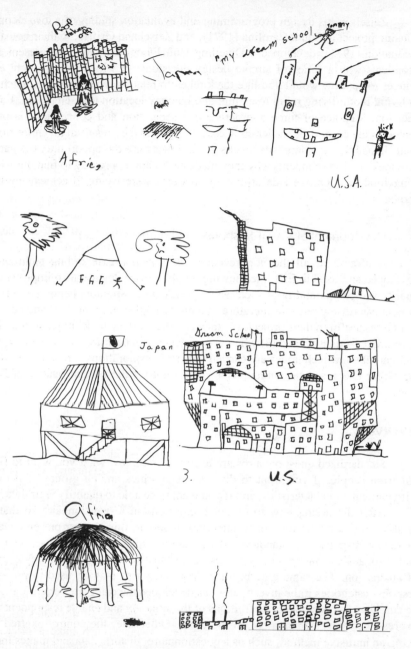

Drawings by children participating in the design charrette for the Wallace O'Neill Alternative School, Pinehurst, North Carolina. (From "An Alternative Strategy for Planning an Alternative School," by H. Sanoff and G. Barbour. In G. T. Coates (Ed.), *Alternative Learning Environments*. Copyright 1974 by Dowden, Hutchinson & Ross, Inc. Used by permission.)

Zeisel, in his design programming and evaluation studies of a low-income housing project in South Carolina (1971), and Zeisel and Griffin, in their housing evaluation (1975), developed a Dwelling Unit Floor Plan Game to present respondents with a series of simple design decisions: in which rooms ought entrances to be; how would you like the kitchen to relate to where you eat; kitchen to living room; living room to eating; and balcony location (Zeisel, 1971). Each decision, a choice of three alternatives for separation and connection, is presented in the context of earlier choices. All together they result in an entire floor plan. In addition to composite results, interviewers use the opportunity the game provides to ask respondents why they made each choice, probing to find out what behavioral or cognitive side effects respondents were trying to achieve by the choice.

Development of Visual-Response Techniques

A catalog of all the nonprecoded visual-response recording techniques developed and used in E-B interviewing would be very lengthy. To improve the quality and comparability of such techniques, (1) investigators beginning a new project can review relevant literature to identify response, recording, and coding categories useful to their project; (2) they can then test each technique in practice to improve its quality; and (3) when experiments with new uses of old techniques and entirely new techniques are carried out, such explorations can be reported to the larger E-B research community to help improve the overall quality of E-B research.

OVERVIEW

Standardized questionnaires are useful if you know what you want to find out from people, if you want to discover regularities among groups of people with particular characteristics, and if you want to be able to quantify your data.

After discussing how to organize questions in a questionnaire so that it establishes a nondefensive, open interview situation, this chapter presents ways to record responses to standardized questions. Open-ended responses can be coded for analysis into mutually exclusive, exhaustive categories at a single level of abstraction. The same criteria for coding categories may be used to precode response categories if the investigator has developed the categories empirically to be sure they fit respondents' definitions of the situation and enable respondents to express themselves adequately on the topic. Otherwise, the control exerted by using an intrusive method, such as a questionnaire, distorts data and makes them worthless.

Some data, particularly visual data useful in assessing respondents' "cognitive maps," cannot be precoded. Response categories for such data include visual presentations by respondents of freehand maps, additions to base maps, drawings, photographs, and games. The visual character of such data makes them available both for quantitative analysis and for qualitative visual presentation on composite maps or charts.

Used together with observation methods and focused interviewing, standardized questionnaires are particularly useful to gather information about such topics as people's perceptions, their attitudes, their values, and the meaning the environment holds for them.

The next chapter presents E-B topics particularly suited to questionnaire and interview investigation and discusses some rules of thumb for asking questions.

Chapter 11

ASKING QUESTIONS: TOPICS AND FORMAT

The quality of interview data rests heavily on whether questions address topics salient to respondents and to the researchers' purpose and on whether questions are asked so that answers may be clearly understood. This chapter first analyzes topics particularly relevant in environment-behavior research.

```
Topics

Actual and Abstract Environments

        Physical
        Administrative
        Behavioral

People's Responses

        Seeing
        Feeling
        Doing in
        Doing to
        Knowing

Linking and Using the Categories

        The question matrix
```

Then the chapter describes how using several straightforward rules of thumb for asking questions can improve a researcher's ability to compare answers with one another.

Format
Simplicity
Can respondents understand questions?
Precision
Can we assume that respondents understand questions in similar ways?
Neutrality
Do questions avoid implicitly influencing the direction of respondents' answers?

TOPICS

Whether E-B researchers use interviews focused on an individual's definition of the situation or questionnaires that standardize an inquiry over people, they want to know how people respond to environments. Questions are asked to find out what people can verbalize and otherwise express about themselves in their surroundings.

One way to approach the question of what to ask people is to ask ourselves what we might want to do with the data. We may, for example, want to effect changes in environments. We may also want to increase the visibility of possible side effects of such changes on people. Environment-behavior research illuminates both these purposes simultaneously, showing the interrelationship between environment and people. Table 11-1 (pp. 184–185) gives an overview of the complex relationships between various types of environments and people's responses to them.

Actual and Abstract Environments

Environments to which people react include those they actually experience daily—places of work, homes, open spaces for play. Their reactions to these settings affect their behavior not only in those particular settings but in others as well. Past experience in environments also affects behavior—for example, the place where you were brought up or a street you used to know. Even if memories of past settings are gilded or perceptions of present ones distorted, the environments themselves are or were actual ones.

People also change the way they behave in the light of pictures they have in mind of future environments they plan to be in and ideal ones they dream about. To understand how people relate to environments and to be able to make design decisions about those settings with control over behavioral side effects, we want to know how people respond to abstract environments as well as actual ones.

Physical, Administrative, and Behavioral Environments

To make decisions about a setting and improve our understanding of side effects of decisions on people, we must speak of environments as more than physical settings. We must also take into account the behavioral and administrative surroundings of people in a setting.

Environments

Physical

    Objects
    Places
    Relations between places
    Qualities

Administrative

    Formal rules
    Informal rules

Behavioral

    Characteristics of people
    Activities
    Relationships between people

A drugstore, for example, is a physical setting in which there may be such things as a soda fountain, a counter with two sides, stools on one side of the counter, a prescription counter, a book rack, pharmacy shelves, storage cabinets, and a glass storefront with a sign over it. A drugstore also comprises an administrative environment: rules about who may go behind the counter or take things off shelves; who may handle drugs; whether local schoolchildren are allowed into the store during school hours. Changes in either of these environments will necessarily have side effects on the other.

Of course, both physical and administrative environments are related to the behavioral environment: types of people who frequent the drugstore; their familiarity with the druggist; whether kids can comfortably hang around to read comic books and adults to browse through magazines; whether teenagers hang around outside the front entrance.

To be able to act on environments with greater awareness and control of side effects, it is useful to distinguish among elements of physical, administrative, and behavioral environments. Understanding each separately can improve our knowledge of how they relate to one another in an E-B system.

- *Physical environments* include *objects* in a setting; *places,* such as street corners, tot lots, rooms, and stairwells; *relations between places* created by such things as walls, distance, windows, barriers, adjacencies; and *qualities* of the setting, such as light and sound.
- *Administrative environments* include *formal* rules governing such things as use of a setting, contractual arrangements for use, and procedures required to get in. Also included are *informal* rules about, for instance, what it is appropriate or inappropriate to do there and when it is all right to break rules.
- *Behavioral environments* include *characteristics of people* there (both individuals and groups), their *activities* there, and *relationships* between people.

People's Responses to Environments

Environments and changes to environments affect what people do. How people see and interpret their surroundings mediates environmental effects. Effects also are tempered by experiences people have had with past surroundings and their intentions for future ones. Hence, the more you know about how people see environments and what people know about environments, the more you will understand their behavioral and emotional reactions to them.

People's Responses to Environments

What They See in Environments

    Perception
    Meaning

What They Feel about Environments

    Opinion
    Value

What They Do in *Environments*

    Place
    Path
    Relation

What They Do to *Environments*

    Adaptations
    Displays
    Messages

What They Know about Environments

    Knowledge
    Data

What people see in environments. People make sense of their surroundings by observing them with all their senses and then organizing and interpreting what they observe. This interpretation in turn has consequences for what they do in an environment and to it. The better designers understand this process, the better able they are to understand the side effects on people of decisions they make about environmental design. The better E-B researchers understand what sense people make of their surroundings and how, the better they themselves can interpret other people's behavior.

Making sense of environment is a process of *perception:* the way persons select and organize what they are aware of in a situation through all their senses (Goodey, 1971: 2–3; Theodorson & Theodorson, 1970: 295). The interpretation people give to what they perceive is its *meaning* to them. The ascribed meaning of things that often holds unforeseen consequences for people making decisions about environments is what linguists call "connotative meaning." Connotative meanings reflect the personal associations things call up, the emotionally toned inferences drawn (Manis, 1966; Theodorson & Theodorson, 1970). The connotative meaning of an object can be distinguished from the explicit, dictionary "denotative meaning."

The meanings of and difference between perception and meaning are apparent in the following statements:

Perception: "Streets in European cities appear to be cleaner than streets in U.S. cities."

Meaning: "When people sit on the front steps of their house, it means they are lower-class."

What people feel about environments. The attitudes people hold toward an object, person, situation, or environment—the way they evaluate it—influence how they respond to it. Environment-behavior researchers therefore ask questions to find out people's *opinions* about things: conscious verbal expressions of their feelings about particular places, objects, persons, events. Underlying opinions about things are people's *values:* commitments to larger, abstract ideals (Theodorson & Theodorson, 1970).

Opinion: "The rules in this factory about work assignments are unfair."

Value: "It is a bad thing to have too many rules for children in a kindergarten."

What people do in environments. Observing behavior tells you about what you see—externalized activities and their externalized consequences. Asking people questions about their environmental behavior tells you other essential things, such as what effects they expected their actions to have, what they intended to do but never did, and what they still intend to do. Questions about what people do may be useful to augment direct observation of behavior, especially when the activities studied are infrequent ones, when investigators want to know about only certain activities of a great number of people, and when the activities of interest are nonillicit behaviors in private settings inaccessible to investigators. Comparing observational data with interview data about the same activity provides investigators with information unavailable using only one method: the relation between a person's conscious perception of himself and its external expression.

To make informed design decisions that separate and connect a set of places, it is useful to distinguish *place* activities, situated in one bounded physical setting, from *path* activity, aimed at getting from one place to another and finding one's way. For the same design purpose it is useful to ask people about their *relations* to others when they do something.

Place:	"When friends drop in in the evening, we usually sit around the kitchen table."
Path:	"Visitors tend to get lost when they first try to find their way around this building."
Relation:	"Whenever my daughter wants privacy on the telephone, she takes the phone into the bathroom and closes the door."

What people do to environments. Observing physical traces tells you something about changes people have made in their surroundings. Asking questions about the same topic tells you about unfulfilled desires to make changes; perhaps someone would like to build a pass-through between kitchen and living room but does not because the separating wall contains the plumbing or because the project seems too expensive. Questions can tell you about the intended effects someone had in mind when making adaptations. Questions can tell you about expectations for future adaptations and the conscious reasoning behind past displays of self.

In the same way that reports of behavior in environments can be usefully compared with observations, reports about what a person does to his surroundings may be usefully compared with observations of physical traces. Questions about environmental change can be grouped into the same categories as observation of changes: adaptations, displays of self, public messages. And for each of these categories the same subsections hold as well (see Chapter 8).

Adaptations:	"If the room were bigger, I would build a wall between the living room and dining area."
Displays:	"I put that bronze American eagle over my front door because it lets other people know I love this country."
Messages:	"If I wanted to buy a used sofa, I would look first at the notices on the window at the corner laundromat."

Table 11-1. E-B questions: Illustrative examples

Present and Past Actual Environments

		Physical	Administrative	Behavioral
People's Responses				
Meaning — Perception	SEES	Streets in European cities seem cleaner than streets in U.S. cities.	Around here, everyone is really free to do as he or she likes.	Most people who use this park seem to take care of it.
Meaning — Perception		The glass and steel in this building make it seem like a factory.	The many signs in this park make it seem like a prison yard.	When my neighbors sit on their front stoop, they make the neighborhood lower-class.
Meaning — Opinion	FEELS	I like the colonial-style house we have.	The rules in this factory are unfair.	The new residents here are making a mess of the place.
Meaning — Value		*Does Not Apply:* Values applied to actual environments are opinions		
Place	DOES IN	My family usually eats dinner at the kitchen table.	No one in this office obeys the rule about no smoking at one's desk.	The secretaries all take a coffee break at 10 o'clock.
Path		Going to the store, I jump over the fence and run down an alley.	Residents in this home for retarded adults aren't allowed to go to their bedrooms during days.	Visitors tend to get lost when they first come to this building.
Relation		I sit on the front porch so I can watch people go by and can say hello.	People here are expected not to bother each other when they're working.	My neighbor drops by to chat at least once a day.
Adaptation	DOES TO	I cannot finish my basement as a playroom because it costs too much.	If you change your apartment at all, you have to return it to the original condition when you move.	Nobody can look into my living room now that I've planted bushes in the yard.
Display		I put all my diplomas on the wall only because there was no room in the closet.	You are not allowed to pin up or tape posters to the wall in this dorm room.	All anyone has to do is look at our souvenirs to know we travel a lot.
Message		When my cat ran away, I pasted reward posters on lampposts all over the neighborhood.	The police don't mind if you put posters up on windows of vacant stores.	While people wait for their Xeroxing, they usually read messages on the wall.
Knowledge	KNOWS	I think this park was designed by Frederick Law Olmsted.	I think people are not allowed to bring dogs into this building.	Approximately 300 people work in this hospital, I think.
Data		There are 3 rooms and a bath in this house.	There is a 24-hour doorman in this building.	I am 33 years old and have one child.

Table 11-1 (cont.)

Ideal and Future Abstract Environments

		Physical	*Administrative*	*Behavioral*
		SEES		
Meaning	Perception	*Does Not Apply:* Perception of abstract environments does not occur		
Meaning	Perception	If a house is made of brick, it means it is well built.	Strict teachers teach well.	Men who hang around street corners are just there to bother others.
		FEELS		
	Opinion	The new sports facility will be really comfortable.	Adventure playgrounds probably stimulate children's imagination more than regular ones.	It's nice when people from different backgrounds live together.
	Value	Buildings are better if designed to fit visually into their context.	Too many rules for schoolchildren is a bad thing.	People living in single-family houses are better than apartment-dwellers.
		DOES IN		
People's Responses	Place	My ideal house would have a special room for smoking cigars.	In good playgrounds there are no rules about what kids can and cannot do.	In progressive schools, dormitory bathrooms are all coeducational.
People's Responses	Path	At a well planned university campus people in wheelchairs can get into every building and room.	Ideally, street signs keep tourists from driving through residential areas.	Crowds in hallways can be a hazard to getting out if there is a fire.
People's Responses	Relation	In modern jury rooms everyone can see and hear each other easily.	In high-income areas people frown on too much dropping in.	I would choose to live in a place where people look after each other's unoccupied houses.
		DOES TO		
	Adaptation	In any new house I would want to build a pigeon coop.	I hope they won't enact any laws against keeping pigeons in your home.	People generally don't have the skill to make their own home improvements.
Display	Display	It is hard to put up pictures on walls in houses with concrete walls.	If I painted my name on the door, I'd probably be fined by my boss.	When I buy a new car, I want everyone to see it in my driveway.
	Message	In elevator buildings you usually have a ready-made place to leave notices—the elevator.	I wish the city would make a law against people who write political graffiti on public walls.	People get to know about their neighbors when they read "lost dog" and "for sale" notices.
		KNOWS		
	Knowledge	It is impossible to build a house out of concrete.	Next year's tax bill will allow deductions for energy-saving insulation.	The new subway stop should be completed in two years.
	Data	The next house I buy will have wall-to-wall carpets.	Next year I am going to develop a tight budget for running this household.	My mother will be coming to visit over Christmas.

What people know about environments. One reason to ask someone questions about her surroundings and herself is to assess what she knows—to assess her *knowledge*. Knowledge questions inquire how much respondents know about a situation, how they found out about an event, what they think occurred. To interpret the answers—to assess someone's knowledge—it is helpful to have used other methods as well to observe and find out about what happened.

Another reason to ask such questions is to ascertain *data* which the respondent has and which it is more efficient to ask about than using other methods to find out—for example, availability of different types of public transportation. This topic area also includes what are generally called "demographic data," such as a respondent's residential history, marital status, family size, age, and other personal characteristics.

Knowledge: "I think that they close the gates to the park at sunset."

Data: "My parents were brought up on a farm in Kentucky."

Linking and Using the Categories

The matrix of topics in Table 11-1 shows how environmental concerns can be linked by questions to people's responses. Each box in the matrix represents a potential link between environment and behavior. For each link (box) an illustrative statement is presented to convey concisely what is meant by the intersection of categories.

You can use this list of topics as part of a focused interview guide to probe respondents' definition of a situation. You could use this system of categories like scissors to help cut out the picture of what people have in mind. If your goal is to find out about groups or types of people without focusing on individuals, you might use the categories outlined here to suggest possible questions. You would generate those questions you thought would be most useful in solving your particular problem.

FORMAT

If you want to compare answers to the same questions from different respondents, respondents must understand the questions, they must understand them in the same way, and questions must not unwittingly influence the direction of respondents' answers (Payne, 1951). Simple, precise, and neutral questions achieve these ends. The nine pitfalls listed in Table 11-2 frequently stand in the way of simplicity, precision, and neutrality. As a rule of thumb for writing useful questions, avoid these pitfalls.

In writing and asking interview questions these rules of thumb can help experienced and inexperienced researchers avoid invalid or unreliable questions. But, like many such rules, they cannot ensure that all questions will cut through irrelevant concerns to focus on important concepts. This ability lies with researchers' skill and with their having enough personal insight to apply the rules strictly where necessary and to bend them when useful.

Be Simple

Avoid double-barreled questions. Frequently researchers think they are offering respondents alternative response categories when they are actually combining two questions into one. An example is this discarded question from the Howell and Epp survey (1976):

> *Qu:* Do you ever see people on your floor whom you don't recognize or who don't seem to live here?
>
> Yes ☐   No ☐

A respondent might answer yes because he sees people all the time whom he does not recognize because he does not see very well and has lived in the building only a short time. Another respondent might answer yes referring only to the second

Table 11-2. Rules of thumb for asking questions

Purpose	Pitfalls to Avoid
So that respondents understand questions	Overcomplexity: • Double-barreled questions • Words and phrases outside respondents' experience • Questions assuming knowledge respondents might not have
So that different respondents understand questions in the same way	Imprecision: • Complicated words with multiple meanings • Simple words with implicit double meanings • Questions about general times and places rather than specific ones
So that questions do not unwittingly influence the direction of respondents' answers	Loading: • One-sided alternatives • Emotionally charged words • Embarrassing answers

part of the question, meaning that she sees people on her floor whom she recognizes as children from the surrounding neighborhood (who come into the building through the unlocked fire-exit door). These two "yes" answers would actually be answers to two separate questions.

There are several strategies to correct double-barreled questions. First, one can simply ask two single-barreled questions:

> *Qu:* Do you ever see people on your floor whom you don't recognize?
>
> Yes ☐   No ☐
>
> *Qu:* Do you ever see people on your floor who don't seem to live here?
>
> Yes ☐   No ☐

Second, one can separate the double-barreled question into one question with follow-up questions:

> *Qu:* Do you ever see people on your floor whom you don't recognize?
>
> Yes ☐   No ☐
>
> (If "yes," ask:)
>
> *Qu:* Why is this? Is it because
>
> 1 _____ They do not seem to live here?
> 2 _____ You know only a few people in the building?
> 3 _____ The light on the floor is not strong enough?
> 4 _____ . . . .
> 5 _____ . . . .

Data obtained using double-barreled questions are virtually impossible to analyze.

Use words and phrases within respondents' experience. First, this means that researchers must not use jargon. Professionals in environmental design and research often use terms that have little or no meaning to most people, such as *layout, ambiance, facade, cluster.* Questions including these words or concepts may elicit misleading responses:

> *Qu:* If you could suggest to the designer changes in the layout of apartments like this, what would you suggest?
>
> None, I like it just as it is _____ 1
> Suggestions to be coded _____ 2

Probing respondents in a pretest will likely show that many of those who say "I like it just as it is" are actually saying that they do not know what the word *layout* means. Sometimes the word can be replaced by an explanatory phrase: "*Layout* means the way the rooms are arranged" or "*Ambiance* means the way the place feels to you." But as often as not such phrases will be as confusing to respondents as the original terms, not because they do not understand the words but because the sentiment expressed by the phrase is outside the respondents' cognitive experience.

Two blatant examples will be instructive. In a study of family housing (Zeisel & Griffin, 1975), researchers tried to find out whether residents noticed or could identify that the architect had planned the buildings to create three interior courts in the project, as illustrated below. They asked the following question:

Qu: Do you think the buildings in Charlesview are grouped together in any way?

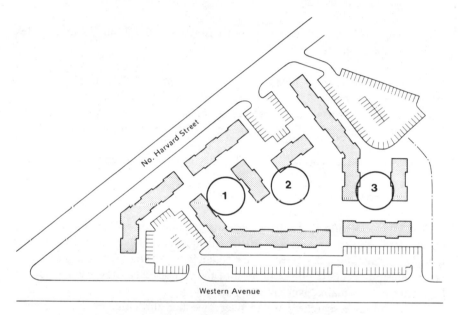

Site plan of Charlesview, showing three interior courts. (From *Sociology and Architectural Design,* by John Zeisel. © 1975 by the Russell Sage Foundation, New York. Reprinted by permission.)

Most respondents registered confusion to this question, answering "I don't know." One interpretation of this result is that the architect's intention of clustering was not achieved, but an equally valid interpretation is that the phrase "buildings grouped together in any way" was beyond residents' conscious experience and that they just did not understand what was being asked of them.

In this case the researchers might have been better able to get at what they wanted by asking an open-ended question and recording whether residents spontaneously mentioned the planned space:

Qu: How would you describe to a friend the arrangement of buildings in Charles-view?

Researchers might also have explained the architect's intent to residents, using drawings, and asked their reaction.

Another question, in the Howell and Epp study (1976), which was pre-tested and then dropped, aimed to find out whether older residents felt disoriented if they had no view of the outside when they stepped off the elevator onto their floor. The question included phrases asking respondents to think in ways un-familiar to them:

Qu: When you get out of the elevator on your floor, do you ever feel as if you are closed up inside the building or don't know where the front is?

This example also shows that it is not easy to ask questions about complex environmental design phenomena.

Do not assume respondents have much information. If a question requires information available only to some respondents, the answers will not reflect informed opinion. Answers will reflect an indistinguishable mixture of opinion and amount of knowledge. For example, researchers might ask housing residents:

Qu: Do you feel that the amount of money being spent on grounds maintenance ought to

be increased? ☐   be decreased? ☐   remain the same? ☐

This is a fair question if it reflects resident attitudes toward quality of mainte-nance. If, however, an increase in the maintenance budget would require an increase in rents, then the question has an altogether different meaning. And the real confusion occurs if only a portion of the respondents know the connection between rents and maintenance costs.

Sometimes researchers try to overcome this difficulty by using a short introduction to provide an informational frame of reference for respondents:

Qu: Management says that if grounds maintenance costs increase, management will have to raise rents. Given this possibility, do you feel . . .

Although such introductions begin to resolve the confusion, researchers must avoid creating additional confusion by providing only a partial frame of reference that does not fully close the knowledge gap between respondents. For example, if some informed residents know that the rent increase would be on the order of 50 cents a month, their answers to the question above will not be comparable to those of residents who think the researchers' introduction means larger rent increases.

Be Precise

Avoid complicated words with multiple meanings. Often we use words that can be understood in various ways. Such words as *territory, privacy, satisfaction,* and *bother* mean different things to different people. To some, *privacy* means being able to be alone if one wants to. To others, it means not being overheard or overseen by others—even by neighbors through thin walls. To still others, it means being able to avoid being the topic of neighborhood gossip. Researchers will have difficulty analyzing answers to the following question:

> *Qu:* Do you have enough privacy in your backyard?

The main point to remember in using this rule of thumb is that one can best compare answers to questions if respondents have generally understood the questions in the same way. This problem does not occur only with complicated words; seemingly simple words can subtly have multiple meanings as well.

Explicitly define even simple terms. Older residents were asked the following question in a pretest:

> *Qu:* Do you find the trip from the building's front door to your apartment to be too long a trip?

The question was discarded because although many residents answered yes, they showed by their verbal elaboration that they interpreted the term *too long* in two ways: (1) too far to carry groceries and heavy objects and (2) too long for people in wheelchairs and walkers because the ramp in the lobby is too difficult.
In reformulating this question, the researchers might have explained:

> *Qu:* Do you ever get tired going from the building's front door to your apartment because one is so far from the other, just in terms of distance?

One could then follow up with specific questions on whether barriers present special difficulties and whether there are special conditions, such as carrying groceries, which make a trip strenuous that otherwise is not tiring.
In E-B research there are some typical terms that seem precise but often prove to be more complicated. *Eating* may mean eating breakfast, lunch, dinner, or snacks; eating alone, with family members, or with friends. *Talking* may mean chatting, having a deep private conversation, or just hanging out. *Food shopping* may mean going daily to the store for a loaf of bread and quart of milk or doing weekly grocery shopping. *Children's safety* may mean safety from car traffic, from bigger children, from dangerous play equipment, or from child molesters. This list could go on and on, but the point is made. Even simple concepts have several dimensions, and researchers must use phrases that describe most precisely what phenomenon they are interested in.

"I guess I'm a conservative, if you mean do I
put up a lot of jams and jellies."

Drawing by Weber; © 1976 The New Yorker Magazine, Inc. Reprinted by permission.

Be specific about time and place. If researchers want to find out how often or where respondents do something, there are several types of questions they can ask. As a rule, the more specific are the response categories and the event being queried, the more likely are respondents to be able to answer the questions and the more likely are the answers to be comparable. A common type of question asks:

Qu: How many machine loads do you wash each month at the laundromat?

Such questions often elicit a high proportion of "don't know" responses, not because respondents have no idea of the answer but because they do not know how to figure out the answer precisely. They do not usually think about laundromat use in terms of months. In such cases researchers can help them by asking two separate and more precise questions:

Qu: About how often do you use the laundromat?

☐ More than once a day
☐ Once a day
☐ About every other day
☐ Once a week
☐ Less than once a week

Qu: When you use the laundromat, generally how many loads of laundry do you wash each time?

☐ One   ☐ Three
☐ Two   ☐ Four or more

This series of questions helps respondents calculate monthly loads and provides researchers with additional information about frequency of use. Introducing such questions with words such as *about* allays respondents' fears about not having precisely the right answer and thereby reduces the number of "don't know" answers.

Another way to make such questions more precise is to ask about specific recent events at specific times.

Qu: Yesterday, did you pass by or go into the following rooms:

	Pass by		Go into	
Recreation room	☐ Yes	☐ No	☐ Yes	☐ No
Pool room	☐ Yes	☐ No	☐ Yes	☐ No
Sitting room	☐ Yes	☐ No	☐ Yes	☐ No

Questions put this way are more likely to be understood than questions asking respondents to report whether they frequently, sometimes, or seldom use some place. More important, responses will be more comparable because it is not up to respondents to interpret "frequently, sometimes, or seldom."

The same rules of thumb about specificity apply to questions about place. To avoid misunderstandings in analysis, it will always be more fruitful to ask about specific rooms, street corners, or events than to construct a general question.

Be Neutral

Avoid one-sided questions. It is essential that researchers not "lead" respondents, as television lawyers sometimes do, by asking respondents to agree or disagree with only one side of an issue:

Qu: Do you think this place is a good place to raise children?

Yes ☐   No ☐

Qu: In the project at night, is the outside lighting too low?

Yes ☐   No ☐

Such questions tend to pressure respondents to answer in the affirmative because it is the easiest answer to give. They choose the most convenient alternative explicitly offered them, rather than choosing one of several implied alternatives. Researchers analyzing answers to such questions would have difficulty distinguishing between "yes" answers from people who felt strongly that the environment was a good place to raise children or that the lighting was too low and "yes" answers from respondents who did not care but felt this was the "correct" response.

In the actual survey in which researchers were interested in these answers (Saile et al., 1972), they avoided one-sided questions by making alternatives explicit:

Qu: Do you think this place is *better* than most places to raise children, is it *worse,* or is it *about the same* as anyplace else?

Qu: In the project at night, is the outside lighting *too bright, about right,* or *not bright enough?*

Avoid emotionally charged words. Blatant stereotypes implied in questions obviously sway respondents in their answers. Asking school principals about "vandals" or nurses about "chronic complainers" arouses emotions that almost certainly take respondents outside the frame of reference of the question. Cautious researchers can avoid this pitfall by describing people, situations, and places in simple, less inflammatory words: "people who knowingly damage property," "patients who complain a lot."

This pitfall can subtly trap even cautious researchers when interviewing people for whom quite normal, seemingly neutral terms are loaded with meaning. This usually happens, for example, when asking questions about "teenagers," unless the respondents happen to be teenagers. Researchers Howell and Epp (1976) found a similar situation in their study on older tenants' use of certain shared spaces in buildings. They wanted to find out whether residents knew that these large rooms were sometimes used for activities in which both the building residents and older residents of nearby buildings participated, such as Bingo, federally financed meal programs, or meetings of neighborhood senior citizens' clubs. They asked:

Qu: Are there ever activities in the community room to which people from the neighborhood are invited along with the people who live here?

Although the investigators knew such programs were carried out there, they found that over 50% of residents in all four buildings studied reported no such shared programs. On further probing in the pretest, the researchers found that residents had been involved in several disputes over who controlled their shared spaces—they or the public housing authority. To them the term *people from the neighborhood* raised the specter of "public events" attended by strangers of all ages at the invitation of management. When such hidden stereotypes are not discovered either through pretests or through thoughtful analysis of questions, they can invalidate crucial questions during later analysis.

Avoid embarrassing answers.   Respondents tend to avoid giving answers that they feel put them in a bad light, especially in face-to-face interviews. As with emotionally charged words, it is particularly difficult to avoid this problem in its subtle forms. People are embarrassed by the strangest things!

The best-known example of this problem comes from political polling. After an election, when pollsters ask a random cross-section of the population whom they voted for for president, a higher percentage say they voted for the winner than actually did (Zeisel, H., 1968: 202). The difference comprises people who are embarrassed to admit they voted for the loser or who want to be seen as winners. There are many possibilities for such problems to arise in E-B research. Researchers trying to find out whether color-coded walls on different floors help older residents find their way asked:

Qu: Have you ever got off on the wrong floor?

Although many residents admitted having done so, there is no way to tell how many said they had not done so because they felt it would be admitting absent-mindedness or senility.

The same is true for persons embarrassed to admit that they usually use the back (kitchen) door instead of the formal front door, which they know a professional architect planned for them to use. Well-to-do respondents may have the same reaction to questions about income because they are embarrassed that they make so much money.

When researchers realize they might run into such problems, they can provide a face-saving way out within the question itself:

Qu: In many buildings it is difficult for people of all ages to find their way and even to recognize the floor they want. Have you ever got off on the wrong floor of this building?

Qu: Many people living in apartments tend to use the back door most often, while many others use the front door. Which door do you tend to use most often when you are going out to the store?

Embarrassment may also be reduced by handing respondents a card on which answers are labeled with letters. Interviewers can then ask respondents to say which group describes them best, "a, b, or c." This is often done with categories of income to make it easier for both high- and low-income respondents to tell interviewers what their income is.

OVERVIEW

You want to ask questions that help you solve your problem. You do that by asking questions which focus accurately on the topics you are interested in and which are formulated so that answers can be usefully interpreted. This chapter suggests that to achieve these ends in E-B inquiry, you ask yourself the following quality-control questions as you construct interviews.

To improve the topical relevance for your E-B problem, ask yourself:

- Have I generated questions about behavioral and administrative environments as well as physical ones?
- Have I asked about both actual past and present environments and abstract environments pictured in respondents' minds?
- Have I asked about respondents' reactions to an environment in breadth—what they see in it, feel about it, do in it, do to it, and know about it?
- Have I linked people's environmental responses to the various types of environments and environmental elements I need to know about to solve my particular problem?

To remind yourself of significant rules of thumb for formulating usable questions, ask yourself:

- Are my questions simple enough for respondents to understand?
- Are my questions precise enough so that respondents generally will understand them the same way?
- Are my questions neutral enough so that they do not influence the direction of respondents' answers?

Sometimes we face E-B problems for which there are no respondents to interview, no people to observe, and no physical traces to record. When this is so, we may approach our problem by analyzing documents and data that others have compiled in the past—archives. We may also turn to archives to augment results from other methods. This is the topic of the next chapter.

Chapter 12

ARCHIVES

If you borrow a friend's ill-equipped country house for a winter weekend and find that the front door does not close, you might look in the basement for a screwdriver and machine oil. If these were not available and nearby stores were closed, you would find another way to close the door: an old knife and cooking oil in the kitchen, picture wire, a large nail to replace the hinge bolt. What you uncover may serve your purposes better than the tools you originally thought you needed.

Environment-behavior researchers are often caught in old, cold houses without a screwdriver—as when they study historical problems or past events about which they can neither interview participants nor observe behavior. For example, when Goffman (1963) wanted to see how ideas of "public" places and "public order" developed during the past several centuries, he turned to histories of medieval England, 19th-century etiquette books, and published historical letters. Interestingly, he found many parallels: today's laws "that a householder is obliged to maintain his walks and roads in good repair and to keep his town land free of noxious refuse" (p. 9) are presaged by medieval ones to "keep one's pigs out of the streets, even though there was much available there for the pigs to eat" (p. 8–9).

Researchers such as Keller who want to find out what decisions designers made and when during a particular design project might turn for data to archives of drawings. In her study of Twin Rivers (1976), she analyzed architects' plans in the project files of three design offices that had worked on this large project before its final stage. From the plans she gleaned what the designers' original intentions had been and when design changes had been made—essentially, how the final design had emerged. For example, early planners originally wanted the community to be primarily pedestrian. They planned footpaths connecting such places as home and school and did not provide car dropoff or pickup areas around the school. When other planning teams eventually acknowledged that cars were inevitable, they made some changes but did not redesign the schoolyard; "the ensuing chaos culminated in one child being knocked down in 1975 and stringent restrictions being put on cars in those areas" (1976: 43).

Institutional records also serve as sources of data. Snyder and Ostrander (1974) wanted to find out what kinds of people lived in the existing nursing home they were studying, to augment their observation and interview research. When they analyzed files that the institution had collected for administrative purposes, they found a much higher proportion of handicapped residents recorded than they observed personally. They looked for an explanation. Were patients recorded as more severely ill than they actually were? Were handicapped residents stopped from moving around the building? Or did investigators not know how to recognize the severity of residents' handicaps?

Each of these researchers turned to archival data sources to solve his or her problem. In archival research investigators find data someone else has gathered for one purpose and turn them into information useful for another. In some research situations—for example, Goffman's and Keller's—archives may be the only source of data. Other investigators—for example, Snyder and Ostrander—choose to use archives because it is more efficient than to collect virgin data.

This chapter presents some characteristics of archival methods, approaches to identifying useful document files, and operations researchers may find helpful in analyzing contents of documents—words, numbers, and especially nonverbal representations, such as architectural plans.

Archives

Qualities

    Pragmatic
    Imaginative
    Historical

Using Archives

Document Files

    Differential accessibility
    Deposit and survival
    Definition of the situation

Types of Data

    Words
    Numbers
    Nonverbal representations

Behavioral Plan Analysis

QUALITIES

In reusing data designed or recorded for other purposes, investigators *imaginatively* and *pragmatically* mix and match available data. For *historical* topics out of the reach of such methods as direct observation and interviews, archives may be the only available source of data. Because archival methods are one remove from the people, activities, and settings a researcher is studying, using such methods requires that investigators take into account the potential bias introduced by those who originally collected the data.

Pragmatic

Researchers approach archives much as architects approach an old building on a site where they have chosen to build. If the old building is totally incompatible with the intended use of the new one, it might be razed. If the building or any of its parts can be reused, the designer might do so; or the designer might make major changes to creatively adapt the existing building to new uses.

The designer's approach is pragmatic. Can he use what is already there to meet his needs, or is it more efficient to tear it down? If a regulation prohibits his razing a building—as historical topics might prohibit researchers from carrying out basic data gathering—the designer asks how he can use what is there.

Archives present researchers the opportunity to adaptively reuse data—to make it do double duty. Less adaptation is needed when a researcher wants to analyze data as they were originally meant to be analyzed. For example, if researchers want to study problems related to population shifts, changes in the quality of housing stock, or types of family organization, they can select and analyze census data collected by others for this purpose.

More adaptation is necessary when the original data were meant to be analyzed for purposes different from those of the researcher. This occurs often when investigators use data from records that institutions or public agencies keep for housekeeping purposes. For example, when Wilner et al. (1954) used public school and housing authority records to find out how children from new and old public housing projects performed in school, they first had to sample existing archives to find out what was there, analyze the coding categories used to organize data, and create new records tailored to their own research purposes. When reusing institutional records, investigators have to make sure they understand how the institution defines the recorded events (Kitsuse & Cicourel, 1963). For example, does an industrial plant include worker suggestions for environmental improvements under "complaints"? If an investigator still finds the records useful, she can consider part of her data collection carried out for her. She is then like the designer who finds that the heating system and floors of an old building can be reused as part of a new one.

Imaginative

Researchers who want to draw information from archives not meant at all to be analyzed as part of a systematic research project must approach their problem *imaginatively*. They must reimage the data and their source; they cannot merely reanalyze them. For example, Günter et al. (1978) carried out a behavioral study of a large open space in Rome called the Spanish Steps—a cascading series of steps and landings built between 1721 and 1726. The steps are used very much the way streets and plazas in Rome and other cities are used: by craftspeople and painters selling their goods; by people promenading to see other people and be seen; by families; by lovers; by guitar players and singing groups. Günter et al. combined a behavior study with a historical perspective to show "that architectural science is a specific type of social science . . . [and] that use is an essential part of architecture" (1978: 2; my translation).

To show how the steps were used during the past three centuries, these E-B researchers analyzed the behavior of people depicted in paintings and prints of the Spanish Steps. The authors propose that the paintings from 1730 to the early 1800s indicate the historical use of the steps. They analyze as follows an 1835 painting by Moscheti of the steps and the plaza at their foot (1978: 80; my translation):

- No one stands alone—rather, always together in groups.
- There are particularly many large groups (over four persons).
- There is some interaction between groups.
- The groups appear to move along invisible parallel lines. (We can draw no conclusions about movement from this observation. It appears, rather, to reflect one of the artist's presentation principles.)
- Most people are walking.
- Some are riding.
- Some are being drawn in a carriage.

Imagination is required to redefine data sources in this way.

In their classic *Unobtrusive Measures* (1966), Webb et al. present a host of archival studies that "reveal the power of insightful minds to see appropriate data where associates only see someone else's records" (1966: 86). Such an approach means being able to see maintenance reports in a hospital as indicators of which places are most used and what materials were least well specified for the use they get. Union grievances recorded at a state labor relations board about the discomfort caused by poor air conditioning and heating systems might indicate that this is a major concern among service workers. An E-B researcher could use suggestion-box submissions as a substitute for survey information.

To the category "records" one can add paintings, correspondence, news reports, and other archival files. Keller's "insightful mind" turned newspaper reports of a garden competition into surprisingly appropriate information. As part of her multimethod study of the Twin Rivers planned unit development (1976), she wanted to find out what residents "who had a special esthetic sense" felt about their surroundings. Because it would have been difficult and expensive to identify such people through interviews, Keller would have had to abandon this part of the study had she not found a news article reporting on winners of a local garden contest—including names and addresses. Assuming these gardeners to be particularly interested in how nice their physical environment looked, she focused her environmental-esthetics interviews on them and other people they identified as having similar esthetic attitudes.

These examples do not merely demonstrate good intuition. They reflect minds trained to see similarities in seemingly disparate events, minds that can identify qualities of useful information implicit in other people's data, and practical minds willing and able to transform what is at hand into something useful.

Historical

Past use and perception of environments can be essential *contexts* for understanding present use and perception. Goffman (1963) studied hundred-year-old etiquette books to get a sense of middle-class norms about what was appropriate public and private behavior at that time. He used these historical documents to describe the background of present-day behavior. Commonly accepted past definitions of situations provide clues to how present-day definitions have evolved.

When investigators are able to interview past participants to uncover historical data, they must take into account the gilding of events that takes place over time. Records kept of daily events at the time of those events may be written with an eye to establishing history in a certain way, but they are not rewritten or changed with hindsight. The recent past is also sometimes most validly studied through archival methods—as is shown by recorded election results that post-election voter interviews cannot reconstruct: more respondents say they voted for the winner than actually did.

To establish what appeals developer and residents made to each other as the Twin Rivers community was being debated years before, Keller used verbatim public records of planning-board hearings. She found that when the builder had requested zoning revisions, he talked about providing low-income housing, about building an impressive community center, and about other community facilities he would develop simultaneously with the housing. The planning-board records show that local community residents expected that these promises would not be fulfilled. When Keller's data from news analysis and interviews later revealed the complaints Twin Rivers residents had about these issues, Keller could demonstrate the way such potential problems were dealt with during the adversary planning process. As an added and unexpected benefit, the hearing records provided Keller and her team with names and addresses of professional consultants called in at the time by both builder and residents: physical planners, tax experts, lawyers. They were not mentioned in other documents because their part in the project was so temporary. She later carried out focused interviews with these persons to fill in details about Twin Rivers' evolution.

Archives resulting from records kept over time—for a society, an institution, or a project—enable investigators to study *patterns of activity* and *change*. Visual records can show how uses of a building, street, or plaza evolve slowly over centuries (Günter et al., 1978); news articles can reflect how complaints grow from isolated incidents to public issues in a new town (Keller, 1976); and two-dimensional plans can reflect how a design emerges through several phases of planning, each developed by a different planning firm (Keller, 1976).

In sum, investigators with the imagination to see opportunities where others see waste can use archival methods to adapt other people's data to new E-B purposes. Such methods are particularly well suited for studying past E-B events and things that change. This opportunity is often worth the risk that results from using data gathered by someone else with different ends.

USING ARCHIVES

The key to using archives is locating and gaining access to *document files:* the groupings into which other people have deposited documents. A file of paintings may be a museum room; files of school-attendance records may be computer tapes; files of documents relating to a particular design project may be a drawer of a file cabinet. Once you have access to a file that you think meets your research needs, you will want to look more closely at the kinds of *documents* it contains: letters and plans, reports, accountings, pictures. To plan a strategy for analyzing the documents, you must in turn determine what *type of data* you have to analyze—words, numbers, or nonverbal representations—because each type requires different handling operations and analytic procedures. Within each type you can choose the *analytic unit* most appropriate for your research purposes.

For example, analysis of a newspaper might focus on headlines, articles, letters to the editor, or announcements; within any one of these categories— articles, for instance—a researcher might decide to record the theme of the article, the structure of every sentence, or the number of times a certain word appears. If the documents are design plans for a building, a researcher who wants to see how spaces were pared down to reduce costs might record square-footage changes for a particular room in successive plans. But if she is interested in the designer's behavioral intentions, she might analyze the possibilities the plan provides for relationships among people who eventually might use the building. All such choices depend on what a researcher wants to find out—his or her purpose.

DOCUMENT FILES

Someone puts documents into archival files, and someone keeps the files: a census organizer, an editor, an office administrator. Although this fact can provide efficiencies for an investigator, it also presents problems of data accessibility, completeness, and relevance.

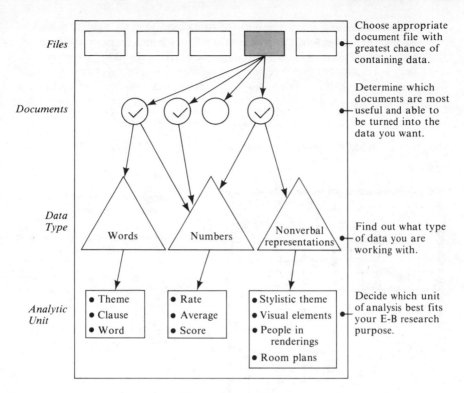

Files		Choose appropriate document file with greatest chance of containing data.
Documents		Determine which documents are most useful and able to be turned into the data you want.
Data Type	Words Numbers Nonverbal representations	Find out what type of data you are working with.
Analytic Unit	• Theme • Clause • Word • Rate • Average • Score • Stylistic theme • Visual elements • People in renderings • Room plans	Decide which unit of analysis best fits your E-B research purpose.

Steps in using archives

Differential Accessibility

The more public a file is, the more likely it is to be available for research. Public archives include, for example, census data, published research and other books, newspapers, public announcements and records, and records of publicly sponsored competitions.

Some public files, although accessible, still need to be ferreted out by investigators. For example, Zeisel et al. (1978) used published research documents as data to generate research-based performance criteria about older people. To demonstrate how designers meet the needs of older people in their designs, the research team located and analyzed microfilms of submissions to a statewide architectural competition.

From published research they generated—and had a panel of experts review—performance criteria, such as the following one for the degree of control that residents need over "backstage" areas.

> With increasing problems of agility and balance, easy accessibility between different areas in the apartment becomes more important for older persons. Areas difficult to reach not only create inconveniences but can also be hazardous to residents' safety and well-being. However, easy physical access must not be

achieved at the expense of visual privacy in "backstage" areas such as bedrooms, bathrooms, and kitchens. To maintain their dignity with visitors, residents need to control visual access to these "backstage" areas where the more private activities such as personal hygiene, sleeping, and cooking, take place. As a result, careful consideration must be given to minimizing physical distance and barriers between public and private areas in the unit while maximizing visual privacy [Zeisel et al., 1978: 30].

They accompanied this guideline with annotated examples from the competition (see figure).

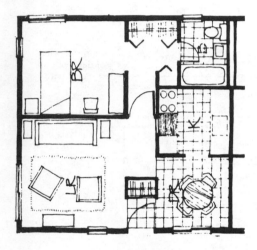

+ bedroom is not visible from pub-lic areas in the apartment

+ kitchen is visually separate from the living room

+ bedroom door location allows private access between bedroom and bath

— there is a partial view into the bedroom from the hallway

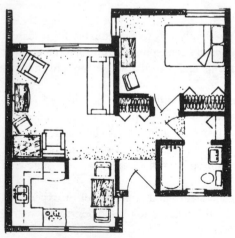

+ bathroom is accessible without going through the bedroom

+ kitchen has visual privacy from living room and entry

+ location of linen closet adds to visual privacy in the bathroom

+ bedroom door swings against wall and in direction of travel

— there is a partial view into the bedroom from the entrance hallway

Annotated plan from design competition, showing comments on control of backstage areas. (From J. Zeisel, G. Epp, and S. Demos, *Low-Rise Housing for Older People: Behavioral Criteria for Design.* Washington, D.C.: U.S. Government Printing Office, 1978.)

Institutional records may be accessible only to researchers who can show that their purposes are scientific or benign and that anonymity is ensured for people the data represent. Such records may be closed by officials of an organization who feel that merely identifying the organization is an invasion of the privacy of their clients. Clearly, when the institution is itself a client for the research, as was the Oxford nursing home for Snyder and Ostrander (1974), records may be easier to acquire.

Private files such as personal letters and diaries are the least accessible unless they have somehow been made public—for example, by being donated to a library or by being published. Private files in the public realm often represent historical figures and times past.

Deposit and Survival

Once an investigator gets hold of a document file, she must determine which out of all possible documents are included in the file. Are all significant documents there? Have some been excluded or suppressed? Have some been weeded out? Selective deposit, self-selective deposit, and selective survival are processes influencing what is deposited into document files and what survives over time. Each reflects the fact that any available file in some way is an edited sample of actual documents. To use a file for her purposes, each investigator must be able to assess how that particular file has been edited.

Selective deposit (Webb et al., 1966) refers to the fact that what is put into files depends not only on what documents are generated but also on which documents someone decides to keep. In a single complex office transaction—for example, a meeting between architect and client—participants might generate a host of documents (Zinnes, 1963):

- A meeting report (which may not be reproduced)
- Annotations in the margins of the report by participants (which may just be left on the table to be thrown out)
- Preliminary and follow-up phone conversations (which may or may not be recorded on memoranda for the file)
- Internal office memoranda (which may be destroyed either carelessly or by design)
- Casual conferences among participants (which may be confirmed by letter or not)
- Secret or embarrassing letters (which are purposely destroyed)
- Preliminary drafts of reports or plans (destroyed as a matter of course after the final draft is accepted)

An editor, archivist, or clerk might screen which documents are filed. An investigator who overlooks such a systematic bias can easily carry out an unbiased analysis of thoroughly biased archival data. In her newspaper analysis for Twin Rivers, Keller (1976) was able to put this realization to work for rather than against her. In initial interviews, she found that when Twin Rivers residents first moved to the area, they were dissatisfied because the reality of a suburban planned community was not like the suburban dream they held. Although residents told Keller that they complained vociferously to officials, the editor of Twin Rivers' 8–10-page mimeographed "newspaper" did not report all their outbursts: he felt that to publish short-lived complaints would merely fan flames of discontent. Sometimes, however, the editor reported problems the community faced as a whole although individual respondents did not mention them spontaneously to interviewers. For example, the paper reported dangerous problems of access to the public school by children and cars. The editor tried to make visible to his readers when an issue, in his view, had reached the scale of a communitywide problem.

Keller incorporated this insight about the editor's point of view into her understanding of the role a small newspaper plays in the development of a new community. To find out how such a community grows was one of her goals. Keller also used the discrepancy between individual reports and news articles to distinguish problems that developed slowly over time, eventually becoming grist for the editor, and transitory problems that the editor never advertised. Keller honored the difference between the data she gathered from the two methods, using their difference as a resource rather than making an inappropriate amalgam of the two sorts of data. They reflected a legitimate discrepancy of perspective, which Keller felt to be a significant part of community life and one that her multiple-method approach was able to catch.

In *self-selective deposit* no intermediary editor or archivist is involved. For example, an investigator of high school life who turns to the yearbook for information about individuals or cliques is likely to find descriptions of students written by themselves. The same is possible for biographies in professional directories, public-relations releases, and other personal announcements.

Self-selective deposit sometimes is determined not by individual volition but by structural constraints in a setting or organization. In a design office, for example, partners and job captains may be the only ones allowed to correspond with clients, consultants, and suppliers; letter files therefore will not directly include the recorded ideas of draftspeople and other members of the design team.

A significant influence on self-selective deposit is the degree to which archives are meant to be evaluated by supervisors. For example, in the study of school property damage (1976a), Zeisel was interested to know how much money was spent on various types of damage, what types of damage were most prevalent, and what proportion of all damage could be called malicious damage versus wear-and-tear damage. Naturally, he looked for this information in "vandalism reports," which custodians requesting repair funds turned over to their superiors. Unfortunately, the reports reflected the custodians' selective presentation of the situation. The custodians knew that their supervisors would come to inspect the damage and would then judge the custodian as well: Did he report minor damage that he could repair himself? Did he report wear-and-tear on which he should have done preventive maintenance? Did he report only "vandalism," as he was expected to do, or did he report other damage as well? The custodians, knowing they themselves were "on the record," modified their reports accordingly.

Blau faced the same problem in his study of worker behavior (1963). Blau wanted to compare the performance of workers in competitive and cooperative offices. To measure placement officers' performance, he decided to use the record the office supervisor kept of how many job placements each officer made. At the same time, Blau observed placement officers' behavior. When calls with job offers came into the office, the officer receiving the call was expected to write down the offer and put it in a basket from which all officers chose jobs for clients. Blau noticed, however, that officers "hoarded" job offers that could be easily filled by putting the phone slips under their desk blotters rather than in the communal basket. In this way, they raised their own placement rate and biased Blau's archives. As Keller did, Blau turned this problem into an opportunity. He used the observation to give him further insight into the informal organization of the office.

Document files are also subject to editing that purges certain documents from the file as time passes: *selective survival*. Housekeeping documents, such as memos, that get into a file may be routinely, systematically, or casually destroyed when the file is transferred onto microfilm for storage or when an office changes location. Records of sensitive transactions and controversial planning proposals may be systematically shredded. As the authors of *Unobtrusive Measures* (1966) point out, "Using archival records frequently means substituting someone else's selective filter for your own" (p. 111).

Environment-behavior researchers who use archival materials face the same dilemmas historians face. You have to figure out what you can do with the available material, and you must determine as well as possible what the material you have represents. How authentic is it? What part of the actual universe of documents do you have? What types of documents are missing? Are key documents represented, or have they been lost? Can you carry out any internal checks of the documents to identify missing documents—for example, seeing whether change orders issued during construction refer to working drawings that are not on file?

Definition of the Situation

The most elusive problem that document files pose for researchers is that the way an editor defines the situation he records may result in records with the same name the investigator uses but containing counts of phenomena different from what the investigator wants (Kitsuse & Cicourel, 1963). When, for example, the official statistical rates are labeled "acts of vandalism" or "substandard housing" and an investigator wants to study these phenomena, can he assume that the rates reflect what he defines to be the problem? Kitsuse and Cicourel argue convincingly that such rates reflect as much the rate keeper's definition of the situation and the institutional process of keeping rates as the number of actual occurrences of events. This is not to say that rate keepers lie—that they record less or more substandard housing in a neighborhood than they observe. Rather, what they see and count is largely determined by the way they look.

This was brought home forcefully to planners when Jacobs' *Death and Life of Great American Cities* (1961) showed that what mortgage banks and municipalities saw as slums, many residents saw as healthy social neighborhoods. The banks called housing in Boston's West End "substandard" because building exteriors were not kept up and plumbing was bad; yet residents kept up the insides of their apartments with their own money. Had Jacobs used only official statistics to assess the degree of "substandard" housing, she would have developed a one-sided picture.

In Zeisel's study of school vandalism, the same situation almost arose. As mentioned earlier, custodians reported only certain acts of property damage because they knew their supervisors would review the reports. These reports had another bias as well: custodians defined all damage as vandalism if it was not obviously wear and tear from normal use. For their purposes, they merely needed to isolate special damage to buildings. If a child's swing was broken because a teenager was swinging on it in the evening, this was "vandalism," not "unintended damage" or "damage from misuse." If windows behind a basketball backboard were broken during a rough game, this was "vandalism," not "incidental breakage." If a door was damaged during the theft of a typewriter, this was "vandalism," not a "professional crime." Custodians who filed reports did not distinguish between different types of damage; to them breakage meant vandalism. Had the E-B research team not seen the difference between its definition and the custodians' definition, it would have been in hot water.

The definition of the situation held by a once-removed recorder can also present opportunities. Brolin and Zeisel (1968) found that Gans' *Urban Villagers* (1962) described life in Boston's West End with a participant-observation perspective they shared. They used this insightful social-planning book as a document in which to locate data about how the predominantly Italo-American residents used their physical surroundings: rooms, streets and street corners, grocery stores, bars. Brolin and Zeisel used these data as the behavioral research basis for a hypothetical building designed to meet some specific needs of these residents (see figure).

TYPES OF DATA

Documents comprise numbers, words, nonverbal representations, or combinations of these. Newspapers are clearly combinations; paintings are not. Each of these types of data found in documents requires different kinds of procedures

2. Perspective through Interior Street

OBSERVATIONS AND REQUIREMENTS

12 OBS: After they are ten years old, boys
are generally unsupervised while
outside, and enjoy the freedom to roam
the neighborhood.
REQ: Many places for pedestrian movement.

13 OBS: Groups of teen-agers of different
sexes spend a lot of time "hanging
around" or looking for something to
do. Often they do this with adults
or teen-agers of the opposite sex.
REQ: (A) Connection between boys' group
and peer groups of other statuses.
(B) Connection between boys' and
girls' outside areas and apartments.

14 OBS: Teen-agers gather on corners near
small stores.
REQ: Areas for informal congregating
outside and around commercial areas.

15 OBS: Although boys meet with boys, and
girls with girls, the girls meet near the
corners where the boys hang out.
REQ: Adolescent girls' areas visible to
boys' areas.

16 OBS: Young teen-age girls take care of
younger children on the streets.
REQ: Adolescent girls' areas near
children's play areas.

17 OBS: Both men and women use dress as a
means of self-expression, spending
much money on clothes.
REQ: General visibility among pedestrian,
apartment, commercial, and
recreational areas.

18 OBS: Men wash their cars on the streets
as often as once a week. For men, the
car is important as a means of
expressing their identity.
REQ: Visibility for areas related to
automobiles.

19 OBS: Bars and luncheonettes are places to
exchange news and gossip, as well as
message centers for regular customers.
REQ: (A) Commercial area connected to
living areas.
(B) Commercial area visible from
street and other commercial areas.

20 OBS: Women socialize while shopping.
REQ: Commercial areas visible to and
from streets.

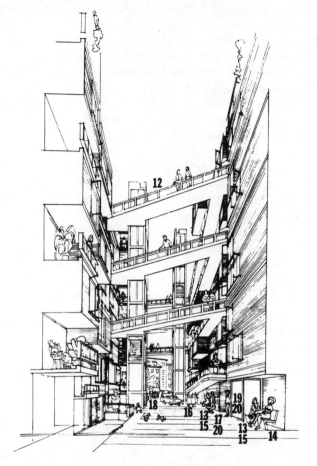

Design for West End, based on behavioral research. (From "Mass Housing: Social Research and Design," by B. Brolin and J. Zeisel, *The Architectural Forum*, July/August 1968, 71. Reprinted by permission.)

to solve E-B problems. You need different analytic skills to analyze an architectural plan than to analyze a newspaper article.

Types of Data
Words: Content analysis
Numbers: Secondary analysis
Nonverbal Representations: Behavioral analysis

Words

What Webb et al. (1966) call "running records"—records kept over time —can be used to find out about such things as changing patterns, past conditions, and particular past events. For example, verbatim transcripts of a public speech could provide clues to the speaker's state of mind, intentions, goals, and perceptions at the time she gave the speech. Heimessen and de Jonge, in another example, used verbal content analysis of poems to find out what teenage students felt about high-rise housing in the Netherlands (1967). Their source for data was the countrywide high school graduation examination given one year. As one of ten questions to choose from, students in that year were asked to write an essay commenting on a modern poem about high-rise housing. The investigators found that 76% of students answering this question were against such buildings, 24% for. Positive attributes the students suggested dealt mainly with green space and play areas; negative attributes mainly with the social and psychological climate in high-rise buildings. Among Heimessen and de Jonge's most interesting findings is that a large majority of the students, both for and against high-rise housing, perceived such housing as inevitable. According to the students, only this efficient building type could meet the housing needs of the rapidly increasing Dutch population. The authors point out that this is a misperception: among 6487 housing units completed in one month in 1967, only 1599 employed labor-intensive industrial building systems.

Subjectivity and context. In interpreting verbal data—especially to determine intentions and perceptions of the writer or speaker—it is difficult to avoid reading your own subjective meaning into the material. For example, when a student writes that a building is "large and imposing," does she mean it positively or negatively? If a designer writes in a letter to a community client that she feels "social concerns are vital to the success of the project," is she catering to the client's desires, or does she mean what she writes?

To avoid subjective ratings and to increase the reliability of such analysis, you can analyze documents in several ways and compare results: have several raters analyze the same documents; develop a definition of a situation by analyzing one sample of documents and then develop another one by analyzing a second sample chosen from the same file.

Another way to interpret what someone means is to know the context of his expressions (George, 1959). This includes *situational* attributes: What is a writer's position? What is the intended reader's position? What events surround the communication? Situational attributes may be summarized by the question "Who is writing to whom under what circumstances?" The answers to these questions may be found in the document file itself, or the investigator may have to find them out by other research means. The same is true for *behavioral* attributes of a writer's context—namely, "the purpose or objective which the specific communication is designed to achieve" (1959: 27). The meaning of the phrase "social concerns are vital" in a letter to a client might be explained by another document in the file—a memo to the writer from her boss telling her to assure the client that everything is all right. Clues to the behavioral context of a phrase may be found in another part of the same letter. In either case, developing a contextual overview of files before analyzing partial units, such as phrases or words, helps to identify data useful in interpreting those partial units.

Frequency and nonfrequency coding. For some research purposes, it can be useful to record how often a theme or a word appears in written documents. For example, Keller (1976) analyzed all articles in the 60 issues the Twin Rivers newspaper had published. She counted the mentions of problems (from design defects and controversial management policies to poor police protection), broken promises (a youth and community center that was never built), and the growth of communitywide organizations. Counting such items alerted Keller to the magnitude and salience of each issue. For example, the lack of promised storm windows turned out to be a much more significant community problem than the research team had expected.

However, frequency content counts might be irrelevant or even misleading for other research purposes. If, for example, a researcher is interested in the types rather than the magnitude of topics covered in a set of letters, counting themes may cause infrequent yet important ones to be disregarded. When a problem mentioned once is as important to an investigator's purpose as a problem mentioned many times, coding frequency does not help. Brolin and Zeisel (1968) used a nonfrequency approach when they translated portions of Gans' *Urban Villagers* into hypothetical housing designs for the Italo-American families Gans described. To develop a culturally responsive behavioral design program, they excerpted from the book each quotation they could find that "described an activity taking place in a physical setting" (p. 68). The two investigators, carrying out this analysis separately and then comparing results, generated over 200 quotations. Brolin, an architect, began to design buildings using the quotations as data. He did not know before he began which quotations would be more valuable and which less. He did not know precisely what it meant to "use" such data. But during the months it took to design the hypothetical buildings, he and Zeisel realized that only 20 of the 200 original quotations were "useful." Those describing relationships between people proved most helpful to Brolin in making design decisions about objects, places, and how places were to relate to one another. Frequency counts would have been at best irrelevant for this content analysis. Counting and measurement are appropriate techniques to use with each research method discussed in Part Two, when the purpose of the particular project requires them.

Coding unit. What words or set of words in a letter or an article should you count or record? Perhaps you should not record words, but rather the theme of the whole document. There is no rule to use in deciding what to record. The best you can aim for is to choose a coding unit that is not too broad to be irrelevant and not too narrow to make the writer's strategy invisible. For different purposes such a coding unit may be a word, a clause or thought unit, a sentence, a configuration, or the composite theme of the entire document.

Numbers

Much information is stored in archives in the form of numerical records: crime rates and turnover rates; student grades and patient illnesses; production figures. Records provide indicators of such things as amount and quality of output, characteristics of a group of people or places, and occurrences of a type of event or action.

A major source of easily accessible numerical archives is the Bureau of the Census, which publishes reports containing data from the Decennial Census of Population and Housing collected every ten years. The Bureau of the Census also makes computer tapes available with more detailed summary statistics about items such as the number of units in particular types of buildings in a geographical area. The ten-year time span is a barrier to studying shorter-span trends with this data, but smaller sample surveys are carried out and reported yearly and even monthly on particular problems.

Institutional and organizational records present investigators with the task of tailoring existing numbers to achieve new ends. Wilner et al., in their 1950s housing experiment (1954), used housing-authority files to determine that their test and control groups of housing residents were comparable on date of birth, length of residence in Baltimore, degree of overcrowding in their former dwellings, and whether their dwellings had hot water and indoor toilet facilities. Similarly, Wilner et al. used public school records to show that children earned higher grades if they lived in newer housing.

However, before Wilner et al. could make these judgments, they had to tailor the data to their own needs—translate them into information for their own purposes. They sampled records to determine the type and format of data they contained as well as their completeness. When did the records begin? What characteristics were left out? How was *overcrowding* defined? Once Wilner et al. determined that these data were suitable for their purposes, they devised forms on which to record precisely those items of data relevant to the study they were engaged in. Only after pretesting and revising these forms did they transfer the data so that they could analyze them appropriately.

When archives offer only composite rates—of vandalism or felonies, for example—investigators may not be able to determine whether the events the rates comprise are the ones they want to know about. The easier it is to disaggregate rates back to an original reporting unit, the more easily the data can be evaluated and—if acceptable—reorganized to fit a researcher's needs. For example, when Zeisel was studying school vandalism in Boston, he was able to analyze individual custodian reports in addition to overall rates. The reports mentioned broken equipment but failed to differentiate between damage from normal use and damage from malicious acts. They mentioned broken glass but did not differentiate between windows located on highly visible streets and windows in out-of-the-way hangouts. Zeisel wanted to find out whether location of damage, intent of the "vandals," and breakage costs were related. The way rate keepers defined vandalism made these records inappropriate for his purposes.

In sum, organized numerical files may reduce the need to collect raw data. But numerical files, as organized, may still require analysis to determine their appropriateness for a researcher's purpose and reorganization to make them useful for this purpose.

Nonverbal Representations

Because behavioral scientists seldom analyze diagrams, photographs, and plans, they usually do so on an ad hoc and common-sense basis. Environment-behavior researchers, in contrast, often find that to understand places and buildings the way they want, a major source of data is analysis of behavioral implications of nonverbal and nonnumerical representations. Analyzing how people and environments are presented in paintings, housing advertisements, and designers' renderings are still exceptional E-B research techniques, but analyzing the behavioral content of drafted plans of physical settings is now common.

Behaviorally analyzing plans means using them to develop tentative predictions, or hypotheses, about what might take place in the environment if it were built. For example, in planning two sets of hospital rooms, Good provided several bedroom and bathroom arrangements, which are illustrated in the figure below (Good & Hurtig, 1978).

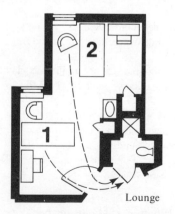
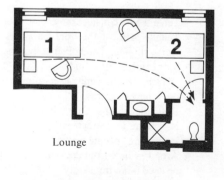

Alternative plans for hospital rooms. In scheme A, patient 2 has his own bed area. When either patient wants to use the toilet, he must walk out of their common room into the shared lounge. In scheme B, the toilet room is near the bed of patient 2. When patient 1 uses the toilet, he must go by the bed of patient 2.

Analyzing plan A might raise such questions as these: Does patient 2 develop a sense of territory about his part of the room because only he has access to it? Will both patients feel that using the toilet requires making themselves presentable because they have to go through a public place—the lounge? You can raise related behavioral questions for plan B: Does patient 1's going to the toilet near patient 2 prevent patient 2 from developing a sense of territory in the room? Does patient 1 feel like an intruder?

There is obviously no limit to the diversity of behavioral questions that researchers and designers can ask of plans. People must decide what type of behavioral plan analysis is best suited to solving their particular problem. For example, for her study of Twin Rivers, Keller (1976) analyzed sets of plans designed and redesigned over a period of years during several phases of planning—each in a different designer's office. The final set of plans was used for construction; the earlier ones were never built. Keller wanted to trace the design process over time: identifying design elements that were planned and later changed, then finding out why the designers made these changes. Keller used behavioral plan analysis as the basis for focused-interview questions with designers about their design intentions.

In their housing evaluation at Charlesview, Zeisel and Griffin (1975) not only used behavioral plan analysis to formulate questions for the architect about his intentions; they also developed behavioral hypotheses from the plan to direct later observational research at the site. For example, the plans showed parking areas located on the street side of most buildings (see figure). Entrances to these buildings are on the same side. At the "backs" of these buildings there are pathways and open grassy areas apparently intended for play. Zeisel and Griffin presented their analysis of these relationships as hypotheses, or tentative predictions:

- Tenants will consider the car location to be extremely convenient.
- Tenants will use the front entrances to the buildings when traveling to and from work, shopping, and other activities.
- Side effects will include use of the "front," parking-area side of buildings as play areas by children and observation areas by older residents—both of whom like to be "where the action is."
- Residents will use the shared "back" open spaces only infrequently because there is nothing to do there and because the doors near parking areas will draw any interesting "people watching" activity to the front of buildings.
- Area 1, where front doors are located on the interior of the housing complex, will be used more frequently.

Such hypotheses served as the basis for an evaluation study using behavior observation, trace observation, and structured questionnaires. This research helped to identify another part of the site where parking and entries behaviorally reinforce each other: area 2, at the right of the diagram.

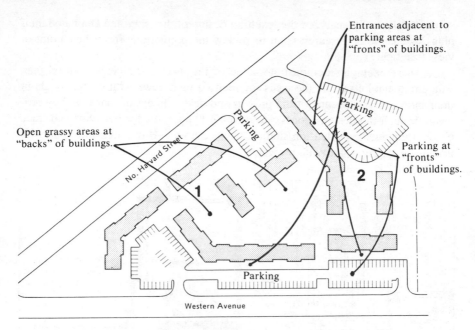

Site plan of Charlesview, showing parking areas and grassy areas

The contradiction at Charlesview between activity generated by entries on the outside of the complex and the architect's apparent desire for activity to take place in the interior of the complex makes visible a significant type of design condition you can look for when analyzing plans: *apparent behavioral inconsistencies and contradictions* in the arrangement of design components (Jones, 1970). If you can identify unintended behavioral inconsistencies in the design of a project, you can improve your understanding of and control over the behavior consequences of design decisions; you can avoid contradicting yourself in design.

Epp et al. (1979) used behavioral plan analysis to still another end—to trace the way designers of housing for older persons used E-B research information about older people in their designs. Firms using an early version of Howell and Epp's research report, *Shared Spaces* (1976), were asked to analyze their own plans and record as annotations on the designs "what they perceived to be important design decisions with an explanation of why each decision was made and the projected impact they expected that decision to have on future elderly residents" (p. 15). Epp et al. (1979) used the designer's annotations to trace what data from the book designers included and how they did so. For example, in one project, in response to what they felt the research implied, designers relocated a main entry door to provide a place for residents to be able to wait and watch for taxicabs or friends picking them up. They also relocated a machine room to enable residents waiting for the elevator to "preview" the community room—to see what is going on there without having to walk into it. The designers themselves behaviorally analyzed the resulting design of the entry and annotated their plans to enable the research team to review the predictions from their point of view (see figure).

These examples demonstrate some of the uses to which behavioral plan annotation can be put: as the basis for focused interviews with designers about their intentions; to document the growth and development of plans as they progress through the design process; to develop hypotheses for behavior and trace observation during evaluation studies; to trace how E-B research information is used in designing a particular project.

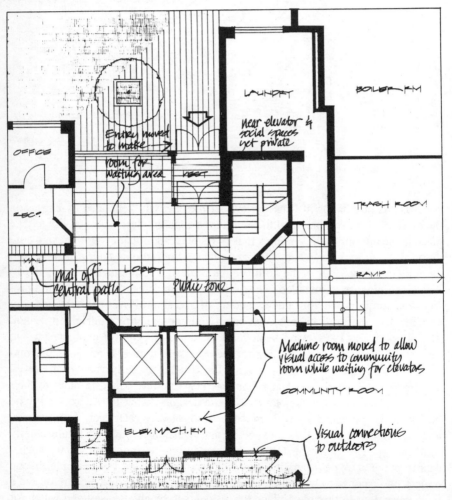

Annotated plan of housing for the elderly, showing uses of behavioral research. (From "Monitoring Environment-Behavior Research," by G. Epp, D. Georgopulos, and S. Howell. *Journal of Architectural Research,* March 1979, 7(1), 12–21. Reprinted by permission of the American Institute of Architects.)

BEHAVIORAL PLAN ANALYSIS

When you watch people analyze, or "read," plans, it can seem like an esoteric skill developed through mystical ritual. Reading behavioral implications of plans is a skill everyone can develop who can (1) imagine things from perspectives that research shows other people have, rather than imagining that other people have one's own perspective, and (2) imagine in three dimensions things drawn in two—including objects and relations between places.

Behavioral Plan Analysis

Other People's Perspectives

    Generic E-B issues
    Generic issues: specific users
    Unique user-group needs

Reading People into Plans

    Research-based scenarios
    Behavioral side effects
    Physical elements

Other People's Perspectives

Generic E-B issues. Environment-behavior research has developed a host of research-based theoretical issues that can help describe how people relate to their physical surroundings. These include the following:

- Degree of privacy: The degree to which people control the access of others to where they are.
- Territoriality: The feeling individuals or groups have that they control what happens in a place—that they can use it as they like and can change it physically to reflect their personalities.
- Personalization: The ways people change their physical surroundings—display, paint, furniture shifts—in order to have those places reflect their personalities, tastes, and identities.
- Backstage behavior: The activities people engage in before and after presenting themselves to others. Nurses present themselves to patients and doctors; job applicants to their potential employers; a host and hostess to their guests. Backstage behavior includes both "getting made up" and "letting down your hair."
- Wayfinding: How people find their way through new, and sometimes familiar, surroundings. The things that help them orient themselves and those that disorient and confuse them.

These concepts do not tell you how each individual will react to a setting or how groups of people tend to react. However, if you keep these E-B issues in mind when you look at a plan, your looking is likely to raise questions that existing knowledge or further research may be able to answer. For example, in Good's hospital-room arrangement, we identified potential problems for patients related to territoriality and privacy. To answer our questions, we need further knowledge of how hospital patients adapt to their surroundings, what their attitudes are toward sharing space with others, and how they feel about modesty in their robes. This information may be available if you search for it; others may have already conducted such research. Or the research may have yet to be done. In either case the heuristic use of generic E-B concepts, such as territoriality and privacy, helps to "get into" a plan and identify issues for further exploration.

Generic issues: specific users. Generic E-B issues applied to a particular plan will refer to particular users, user groups, and settings. For example, questions about territoriality and privacy applied to Good's building refer to the way patients in hospitals behave. Applied to Howell and Epp's problem, they refer to older persons' behavior in elevator buildings. Among the many user groups and settings that have been studied are teenagers in parks, students in schools, patients in hospitals, older persons in housing, families with children in housing, employees in offices, and visitors in any setting.

Research can be used to determine the tendencies of people in certain groups to respond in particular ways to generic issues, such as wayfinding, territoriality, and privacy. For example, one study seems to indicate that patients waiting in various states of undress in cancer-treatment clinics value social contact with relatives and other patients more than privacy from members of the opposite sex (Conway et al., 1977). The more information on this topic designers have, the better the design of such a facility can provide opportunities for social mixing and privacy to meet the needs of the greatest number of patients. Another example is that teenagers in schools tend to take over particular places as their "turf" more than other places: they use as hangouts or clubhouses slightly hidden areas behind schools, and they perch on available planters and walls to watch people in more active areas (Zeisel, 1976a). Designers can use data about teenagers to provide for such informal activity while minimizing property damage to the school resulting from rough play.

Unique user-group needs. Some issues are unique to certain users. For example, older people with limited muscular ability to control pupil dilation and contraction are particularly sensitive to the contrast between dark surroundings and bright light—including sunlight (Pastalan, Mantz, & Merrill, 1973). Designers who maximize southern sun to warm a building might unwittingly be making it uncomfortable for older residents to use that side of a building. As another example, teenagers take part in more show-off and challenge activity than other groups. A hung ceiling in a park's recreation room—meant to be convenient for many maintenance tasks—is likely to present teenage users with an opportunity to show off by seeing who can jump the highest and break one of the panels. The resulting maintenance problems may be worse than the ones the hung ceiling was meant to solve.

(From *Managing Vandalism,* by A. Scott, R. Fichter, and S. King. Illustrated by Kata Hall. Boston: Parkman Center for Urban Affairs, 1978. Used by permission.)

In sum, E-B research provides designers and investigators with the chance to put themselves into someone else's shoes without relying on well-meaning but often misguided empathy and intuition. Such research data include descriptions of (1) generic E-B concepts, (2) generic concepts referring to specific users, and (3) unique user-groups' needs.

Reading People into Plans

Research findings about groups of people may be able to provide data about what some people might tend to do in a setting. Such data do not tell you how the setting will actually be used by individuals with diverse wants and needs.

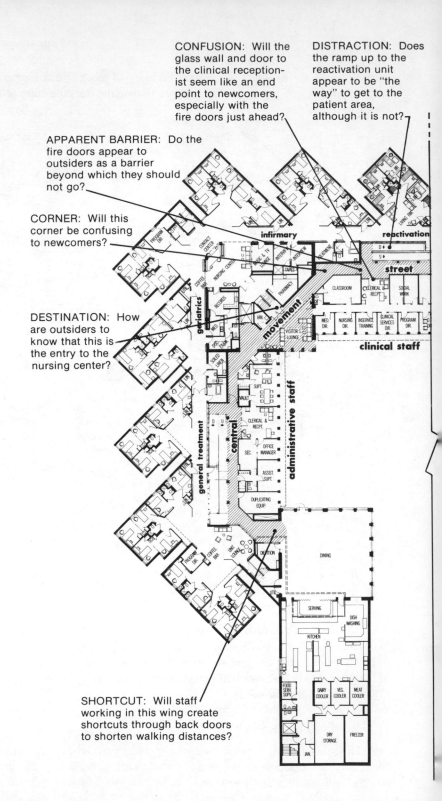

CONFUSION: Will the glass wall and door to the clinical receptionist seem like an end point to newcomers, especially with the fire doors just ahead?

DISTRACTION: Does the ramp up to the reactivation unit appear to be "the way" to get to the patient area, although it is not?

APPARENT BARRIER: Do the fire doors appear to outsiders as a barrier beyond which they should not go?

CORNER: Will this corner be confusing to newcomers?

DESTINATION: How are outsiders to know that this is the entry to the nursing center?

SHORTCUT: Will staff working in this wing create shortcuts through back doors to shorten walking distances?

infirmary

reactivation

street

clinical staff

geriatrics

movement

central

general treatment

administrative staff

DINING

SERVING

DISH WASHING

KITCHEN

FOOD SERV SUPY

DAIRY COOLER

VEG. COOLER

MEAT COOLER

DRY STORAGE

FREEZER

JAN.

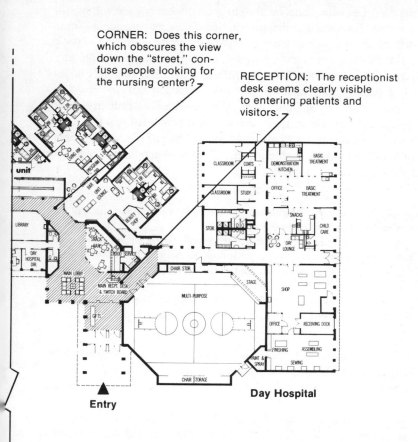

CORNER: Does this corner, which obscures the view down the "street," confuse people looking for the nursing center?

RECEPTION: The receptionist desk seems clearly visible to entering patients and visitors.

Day Hospital

▲
Entry

IPATIENT UNITS-UPPER LEVEL EL. 105'4"
ACTIVITIES, STAFF EL. 100'0"

0	10		50		
	5	20			100

Behavioral annotations raising wayfinding questions for future evaluation of the Norwood Mental Health Center, Wood County, Wisconsin. (Courtesy of Lawrence R. Good, Hougen–Good–Pfaller & Associates, Architects–Engineers.)

Nor can descriptions of environments be used to predict what anyone will or will not do. Environments enable and constrain activities; they can encourage some activities by making them easier to carry out and discourage others by making them difficult. For example, in Good's hospital, one visitor might find his way from the entry to the nurses' center with no difficulty while another gets hopelessly lost until a passing staff member gives her directions. If you want to foresee from a plan some of the things that might eventually occur in a built environment, you must be able to imagine how different people using it will react to its various parts: If a nurse wants to relax, where will he go? If a visitor wants to relax, where does the hospital enable her to sit? To read people into plans in this way, three questions can be helpful:

- What *scenarios* does E-B research indicate particular users might enact in the setting: what will they want to do and need to do?
- What behavioral *side effects* will there be for particular users when they do what they want or need to do in the setting: what does the environment allow or force people to do, see, hear, smell, touch, and perceive on the way to their primary goal?
- What *physical elements* in the setting influence these reactions: what objects, barriers, and environmental attributes (such as size and shape)?

Research-based scenarios. If you want to put yourself in someone else's shoes, one of the easiest persons to imagine is a visitor trying to find his way. You probably have information to do this from personal experience in new places. If you ask yourself "How would I know where to go if I were arriving here for the first time?" you will begin to look for and find wayfinding clues in the design. You will begin to see places where paths are clear and places where they might be confusing. For example, in Good's mental-health clinic you might feel that the receptionist's desk is clear enough but that finding your way to the nurses' station might be confusing, since you will have to pass corners, a ramp going up to your right, a suite of offices to your left, and a set of doors in the hallway before even seeing the steps to the nurses' center.

If you want the design decisions you make to have the effects you want in the eventual setting, you will base scenarios as much as possible on research. To design on the assumption that patients in mental hospitals will spend most of their days in bed is not helpful, especially if research shows they do not. Scenarios used in this way are aids to translating E-B research data into useful design information; they are not mechanisms for making explicit fictitious views of people. Scenarios help to translate research data about what people want, how individuals or groups get what they want, needs people have and how they meet them, particular perceptions people have—all the types of data this book's research methods can help to collect.

Behavioral side effects. Research-based scenarios provide vehicles for reading into plans particular persons doing something: a patient who needs to go to the bathroom; a visitor who wants to find a nursing center; a nurse trying to relax during a hectic day. In different settings users would do these things differently. In one room a patient has to pass close to his roommate to reach the toilet; in the other both patients are forced to be seen by anyone sitting in the adjacent lounge. Good's nursing center is open on all sides to patients, visitors, and other staff members. To relax, nurses there might have to retreat into the nearby "records" room. In nursing centers with some closed-off areas, nurses can disappear more easily.

The possible immediate behavioral and sensory side effects are limited only by the number of possible scenarios; in other words, there are no limits within the constraints research sets for possible scenarios. The environment that physical plans represent provides E-B investigators with data to use to identify what is likely to happen when people use the environment. When, for example, a patient goes to the bathroom, you can read from lines on the drawing what kind of places he must pass through and what he will be likely to see, hear, smell, touch, and perceive on the way. The only question that remains is: what parts of the drawn setting are likely to be most helpful in making this determination.

Physical elements. Plans are models of physical environments—you ought to be able to look at and do things to the two-dimensional drawing as if it were the real setting. Symbols represent objects:

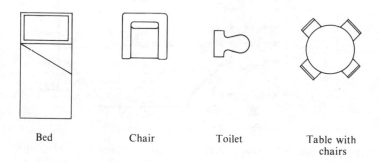

| Bed | Chair | Toilet | Table with chairs |

Other symbols represent types of barriers:

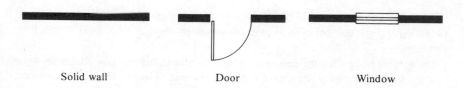

| Solid wall | Door | Window |

Still others represent field attributes of places, such as size, orientation, and shape:

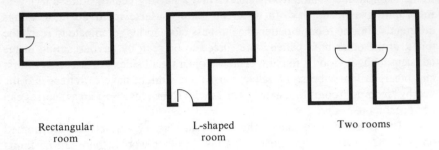

Rectangular   L-shaped   Two rooms
room   room

And some attributes of the environment, such as noise and light conditions, have to be inferred from the way symbols like the preceding ones are put together (see figure).

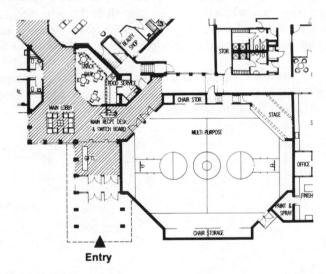

Entry

Identifying behavioral side effects: If a basketball game takes place in the multipurpose room and the doors are open, there might be much noise in the entryway. (Courtesy of Lawrence R. Good, Hougen–Good–Pfaller & Associates, Architects–Engineers.)

With knowledge of a handful of such symbols applied, for example, to Good's plan, you can begin to answer for yourself:

- What *objects* has the designer put into this plan to indicate how spaces are to be used? (Examples are chairs indicating visitors' lounge and cafeteria counter indicating a place to eat.)

- What barriers have been provided between areas: what *connections* (glass between the entry area and the cafeteria; a ramp between the "street" and the "reactivation unit") and what *separations* (doors between entry and multipurpose gymnasium; wall between library and "street")?
- What *fields* does the designer set up by the way he plans and arranges spaces? (Shapes of various patient rooms; potential for noontime sun through the windows into the clinical staff offices.)

These are the same questions suggested in Chapter 8 to help in understanding the behavioral consequences of built environments.

As with every technique dependent on the skill of the person using it, everyone who analyzes the behavioral implications of plans will do it in her own way to meet her own purposes. If your purpose is to put yourself hypothetically into another person's shoes, you can do this successfully, using your own intuition, only for yourself as a user. At other times you must know your limitations and turn instead to E-B research.

OVERVIEW

Archives of documents—from newspapers to institutional records and architectural plans—can provide E-B investigators with readily available data about the past. Investigators who overcome potential problems of access, completeness, and relevance have access to varied types of data: words, numbers, and nonverbal representations. Behavioral scientists engaged in communications research and propaganda studies have long carried out content analysis of verbal documents; those engaged in all sorts of research have analyzed other people's numerical data. Nonverbal representations—especially designers' two-dimensional plans—remain a special source of data for E-B researchers who want to learn from people and apply what they find out about people to designing environments.

In behavioral plan analysis, to foresee how others will react to an environment, you have to use research to gain insight into other people's perspectives. For the same reason, you have to be able to read plans with these perspectives: to understand what effects elements in a particular plan will have on eventual users. These skills will enable people to avoid imposing their own—often misguided—empathy and subjective intuition on their research data and on future users of planned environments.

RECAPITULATING THEMES

Several themes consciously underlay my writing this book. I hope you found others emerge on reading it. The ones I had in mind are these:

I. Research and design are surprisingly similar activities with crucial differences in emphasis; these attributes help in linking the two.
II. If researchers and designers can see environment and behavior as an integrated E-B system, they will be able to identify and solve new types of problems.
III. Multiple-methods research can be an effective way to raise the quality of research, especially for E-B research topics.
IV. Research seen as problem- and situation-specific becomes a tool to achieve someone's purposes rather than an end in itself.
V. Appreciating and using E-B research does not require a set of prerequisite courses.

Some themes are explicit in the book, others implicit. The last theme explains why fundamental topics such as statistics, social theory, philosophy, experimental design, and sampling are dealt with so briefly.

I. RESEARCH AND DESIGN: SIMILARITIES AND DIFFERENCES

Carrying out a research project and designing an environment are similar in that both invent new ways to see the world around us. Research invents organizing concepts; design arrives at plans for future settings. Yet even these differences can be artificial: designers clearly develop concepts, and some researchers arrive at plans for the future. Another similarity is that both activities rely on people's critical faculties to improve and refine concepts once they are presented: sketches, hypotheses, reports, and even buildings. In both research and design, the more someone is able to present and thus share ideas with others—pinning up a drawing, publishing an article—the more others are able to help refine ideas.

Despite their similarities, research and design are not interchangeable. Design training tends to emphasize being able to present concepts; research training emphasizes testing them. Design training emphasizes making decisions; research training stresses the importance of learning from them. Design training teaches people how to take risks; research training, how to minimize them. Curiously, however, if you were to tell a successful researcher that he does not know how to take risks and present ideas, he would laugh. An easy way to insult a designer would be to tell her that she is uncritical or takes uninformed risks. Such differences are ones of emphasis, not kind. Highly skilled researchers and designers probably value many of the same skills. A researcher or designer who presents his ideas well can test them more easily; the more effectively an idea is tested, the better informed later decisions will be; and so on.

So what? When designers want to gather data about people to make good decisions, they need to know how to do research. When researchers, especially applied researchers, need to make risky decisions in order to be able to gather the data they want, they had better know how to do so. For example, if an E-B researcher is asked to advise someone how to plan alternative apartments so that they can be evaluated later, she needs to know about room sizes and door openings as well as what decisions are possible in that particular design situation.

In sum, if researchers and designers know how to judge what skills are appropriate to a particular situation, and if they have a range of skills, they can best solve their problems. Their real skill, then, is to be able to use the most appropriate tools, whether they come out of the tool kit traditionally called "research" or the one called "design."

II. ENVIRONMENT AND BEHAVIOR: MUTUAL EFFECTS AND PROCESSES

For some purposes environment and behavior need not be treated as interdependent. If you want to build a physical shell of a house only to find out how a particular mechanical connection is made, it may be counterproductive to think about what people might do in and think about the shell. And if you want to study how people generate visual concepts, it may be irrelevant to think about any physical environment other than the experimental setting you are trying to control. In such situations it may be most useful to think of environment and behavior separately.

Environment-behavior investigators and designers, however, face situations in which this view is dysfunctional—it works against their own declared goals. For example, if you want to design a house in which mentally retarded residents feel comfortable and independent, you have to think about the building and people at the same time. The reverse is also true: to provide certain social services effectively, environmental concerns are crucial.

So what? Once the effects of environment and behavior on each other become readily apparent, you can begin to look more thoroughly at secondary E-B effects. For example, you may be better able to design a home for mentally retarded residents if you consider as well the reactions of neighbors and local politicians who might stand in the way of its getting built. Perceptions held by residents' relatives may well determine what kinds of residents finally live there.

Just as significant as such secondary E-B effects are questions about E-B process. What happens to environments and to people when users participate in designing environments? Do different forms of participation result in different changes? If users of a place manage and maintain it, do they develop special relationships to it, or do they first get more disgusted with it? How do reactions differ when situations and people differ? If environmental management, environmental maintenance, environmental participation, and other such topics are included in the realm of E-B studies, the job environmental designers and researchers have ahead becomes more and more intriguing.

III. MULTIPLE RESEARCH METHODS: RESEARCH QUALITY

Among the ways to achieve higher-quality research is to use several methods to attack one problem. The simplest way to present the idea of multiple-method research is to say that because each method you might use has its own bias, using several methods ought to improve your chances that the bias of one is canceled by the others.

The theme of multiple methods underlies not only the chapter on research quality (Chapter 6) but also the organization of the book. Although each method described in Part Two is treated separately, most case-study examples are multiple-method; for this reason the same case studies reappear in various chapters —giving the reader a broad picture of the case study only after several chapters. These excellent case studies—Howell and Epp (1976), Keller (1976), Snyder and Ostrander (1974), and others—serve two ends: first, to show how to use one method to achieve a purpose efficiently and effectively; second, to show that to arrive at a multifaceted picture of a complex E-B problem, an investigator may want to use a multiple-method approach.

So what? Getting a full picture of a problem is not enough by itself; the picture must also be valid—people must be able to act on the basis of that picture with the results they want and with the fewest uncontrolled effects. For example, if you want to design furniture in an airport waiting lounge so that travelers will rearrange it for their own needs (grouped for chatting families and friends, isolated for people who want to be alone, and so on), you need to understand such people. If you base your design on what people say they want to do, you might overlook inhibitions they have against actually moving furniture in public. If you look only at behavior of people waiting, you may identify a need but not know how to meet it; if only at physical traces after a plane has departed, you might design furniture which moves but which antagonizes airport personnel

—an uncontrolled side effect. The appropriate mix of methods will be the one that enables you to achieve your ends with greatest control over side effects. A significant theme of this book is that E-B researchers and decision makers who use a multiple-method research approach will best be able to use what they find out to do what they want to do.

IV. RESEARCH SPECIFIC TO PROBLEMS AND SITUATIONS: MEANS, NOT ENDS

Throughout this book I have included examples of how someone used research techniques and methods to solve a particular problem in a particular situation. I discuss techniques in terms of how to make them serve your purposes rather than what they are meant to do generally. Wherever possible I use, or imply, "if . . . then" phrases to demonstrate possible consequences of using one or another research procedure, so that you can decide whether the procedure is right for you rather than learning that it is good in general. For example, in discussing research quality (Chapter 6) I did not say that the more testable a hypothesis is, the better it is, but rather that if you want to learn something from testing a hypothesis, the greater the chance you give it of being proved wrong if it is wrong, the more you can learn.

If you see research methods as nothing but a set of clearly defined and highly valued rules, you can easily begin to carry out research as an end in itself—that is, as if the rules had intrinsic value. However, if you realize that methods, quality criteria, techniques, and rules of thumb have been made explicit so that they can be used selectively, then they become useful tools. For example, if you learn that it is always better to share research with colleagues than to leave research ideas fuzzy, you might begin to present your thoughts clearly before they are developed enough to do so. Clarity would then become a counterproductive end in itself rather than a means to share what you know and in turn improve its quality.

So what? Either view—research as end or as tool—is a static view. In dynamic problem-solving situations, investigators must be ready to modify any view; to stretch the applicability of methods; to invent others. Particular situations can present investigators with research problems requiring new inventions or modifications. Particular problems become resources to help us improve not only our research skills but also—by questioning—to improve research itself. If researchers use and refine their tools to solve particular problems, they will be able to benefit from the diversity that problems provide. Seeing research as a set of tools is a necessary first step toward improving the whole tool chest in this way.

V. RESEARCH AS A POINT OF VIEW: NO PREREQUISITES

To carry out an E-B research project, you may find that you need to know more about such topics as statistics, sampling, and experimental design than are presented in this book. To analyze the data you collect in questionnaires, you will need to know how to evaluate whether the statistical significance of answers is sufficient for your purposes. To choose a group of people to interview, you will want to know what different sampling procedures can do for you. If you want to experiment with various apartment configurations, you will need to know how to assess the factors that might confound your findings. All this is necessary to carry out a research project.

To carry out some E-B research, however, none of it is needed. You can do E-B research just by looking around you; by seeing physical traces as reflections of people; by interpreting shapes of rooms in terms of their behavioral implications; by recording how two people sit next to each other. You can do E-B research by developing tentative hypotheses about what such observations mean and then by evaluating and refining the hypotheses. You can apply E-B research by gently making and evaluating design decisions on the basis of what you have seen. The more you want to know, the more you want to be sure about what you know, the more efficiently you want to carry out your research—the more you will have to learn from other books.

When you begin to study further, you may find that for each topic you want to read several books. I have briefly presented some of these topics and have merely used others to explain how one might apply a research technique. For example, sampling is not covered extensively but is referred to in most methods chapters. I assume throughout that E-B researchers or designers will find the appropriate books when they want to do something for which they need to know more about various types of sampling, analytic logics, experimental designs, and significance tests.

Another set of topics not dealt with in detail in the text are philosophical ones: What does it mean that design and research are both essentially creative acts (Koestler, 1976)? How does scientific knowledge develop (Popper, 1972)? How do the artistic and private aspects of knowing fit into science (Polanyi, 1958)? Why don't we just leave research to individuals instead of creating complex "inquiring systems" with rules and logics and methods (Churchman, 1971)? Where does more and more knowledge lead us (Morison, 1974)? What would society be like if public officials made decisions knowing they are to be evaluated and could be proved wrong (Campbell, 1969)? Each topic leads the inquiring reader to search out a series of books that might provide some explicit guidance in answering such questions.

So what? With fewer obstacles in the way, readers may be able to get to the business and pleasure of doing research more quickly. Once you start doing

E-B research, you can identify what you need to know and the resources you need to continue doing the kind of research you want to do.

INQUIRY BY DESIGN

Research is a purposeful, systematic way to improve knowledge. Design can also contribute to a body of knowledge when designers commit themselves to share what they know, when they approach design problems as opportunities to learn what they do not know, and when they make design decisions that contribute to inquiry.

REFERENCES

Alexander, Christopher. *Notes on the Synthesis of Form*. Cambridge, Mass.: Harvard University Press, 1964.

Altman, Irwin. *The Environment and Social Behavior*. Monterey, Calif.: Brooks/Cole, 1975.

Altman, Irwin, Patricia A. Nelson, & Evelyn E. Lett. *The Ecology of Home Environment*. Washington, D.C.: U.S. Dept. of Health, Education and Welfare, 1972.

Amarel, Saul. "On Representations of Problems of Reasoning about Actions" in *Machine Intelligence 3*, D. Michie (Ed.). New York: American Elsevier, 1968.

Archea, John, & Aristide H. Esser. "Man-Environment Systems: A Statement of Purpose." *Man-Environment Systems, 1*, No. 2 (January 1970).

Archer, L. Bruce. "The Structure of the Design Process" in Broadbent & Ward (1969).

Argyris, Christopher. *Learning in Design Settings*. Mimeo, Harvard Graduate School of Education, 1977.

Asimov, Morris. *Introduction to Design*. Englewood Cliffs, N.J.: Prentice-Hall, 1962.

Barker, Roger. *Ecological Psychology*. Stanford, Calif.: Stanford University Press, 1968.

Barnett, H. G. *Innovation: The Basis of Cultural Change*. New York: McGraw-Hill, 1953.

Barton, Alan, & Paul F. Lazarsfeld. "Some Functions of Qualitative Analysis in Social Research" in McCall & Simmons (1969).

Bechtel, Robert B. *Enclosing Behavior*. Stroudsburg, Pa.: Dowden, Hutchinson & Ross, 1977.

Bell, Paul A., Jeffrey D. Fisher, & Ross J. Loomis. *Environmental Psychology*. Philadelphia: W. B. Saunders, 1978.

Blau, Peter M. *The Dynamics of Bureaucracy*. Chicago: University of Chicago Press, 1963.

Blau, Peter M. "The Research Process in the Study of the Dynamics of Bureaucracy" in Hammond (1964, 1967).

Boulding, Kenneth E. *The Image: Knowledge in Life and Society*. Ann Arbor: University of Michigan Press, 1956.

Boulding, Kenneth E. "Foreword" in Downs & Stea (1973).

Broadbent, Geoffrey. "Creativity" in *The Design Method*, S. Gregory (Ed.). London: Butterworths, 1966.

Broadbent, Geoffrey, & Anthony Ward (Eds.). *Design Methods in Architecture*. London: Lund Humphries for the Architectural Association, 1969.

Brolin, Brent C. "Chandigarh Was Planned by Experts, but Something Has Gone Wrong." *Smithsonian, 3*, No. 3 (June 1972), 56–63.

Brolin, Brent C. *The Failure of Modern Architecture*. New York: Van Nostrand Reinhold, 1976.

Brolin, Brent C., & John Zeisel. "Mass Housing: Social Research and Design." *Architectural Forum, 129* (July/August 1968), 66–71.

Brower, Sidney. *The Design of Neighborhood Parks*. Baltimore, Md.: City Planning Commission, Dept. of Planning, 1977.

Bruner, Jerome S. *Beyond the Information Given: Studies in the Psychology of Knowing* (J. M. Anglin, Ed.). New York: Norton, 1973.

Campbell, Donald T. "Reforms as Experiments." *American Psychologist, 24*, No. 4 (April 1969), 409–429. Reprinted with modifications in *Readings in Evaluation Research* (2nd ed.), F. G. Caro (Ed.). New York: Russell Sage Foundation, 1977.

Campbell, Donald T. "Quasi-Experimental Designs" in *Social Experimentation: A Method for Planning and Evaluating Social Intervention*, H. W. Riecken & R. F. Boruch (Eds.). New York: Academic Press, 1974.

Campbell, Donald T. "Degrees of Freedom and the Case Study." *Comparative Political Studies, 8*, No. 2 (July 1975), 178–193.

Campbell, Donald T. "Qualitative Knowing in Action Research." *Journal of Social Issues,* in press. (Kurt Lewin Award Address, Society for the Psychological Study of Social Issues, meeting with the American Psychological Association, New Orleans, 1974.)

Campbell, Donald T., & Donald W. Fiske. "Convergent and Discriminant Validation by the Multitrait-Multimethod Matrix." *Psychological Bulletin, 56*, No. 2 (1959), 81–105.

Campbell, Donald T., & Julian C. Stanley. *Experimental and Quasi-Experimental Designs for Research*. Chicago: Rand McNally, 1966.

Canter, David. *The Psychology of Place*. London: Architectural Press, 1977.

Carp, Frances. *A Future for the Aged: Victoria Plaza and Its Residents*. Austin: University of Texas Press, 1966.

Chapin, F. S. "An Experiment on the Social Effects of Good Housing." *American Sociological Review, 5* (1940), 868–878.

Christopherson, D. G. "Opening Address: Discovering Designers" in Jones & Thornley (1963).

Churchman, C. West. *The Design of Inquiring Systems*. New York: Basic Books, 1971.

Conway, Donald. *Social Science and Design: A Process Model for Architect and Social Scientist Collaboration*. Washington, D.C.: American Institute of Architects, 1973.

Conway, Donald, John Zeisel, & Polly Welch. "Radiation Therapy Centers: Behavioral and Social Guidelines for Design" (Report). Washington, D.C.: National Institutes of Health, 1977.

Cook, Barbara E. "Survey Evaluation for Low Cost Low Rent Public Housing for the Elderly, Pleasanton, California." Mimeo, Berkeley, Calif.: Hirshen & Partners, Architects, 1971.

Cook, Barbara E. "Initial Evaluation of Koffinger Place, Pleasanton, California." Berkeley, Calif.: Hirshen & Partners, Architects, 1973.

Cook, Thomas D., & Donald T. Campbell. *Quasi-Experimentation: Design and Analysis Issues for Field Settings*. Chicago: Rand McNally, 1979.

Cooper, Clare. *Residents' Attitudes toward the Environment at St. Francis Square, S.F.* (Working Paper #126). Berkeley: Institute of Urban and Regional Development, University of California, 1970.

Cooper, Clare. "St. Francis Square: Attitudes of Its Residents." *AIA Journal, 56* (December 1971), 22–27.

Cooper, Clare. *Easter Hill Village*. New York: Free Press, 1975.

Cooper, Clare, & Phyllis Hackett. "Analysis of the Design Process at Two Moderate-Income Housing Developments" (Working Paper #80). Berkeley: Institute of Planning and Development Research, University of California, 1968.

Davis, Gerald, & Virginia Ayers. "Photographic Recording of Environmental Behavior" in Michelson (1975).

Downs, Roger M., & David Stea (Eds.). *Image and Environment: Cognitive Mapping and Spatial Behavior*. Chicago: Aldine, 1973.

Ellis, William R., Jr. "Planning, Design and Black Community Style: The Problem of Occasion-Adequate Space" in Mitchell (1972).

Ellis, William R., Jr. "The Environment of Human Relations: Perspectives and Problems." *Journal of Architectural Education, 27*, Nos. 2 & 3 (June 1974), 11–18, 54.

Epp, Gayle, Diane Georgopulos, & Sandra Howell. "Monitoring Environment-Behavior Research." *Journal of Architectural Research, 7*, No. 1 (March 1979), 12–21.

Felipe, Nancy Jo, & Robert Sommer. "Invasions of Personal Space." *Social Problems, 14*, No. 2 (1966), 206–214. (Reprinted in Gutman, 1972.)

Festinger, Leon S., Stanley Schachter, & Kurt Back. *Social Pressures in Informal Groups*. New York: Harper, 1950.

Finnie, W. C. "Field Experiments in Litter Control." *Environment and Behavior, 5* (1973), 123–144.

Foz, Adel T. K. *Some Observations on Designer Behavior in the Parti* (Master's Thesis). Cambridge, Department of Urban Studies and Planning, Massachusetts Institute of Technology, 1972.

Fried, Marc. "Grieving for a Lost Home" in *The Urban Condition*, L. J. Duhl (Ed.). New York: Basic Books, 1963. (Reprinted in Gutman, 1972.)

Fried, Marc, & Peggy Gleicher. "Some Sources of Residential Satisfaction in an Urban Slum." *Journal of the American Institute of Planners, 27*, No. 4 (1961), 305–315.

Galtung, Johan. *Theory and Methods of Social Research*. New York: Columbia University Press, 1967.

Gans, Herbert J. *The Urban Villagers*. New York: Free Press, 1962.

Gans, Herbert J. *The Levittowners*. New York: Pantheon, 1967.

Gans, Herbert J. "The Potential Environment and the Effective Environment" in *People and Plans*, H. J. Gans (Ed.). New York: Basic Books, 1968.

George, Alexander L. "Quantitative and Qualitative Approaches to Content Analysis" in *Trends in Content Analysis*, I. Pool (Ed.). Urbana: University of Illinois Press, 1959.

Goffman, Erving. *The Presentation of Self in Everyday Life*. New York: Doubleday, 1959.

Goffman, Erving. *Behavior in Public Places*. New York: Free Press, 1963.

Good, Lawrence, & William Hurtig. "Evaluation: A Mental Health Facility, Its Users and Context." *AIA Journal, 67*, No. 2 (February 1978), 38–41.

Goodey, Brian. *Perception of the Environment*. Birmingham, England: Centre for Urban and Regional Studies, University of Birmingham, 1971.

Gordon, W. J. J. *Synectics: The Development of Creative Capacity*. New York: Harper & Row, 1961.

Gould, Stephen Jay. "This View of Life: Bathybius Meets Eozoon." *Natural History, 87*, No. 4 (April 1978), 16–22.

Guerra, G. "A Geometrical Method of Systematic Design in Architecture" in Broadbent and Ward (1969).

Günter, Roland, Wessel Reinink, & Janne Günter. *Rom-Spanische Treppe*. Hamburg: VSA-Verlag, 1978.

Gutman, Robert. *People and Buildings*. New York: Basic Books, 1972.

Habraken, John. *Supports: An Alternative to Mass Housing*. New York: Praeger, 1972.

Hall, Edward T. *The Hidden Dimension*. Garden City, N.Y.: Doubleday, 1966.

Hammond, Phillip E. (Ed.). *Sociologists at Work*. New York: Basic Books, 1964; Anchor Books, 1967.

Heimessen, C. F. H., & Derk de Jonge. "Eindexamencandidaten over Woningen en Mensen." Delft: Centrum voor Architectuuronderzoek, Afdeling der Bouwkunde, Technische Hogeschool Delft, 1967.

Hillier, Bill, & Adrian Leaman. "How Is Design Possible?" *Journal of Architectural Research, 3,* No. 1 (January 1974), 4–11.

Hillier, Bill, John Musgrove, & Pat O'Sullivan. "Knowledge and Design" in Mitchell (1972).

Hoogdalem, Herbert van. "Some Conceptual Tools for the Analysis of Man-Environment Systems." *Delft Progress Report, 2* (1977), 249–256.

Howell, Sandra C. *Designing for Aging: Patterns of Use.* Cambridge, Mass.: M.I.T. Press, in press.

Howell, Sandra, & Gayle Epp. *Shared Spaces in Housing for the Elderly.* Cambridge, Mass.: Design Evaluation Project, Department of Architecture, Massachusetts Institute of Technology, 1976.

Hutt, Corinne. "Crowding among Children." Mimeo, University of Reading, England, 1969.

Hyman, Herbert. *Survey Design and Analysis.* New York: Free Press, 1955.

Ittelson, William H., Leanne Rivlin, & Harold M. Proshansky. "The Use of Behavioral Maps in Environmental Psychology" in Proshansky, Ittelson, & Rivlin (1970).

Jacobs, Jane. *The Death and Life of Great American Cities.* New York: Vintage Books, 1961.

Jones, J. Christopher. *Design Methods: Seeds of Human Futures.* London: Wiley, 1970.

Jones, J. C., & D. G. Thornley (Eds.). *Conference on Design Methods.* Oxford: Pergamon, 1963.

Jonge, D. de. "Images of Urban Areas, Their Structure and Psychological Foundations." *Journal of the American Institute of Planners, 28* (1962), 266–276. (Also in Gutman, 1972.)

Keller, Suzanne. *Twin Rivers: Study of a Planned Community.* National Science Foundation (Grant NSF G1 41 311) 1976.

Keller, Suzanne. "Design and the Quality of Life in a New Community" in *Major Social Issues: An Interdisciplinary View,* J. M. Yinger & S. J. Cutler (Eds.). New York: Free Press, 1978.

Kitsuse, J. I., & A. V. Cicourel. "A Note on the Uses of Official Statistics." *Social Problems, 11* (1963), 131–139.

Koestler, Arthur. *The Act of Creation,* (Second Danube Edition). London: Hutchinson, 1976.

Koestler, Arthur, & J. R. Smythies. *Beyond Reductionism: The Alpbach Symposium.* London: Hutchinson, 1969.

Korobkin, Barry J. *Images for Design: Communicating Social Science Research to Architects.* Cambridge, Mass.: Architecture Research Office, Harvard Graduate School of Design, 1976.

Kuhn, Thomas S. *The Structure of Scientific Revolutions* (2nd ed.). Chicago: University of Chicago Press, 1970.

Ladd, F. C. "Black Youths View Their Environment: Neighborhood Maps." *Environment and Behavior, 2* (June 1970), 74–99.

Lakatos, Imre. "Falsification and the Methodology of Scientific Research Programmes" in Lakatos & Musgrave (1970).

Lakatos, Imre, & Alan Musgrave (Eds.). *Criticism and the Growth of Knowledge.* Cambridge: The University Press, 1970.

Lang, Jon, Charles Burnette, Walter Moleski, & David Vachon (Eds.). *Designing for Human Behavior.* Stroudsburg, Pa.: Dowden, Hutchinson & Ross, 1974.

Lazarsfeld, Paul F., & Morris Rosenberg. *The Language of Social Research*. New York: Free Press, 1965.

Lazarsfeld, Paul F., William Sewell, & Harold Wilensky (Eds.). *The Uses of Sociology*. New York: Basic Books, 1967.

Le Corbusier. *Towards a New Architecture*. New York: Praeger, 1965.

Lefkowitz, M., R. Blake, & J. Mouton. "Status Factors in Pedestrian Violation of Traffic Signals." *Journal of Abnormal and Social Psychology, 51* (1955), 704–706.

Lenihan, Kenneth J. *85 Vistas*. Bureau of Applied Social Research, Research Report, Columbia University, 1966.

Lewin, Kurt. *Field Theory in Social Science*. New York: Harper & Row, 1951.

Lynch, Kevin. *The Image of the City*. Cambridge, Mass.: M.I.T. Press, 1960.

Madge, John. "Housing: Social Aspects" in *International Encyclopedia of the Social Sciences,* D. Sills (Ed.), vol. 6, 516–517. New York: Macmillan & The Free Press, 1968.

Manis, Melvin. *Cognitive Processes*. Monterey, Calif.: Brooks/Cole, 1966.

Markus, Thomas A. "The Role of Building Performance Measurement and Appraisal in Design Method" in Broadbent & Ward (1969).

Matchett, E. "Control of Thought in Creative Work." *The Chartered Mechanical Engineer, 14,* No. 4 (1968).

McCall, George J., & J. L. Simmons (Eds.). *Issues in Participant Observation*. Reading, Mass.: Addison-Wesley, 1969.

Merton, Robert K. *Social Theory and Social Structure*. New York: Free Press, 1957.

Merton, Robert K., et al. "Crafttown and Hilltown." Unpublished mimeo, 1960.

Merton, Robert K., Marjorie Fiske, & Patricia L. Kendall. *The Focused Interview*. New York: Free Press, 1956.

Merton, Robert K., & Patricia Kendall. "The Focused Interview." *American Journal of Sociology, 51,* No. 6 (1946), 541–557. (Bobbs-Merrill Reprint Series 5–467.)

Michelson, William. *Man and His Urban Environment*. Reading, Mass.: Addison-Wesley, 1970.

Michelson, William (Ed.). *Behavioral Research Methods in Environmental Design*. Stroudsburg, Pa.: Dowden, Hutchinson & Ross, 1975.

Mintz, Norbett L. "Effects of Esthetic Surroundings: II. Prolonged and Repeated Experience in a 'Beautiful' and an 'Ugly' Room." *Journal of Psychology, 41* (1956), 459–466. (Reprinted in Gutman, 1972.)

Mitchell, W. J. (Ed.). *Proceedings of the Environmental Design Research Association, Third Annual Conference, EDRA-3*. Stroudsburg, Pa.: Dowden, Hutchinson & Ross, 1972.

Montgomery, Roger. "Comment on Rainwater's Fear and House as Haven in the Lower Class." *Journal of the American Institute of Planners, 32,* No. 1 (January 1966), 30–35.

Moore, Charles, Gerald Allen, & Donlyn Lyndon. *The Place of Houses*. New York: Holt, Rinehart & Winston, 1974.

Moore, Robin. "Children at Play." Film study presented at conference of Environmental Design Research Association, Blacksburg, Va., 1973.

Morison, Elting. *From Know-How to Nowhere*. New York: Basic Books, 1974.

Nahemow, Lucille, & Gregory Downes. "Collaboration in Architectural Design: A Case Study of the Oxford Home for the Aged." *Journal of Architectural Research, 7,* No. 2 (August 1979).

National Bureau of Standards. *The Performance Concept: A Study of Its Application in Housing*. Washington, D.C.: U.S. Dept. of Commerce, 1968.

Newman, Oscar. *Defensible Space*. New York: Macmillan, 1972.

O'Doherty, E. F. "Psychological Aspects of the Creative Life" in Jones & Thornley (1963).

Orleans, Peter. "Differential Cognition of Urban Residents: Effects of Social Scale on Mapping" in Downs & Stea (1973).

Osborn, A. F. *Applied Imagination*. New York: Scribner's, 1963.

Osgood, Charles, George J. Suci, & Percy H. Tannenbaum. *The Measurement of Meaning*. Urbana: University of Illinois Press, 1957.

Ostrander, Edward, & James Groom. "The Coolfont Design Process Model: A Finer Grain Look" in *Programming for Habitability*, Wolfgang Preiser (Ed.), (Monograph Series). Urbana-Champaign: Department of Architecture, University of Illinois, 1975.

Parsons, Talcott, & Edward Shils (Eds.). *Towards a General Theory of Action*. Cambridge, Mass.: Harvard University Press, 1951.

Pastalan, Leon, R. K. Mantz, & J. Merrill. "The Simulation of Age Related Sensory Losses: A New Approach to the Study of Environmental Barriers" in Preiser (1973), vol. 1.

Payne, Stanley. *The Art of Asking Questions*. Princeton, N.J.: Princeton University Press, 1951.

Perin, Constance. *With Man in Mind*. Cambridge, Mass.: M.I.T. Press, 1970.

Piaget, Jean, & Barbel Inhelder. "The Gaps in Empiricism" in Koestler & Smythies (1969).

Polanyi, Michael. *Personal Knowledge: Towards a Post-Critical Philosophy*. Chicago: University of Chicago Press, 1958.

Polanyi, Michael. *The Tacit Dimension*. Garden City, N.Y.: Doubleday Anchor, 1967.

Polya, George. *How to Solve It: A New Aspect of Mathematical Method*. Princeton, N.J.: Princeton University Press, 1945.

Popper, Karl. *Conjectures and Refutations*. London: Oxford University Press, 1963.

Popper, Karl R. *Objective Knowledge: An Evolutionary Approach*. London: Oxford University Press, 1972.

Preiser, Wolfgang (Ed.). *Environmental Design Research*. (Proceedings of the Fourth Environmental Design Research Association Conference.) Stroudsburg, Pa.: Dowden, Hutchinson & Ross, 1973.

Proshansky, Harold M., William Ittelson, & Leanne Rivlin (Eds.). *Environmental Psychology: Man and His Physical Setting*. New York: Holt, Rinehart & Winston, 1970.

Rainwater, Lee. "Fear and the House-as-Haven in the Lower Class." *Journal of the American Institute of Planners, 32*, No. 1 (January 1966), 23–31. (Reprinted in Gutman, 1972.)

Rapoport, Amos. "Facts and Models" in Broadbent & Ward (1969a).

Rapoport, Amos. *House Form and Culture*. Englewood Cliffs, N.J.: Prentice-Hall, 1969b.

Reizenstein, Jan. "Linking Social Research and Design." *Journal of Architectural Research, 4*, No. 3 (December 1975), 26–38.

Richardson, Stephen A., Barbara S. Dohrenwend, & David Klein. *Interviewing: Its Forms and Functions*. New York: Basic Books, 1965.

Robinson, Ira M., et al. "Trade-off Games" in Michelson (1975).

Roethlisberger, F. J., & W. J. Dixon. *Management and the Worker*. Cambridge, Mass.: Harvard University Press, 1939.

Ruesch, Jurgen, & Weldon Kees. *Nonverbal Communication*. Berkeley: University of California Press, 1970.

Runkel, Philip J., & Joseph E. McGrath. *Research on Human Behavior*. New York: Holt, Rinehart & Winston, 1972.

Saile, D., J. R. Anderson, R. Borooah, A. Ray, K. Rohling, C. Simpson, A. Sutton, & M. Williams. *Families in Public Housing: An Evaluation of Three Residential Environments in Rockford, Illinois*. Urbana-Champaign: Committee on Housing

Research and Development, University of Illinois, 1972.

Sanoff, Henry. *Methods of Architectural Programming*. Stroudsburg, Pa.: Dowden, Hutchinson & Ross, 1977.

Sanoff, Henry, & George Barbour. "An Alternative Strategy for Planning an Alternative School" in *Alternative Learning Environments*, G. T. Coates (Ed.). Stroudsburg, Pa.: Dowden, Hutchinson & Ross, 1974.

Schon, Donald A. "The Design Process." Mimeographed paper available from the author, Massachusetts Institute of Technology, 1974.

Scott, Alvin, Robert Fichter, & Scott King. *Managing Vandalism*. Boston: Parkman Center for Urban Affairs, 1978.

Shaw, Marvin E., & Jack M. Wright. *Scales for the Measurement of Attitudes*. New York: McGraw-Hill, 1967.

Simon, Herbert A. *The Sciences of the Artificial*. Cambridge, Mass.: M.I.T. Press, 1969.

Snyder, Lorraine, & Edward Ostrander. *Research Basis for Behavioral Program: The New York State Veterans Home, Oxford, New York*. Ithaca, N.Y.: Dept. of Design and Environmental Analysis, Cornell University, 1974.

Sommer, Robert. *Personal Space: A Behavioral Basis for Design*. Englewood Cliffs, N.J.: Prentice-Hall, 1969.

Stea, David. "Architecture in the Head: Cognitive Mapping" in Lang et al. (1974).

Steinfeld, Edward. *Barrier Free Design for the Elderly and the Disabled, Part Three: Programmed Workbook*. Syracuse: All University Gerontology Center, Syracuse University, 1975.

Theodorson, George, & Achilles Theodorson. *A Modern Dictionary of Sociology*. London: Methuen, 1970.

Turner, John. "Housing as a Verb" in *Freedom to Build*, J. F. C. Turner & R. Fichter (Eds.). New York: Macmillan, 1972.

Van der Ryn, Sim, & Murray Silverstein. *Dorms at Berkeley: An Environmental Analysis*. New York: Educational Facilities Laboratories, 1967.

Wampler, Jan. " 'La Puntilla' Design Awards." *Progressive Architecture*, January 1968.

Webb, Eugene J., et al. *Unobtrusive Measures*. Chicago: Rand McNally, 1966.

Weiss, Robert, & Serge Bouterline. *Fairs, Exhibits, Pavilions and their Audiences*. New York: IBM Corp., 1962.

Welch, Polly. *Hospital Emergency Facilities: Translating Behavioral Issues into Design* (Graham Foundation Fellowship Report). Cambridge, Mass.: Architecture Research Office, Harvard Graduate School of Design, 1977.

Welch, Polly, John Zeisel, & Florence Ladd. "Social Dynamics of Property Damage in Boston Park and Recreation Facilities." Mimeographed report, Cambridge, Mass., 1978.

Whyte, William F. "The Social Structure of the Restaurant." *American Journal of Sociology, 54* (1949), 302–308.

Whyte, William F. *Street Corner Society* (rev. ed.). Chicago: University of Chicago Press, 1955.

Whyte, William H. *The Social Life of Small Urban Spaces*. New York: Municipal Art Society of New York, 1980. (film)

Wicker, Allen W. *An Introduction to Ecological Psychology*. Monterey, Calif.: Brooks/Cole, 1979.

Wilner, Daniel, et al. *Housing Environment and Family Life*. Baltimore, Md.: Johns Hopkins Press, 1954.

Wilson, R. L. "Liveability of the City: Attitudes and Urban Development" in *Urban Growth Dynamics*, F. S. Chapin & S. F. Weiss (Eds.). New York: Wiley, 1962.

Wiseman, Frederick. *Hospital*. Boston: Zipporah Films, 1970. (film)

Yinger, Milton J., & Stephen J. Cutler (Eds.). *Major Social Issues: An Interdisciplinary View*. New York: Free Press, 1978.

Young, M., & P. Willmott. *Family and Kinship in East London*. London: Routledge & Kegan Paul, 1957.

Zeeuw, Gerard de. "Andragogisch Verbeteringsonderzoek: Commentaar op Problemen" ("Andragogical Improvement Research: Comments on Problems"). Serie Commentaar No. k. Mimeo, Institut Wetenschap der Andragogie, Amsterdam, 1978.

Zeisel, Hans. *Say It with Figures* (5th ed.). New York: Harper & Row, 1968.

Zeisel, John. *Sociology and Architectural Planning*. (Ph.D. thesis.) Chicago: University Microfilms, 1971.

Zeisel, John. "Symbolic Meaning of Space and the Physical Dimension of Social Relations: A Case Study of Sociological Research as the Basis of Architectural Planning" in *Cities in Change*, J. Walton & D. Carns (Eds.). Boston: Allyn & Bacon, 1973. (a)

Zeisel, John. "Technology Is Not Enough." *Progressive Architecture*, June 1973, *54,* No. 6, 109–112. (b)

Zeisel, John. *Sociology and Architectural Design* (Russell Sage Social Science Frontiers Series, No. 6). New York: Free Press, 1975.

Zeisel, John. *Stopping School Property Damage: Design and Administrative Guidelines to Reduce School Vandalism*. Arlington, Va.: American Association of School Administrators, and New York: Educational Facilities Laboratories, 1976. (a)

Zeisel, John. "Negotiating a Shared Community Image." *Ekistics, 42,* No. 251 (1976), 224–227. (b)

Zeisel, John. "Fundamental Values in Planning with Non-Paying Clients" in *Interpreting the Built Environment*. B. Goodey (Ed.). Oxford: Pergamon (in press). Earlier version published in Lang et al. (1974).

Zeisel, John, Gayle Epp, & Stephen Demos. *Low-Rise Housing for Older People: Behavioral Criteria for Design*. Washington, D.C.: U.S. Government Printing Office, 1978.

Zeisel, John, & Mary Griffin. *Charlesview Housing: A Diagnostic Evaluation*. Cambridge, Mass.: Architecture Research Office, Harvard Graduate School of Design, 1975.

Zeisel, John, & Deana Rhodeside. "A Social/Physical Diagnosis of Gund Hall." Unpublished research report, 1975.

Zinnes, Dina A. "Documents as a Source of Data" in *Content Analysis*, R. C. North et al. Evanston, Ill.: Northwestern University Press, 1963.

NAME INDEX

SUBJECT INDEX